ESSENTIALS

Microsoft® Office Excel 2003

Level Two

ESSENTIALS

Microsoft® Office Excel 2003

Level Two

Marianne Fox
College of Business Administration, Butler University

Lawrence C. Metzelaar
College of Business Administration, Butler University

Prentice Hall
Upper Saddle River, New Jersey 07458

Library of Congress Cataloging-in-Publication Data

Fox, Marianne B.
   Essentials Microsoft Office Excel 2003 : level two / Marianne Fox.
      p. cm.—(Essentials)
   Includes index.
   ISBN 0-13-143555-8
   1. Microsoft Excel (Computer file)   2. Business—Computer programs.
   3. Electronic spreadsheets.   I. Metzelaar, Lawrence C. II. Title.
   III. Essentials (Prentice-Hall, inc.)

   HF5548.4.M523F678953   2004
   005.54—dc22   2004001204

Publisher and Vice President: Natalie E. Anderson
Executive Editor: Jodi McPherson
Acquisitions Editor: Melissa Sabella
Editorial Assistant: Alana Meyers
Developmental Editor: Patricia O'Shea
Senior Media Project Manager: Cathleen Profitko
Marketing Manager: Emily Knight
Senior Managing Editor: Gail Steier de Acevedo
Senior Project Manager, Production: April Montana
Project Manager, Production: Vanessa Nuttry
Manufacturing Buyer: Natacha St. Hill Moore
Design Manager: Maria Lange
Interior Design: Kevin Kall
Cover Design: OX Design
Manager, Print Production: Christy Mahon
Composition and Design Services: Kinetic Publishing Services, LLC
Full-Service Management: Thistle Hill Publishing Services, LLC
Cover Printer: Coral Graphics
Printer/Binder: Quebecor World

Credits and acknowledgments borrowed from other sources and reproduced, with permission, in this textbook appear on the appropriate page within the text.

Microsoft, Windows, Windows NT, MSN, The Microsoft Network, PowerPoint, Outlook, FrontPage, Hotmail, the MSN logo, and/or other Microsoft products referenced herein are either trademarks or registered trademarks of Microsoft Corporation in the United States and/or other countries. Screen shots and icons reprinted with permission from the Microsoft Corporation. This book is not sponsored or endorsed by or affiliated with Microsoft Corporation.

Microsoft and the Microsoft Office Specialist Logo are either trademarks or registered trademarks of Microsoft Corporation in the United States and/or other countries. Pearson Education is independent from Microsoft Corporation, and is not affiliated with Microsoft in any manner. This text may be used in assisting students to prepare for a Microsoft Office Specialist (MOS) Exam. Neither Microsoft, its designated review company, nor Pearson Education warrants that use of this text will ensure passing this exam.

Use of the Microsoft Office Specialist Approved Courseware Logo on this product signifies that it has been independently reviewed and approved in complying with the following standards: Acceptable coverage of all content related to the Specialist and Expert Level Microsoft Office exams entitled "Excel 2003" when used in combination with the following books— Essentials Excel 2003 Level 1, Essentials Excel 2003 Level 2, and Essentials Excel 2003 Level 3.

10 9 8 7 6 5 4 3 2 1

ISBN 0-13-143555-8

What does this logo mean?

It means this courseware has been approved by the Microsoft® Office Specialist Program to be among the finest available for learning **Microsoft® Office Word 2003, Microsoft® Office Excel 2003, Microsoft® Office PowerPoint® 2003,** and **Microsoft® Office Access 2003.** It also means that upon completion of this courseware, you may be prepared to take an exam for Microsoft Office Specialist qualification.

What is a Microsoft Office Specialist?

A Microsoft Office Specialist is an individual who has passed exams for certifying his or her skills in one or more of the Microsoft Office desktop applications such as Microsoft Word, Microsoft Excel, Microsoft PowerPoint, Microsoft Outlook, Microsoft Access, or Microsoft Project. The Microsoft Office Specialist Program typically offers certification exams at the "Specialist" and "Expert" skill levels.* The Microsoft Office Specialist Program is the only program approved by Microsoft for testing proficiency in Microsoft Office desktop applications and Microsoft Project. This testing program can be a valuable asset in any job search or career advancement.

More information:

To learn more about becoming a Microsoft Office Specialist, visit **www.microsoft.com/officespecialist**

To learn about other Microsoft Specialist approved courseware from Pearson Education, visit **www.prenhall.com/computing**

Dedication

We would like to dedicate this book to all who use it, in appreciation of your desire to learn how to learn, and your selection of our book to support those efforts.

Acknowledgments

We want to express our appreciation to the entire *Essentials 2003* team—other authors, editors, production staff, and those in marketing who start and end the process of developing and delivering a quality text. Special thanks go to those with whom we were most involved on a day-to-day basis: Jodi McPherson, Executive Editor; Laura Burgess, Editorial Project Manager; Trisha O'Shea, Developmental Editor; Joyce Nielsen and Maurie Lockley, Technical Editors; Vanessa Nuttry, Project Manager; and April Montana, Senior Project Manager. A more dedicated, talented, cohesive, and responsive group of authors cannot be found. We also appreciate the many reviewers whose comments ensure continuous improvements.

About the Series Editors

Marianne Fox—Series editor of *Essentials Microsoft Office 2003* and coauthor of *Essentials Microsoft Office Excel 2003 Level 1, Level 2,* and *Level 3.* Marianne Fox is a CPA with B.S. and M.B.A. degrees in Accounting from Indiana University. For 24 years she enjoyed teaching full-time—10 years teaching accounting in Indiana University's School of Business and 14 years teaching accounting and microcomputer applications in the College of Business Administration at Butler University. Currently she retains adjunct faculty status at Butler University. As the co-owner of a consulting firm, Marianne has extensive experience consulting and training in the corporate and continuing education environments. Since 1984, she has coauthored more than 40 computer-related books and has given presentations on accounting, computer applications, and instructional development topics at numerous seminars and conferences.

Lawrence C. Metzelaar—Series editor of *Essentials Microsoft Office 2003* and coauthor of *Essentials Microsoft Office Excel 2003 Level 1, Level 2,* and *Level 3.* Lawrence C. Metzelaar earned a B.S. degree in Business Administration and Computer Science from the University of Maryland, and an Ed.M. and C.A.G.S. in Human Problem Solving from Boston University. Lawrence has more than 35 years of experience with military and corporate mainframe and microcomputer systems. He has taught courses on computer science and Management Information Systems (MIS) at the University of Hawaii, Control Data Institute, Indiana University, and Purdue University; currently, he is an adjunct faculty member in the College of Business Administration at Butler University. As the co-owner of a consulting firm, he has extensive experience consulting and training in the corporate and continuing education environments. Since 1984, he has coauthored more than 40 computer-related books and has given presentations on computer applications and instructional development topics at numerous seminars and conferences.

Contents at a Glance

Table of Contents

Introduction

Essentials courseware from Prentice Hall Information Technology is anchored in the practical and professional needs of all types of students.

The *Essentials* series is conceived around a learning-by-doing approach that encourages you to grasp application-related concepts as you expand your skills through hands-on tutorials. As such, it consists of modular lessons that are built around a series of numbered, step-by-step procedures that are clear, concise, and easy to review.

The end-of-project exercises have likewise been carefully constructed, from the routine Checking Concepts and Terms to creative tasks in the Discovery Zone that prod you into extending what you've learned into areas beyond the explicit scope of the lessons proper.

How to Use This Book

Typically, each *Essentials* book is divided into eight projects. A project covers one area (or a few closely related areas) of application functionality. Each project consists of six to nine lessons that are related to that topic. Each lesson presents a specific task or closely related set of tasks in a manageable chunk that is easy to assimilate and retain.

Each element in the *Essentials* book is designed to maximize your learning experience. A list of the *Essentials* project elements and a description of how each element can help you follows. To find out more about the rationale behind each book element and how to use each to your maximum benefit, take the following walk-through.

Essentials Series 2003 Walk-Through

Project Objectives. Starting with an objective gives you short-term, attainable goals. At the beginning of each project are objectives that closely match the titles of the step-by-step tutorials. ▶

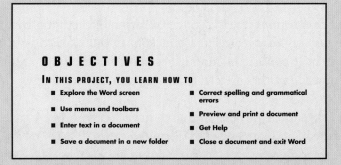

OBJECTIVES

IN THIS PROJECT, YOU LEARN HOW TO

- Explore the Word screen
- Use menus and toolbars
- Enter text in a document
- Save a document in a new folder
- Correct spelling and grammatical errors
- Preview and print a document
- Get Help
- Close a document and exit Word

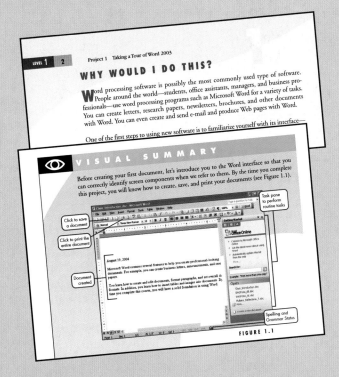

FIGURE 1.1

◀ **Why Would I Do This?** Introductory material at the beginning of each project provides an overview of why these tasks and procedures are important.

Visual Summary. An illustrated introductory feature graphically presents the concepts and features you will learn, including the final results of completing the project. ▲

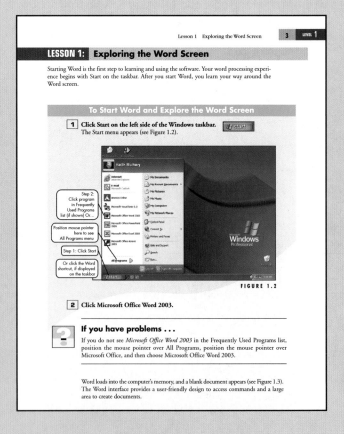

Lesson 1 Exploring the Word Screen **3** LEVEL 1

LESSON 1: **Exploring the Word Screen**

Starting Word is the first step to learning and using the software. Your word processing experience begins with Start on the taskbar. After you start Word, you learn your way around the Word screen.

To Start Word and Explore the Word Screen

1 Click Start on the left side of the Windows taskbar.
The Start menu appears (see Figure 1.2).

FIGURE 1.2

2 Click Microsoft Office Word 2003.

If you have problems . . .
If you do not see *Microsoft Office Word 2003* in the Frequently Used Programs list, position the mouse pointer over All Programs, position the mouse pointer over Microsoft Office, and then choose Microsoft Office Word 2003.

Word loads into the computer's memory, and a blank document appears (see Figure 1.3). The Word interface provides a user-friendly design to access commands and a large area to create documents.

Step-by-Step Tutorials. Hands-on tutorials let you "learn by doing" and include numbered, bold, step-by-step instructions. ▶

◀ If You Have Problems. These short troubleshooting notes help you anticipate or solve common problems quickly and effectively.

◀ To Extend Your Knowledge. These features at the end of most lessons provide extra tips, shortcuts, alternative ways to complete a process, and special hints about using the software.

◀ Creative Solution Exercises. Special icons mark selected end-of-project exercises. The creative solution exercises enable you to make choices that result in a unique solution.

End-of-Project Exercises. Extensive end-of-project exercises emphasize hands-on skill development. You'll find three levels of reinforcement: Skill Drill, Challenge, and Discovery Zone. Accompanying data files eliminate unnecessary typing. ▶

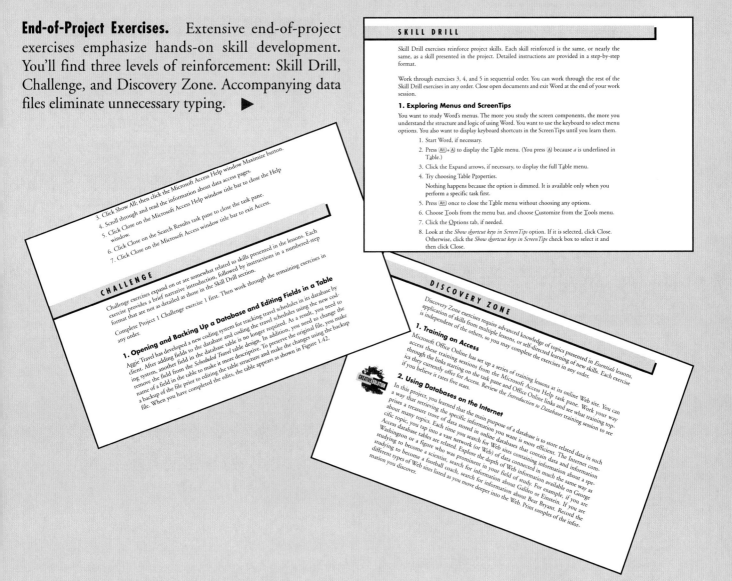

SKILL DRILL

Skill Drill exercises reinforce project skills. Each skill reinforced is the same, or nearly the same, as a skill presented in the project. Detailed instructions are provided in a step-by-step format.

Work through exercises 3, 4, and 5 in sequential order. You can work through the rest of the Skill Drill exercises in any order. Close open documents and exit Word at the end of your work session.

1. Exploring Menus and ScreenTips

You want to study Word's menus. The more you study the screen components, the more you understand the structure and logic of using Word. You want to use the keyboard to select menu options. You also want to display keyboard shortcuts in the ScreenTips until you learn them.

1. Start Word, if necessary.
2. Press (Alt)+(A) to display the Table menu. (You press (A) because *a* is underlined in Table.)
3. Click the Expand arrows, if necessary, to display the full Table menu.
4. Try choosing Table Properties.
   Nothing happens because the option is dimmed. It is available only when you perform a specific task first.
5. Press (Alt) once to close the Table menu without choosing any options.
6. Choose Tools from the menu bar, and choose Customize from the Tools menu.
7. Click the Options tab, if needed.
8. Look at the *Show shortcut keys in ScreenTips* option. If it is selected, click Close. Otherwise, click the *Show shortcut keys in ScreenTips* check box to select it and then click Close.

3. Click Show All; then click the Microsoft Access Help window Maximize button.
4. Scroll through and read the information about data access pages.
5. Click Close on the Microsoft Access Help window title bar to close the Help window.
6. Click Close on the Search Results task pane to close the task pane.
7. Click Close on the Microsoft Access window title bar to exit Access.

CHALLENGE

Challenge exercises expand on or are somewhat related to skills presented in the lessons. Each exercise provides a brief narrative introduction, followed by instructions in a numbered-step format that are not as detailed as those in the Skill Drill section.

Complete Project 1 Challenge exercise 1 first. Then work through the remaining exercises in any order.

1. Opening and Backing Up a Database and Editing Fields in a Table

Aggie Travel has developed a new coding system for tracking travel schedules in its database by client. After adding fields to the database and coding the travel schedules using the new coding system, another field in the database table is no longer required. As a result, you need to remove the field from the *Scheduled Travel* table design. In addition, you need to change the name of a field in the table to make it more descriptive. To preserve the changes using the backup file. When you have completed the edits, the table appears as shown in Figure 1.42.

DISCOVERY ZONE

Discovery Zone exercises require advanced knowledge of topics presented in *Essentials* lessons, application of skills from multiple lessons, or self-directed learning of new skills. Each exercise is independent of the others, so you may complete the exercises in any order.

1. Training on Access

Microsoft Office Online has set up a series of training sessions from the Microsoft Access Help task pane and Office Online links and information access these training sessions from the Microsoft Access Help task pane and information through the links starting on the task pane. Review the *Introduction to Databases* training topics they currently offer for Access. Review the *Introduction to Databases* training session to see if you believe it rates five stars.

2. Using Databases on the Internet

In this project, you learned that the main purpose of a database is to store related data in such a way that retrieving the specific information you want is more efficient. The Internet comprises a treasure trove of data stored in online databases that contain data and information about many topics. Each time you search for Web sites containing information about a specific topic, you tap into a vast network (or Web) of data connected in much the same way as Access database tables are related. Explore the depth of Web information available on George Washington or a figure who was prominent in your field of study. For example, if you are studying to become a scientist, search for information about Galileo or Einstein. If you are studying to become a football coach, search for information about Bear Bryant. Record the different types of Web sites listed as you move deeper into the Web. Print samples of the information you discover.

◄ **Integrating Projects Exercises.** Hands-on activities provide an opportunity to apply skills from two or more projects.

INTEGRATING P R O J E C T S

Essentials 2003: Microsoft Excel

The Integrating Projects exercises are designed to provide additional hands-on practice in working with Excel. Each exercise requires the application of skills from multiple projects; a cross-reference by each exercise title tells you which projects introduced the skills applied in the exercise. The exercises are independent and can be worked in any order.

You follow a checklist as you create and enhance each complete end product. Many of the exercises include opportunities to make decisions about the best approach and features to use in a particular situation.

1   CREATING A TARGET HEART RATE CALCULATOR

Based on Projects 2, 3, and 4

You are beginning an intensive workout program in preparation for a back-packing trip on the Appalachian Trail. You want to train effectively, and you have started an Excel worksheet that computes target heart rates for several activity levels. Now you want to add remaining content, make sure that the worksheet calculates correctly, and add formatting to enhance appearance. Figure EIP.1 illustrates your plans for the completed worksheet. Save your work periodically as you make your changes.

FIGURE EIP.1

File Guides. Convenient reference tables list the student and solution files for each project.

▶

◄ **Task Guides.** These charts, found at the end of each book, list alternative ways to complete common procedures and provide a handy reference tool.

FILE GUIDES

Guide to Files in Essentials: Microsoft Word 2003

Word	Original Student File	Student File Saved As	Related Solution Notes
Project 1			
P1-L1 and L2			No files; explore Word screen, menus, and toolbars
P1-L3 thru L8	New document	Class_Introduction.doc	Create folder and rename it as Project_1_Documents; save file in this folder
P1-SD1 and SD2			No files; explore Word screen, menus, and toolbars
P1-SD3			Create three folders: Project_2_Documents, Project_3_Documents, and Project_4_Documents
P1-SD4 and SD5	New document	Turner_Note.doc Baxter_Note.doc	*Baxter_Note.doc* is a slight revision of *Turner_Note.doc*
P1-SD6			No files; explore Help topics
P1-CH1	New document	Introduction_Letter.doc	Creative Solution exercise
P1-CH2	New document	Project_1_Study_Guide.doc	
P1-CH3			No files; explore Help topics
P1-CH4		Keyboard_Shortcut_Practice.doc	Download a keyboard practice document from Microsoft's Web site
P1-DZ1		Password_Information.doc	Copy a Help topic and save it with the password tOP sECreT
P1-DZ2	New document	Committee_Meeting.doc	
P1-DZ3		Introduction_Letter_and_Envelope.doc	Create an envelope for the letter saved in CH1 as *Introduction_Letter.doc*
Project 2			
P2-L1 thru L9	EW1_0201.doc	Basic_Document_Formats.doc	
P2-SD1-SD5	EW1_0202.doc	Fun_with_Graphics.doc	

P = Project   L = Lesson   SD = Skill Drill   CH = Challenge   DZ = Discovery Zone   IP = Integrating Projects

Creative Solution exercises permit individual choices that produce unique solutions

MICROSOFT WORD 2003 TASK GUIDE

A book in the *Essentials* series is designed to be kept as a handy reference beside your computer even after you have completed all the projects and exercises. Any time you have difficulty recalling the sequence of steps or a shortcut needed to achieve a result, look up the general category in the alphabetized listing that follows, and then quickly find your task. If you have difficulty performing a task, turn to the page number listed in the second column to locate the step-by-step exercise or other detailed description. Additional entries without page numbers describe tasks that are closely related to those presented in the projects.

Word Task	Page	Mouse	Menu Bar	Shortcut Menu	Shortcut Keys
AutoComplete, entering date	124				Type first few letters of current month and ←Enter
AutoCorrect options	257		Tools | AutoCorrect Options | select options		
Bold	198	**B** on Formatting toolbar	Format | Font | Bold		Ctrl+B
Bulleted list, create	169	on Formatting toolbar	Format | Bullets and Numbering	Select text, right-click, Bullets and Numbering	
Change case	245		Format | Change Case		↑Shift+F3
Character spacing	206		Format | Font, Character Spacing tab	Right-click text, Font, Character Spacing tab	
Close document	141	✕	File | Close		Ctrl+F4
Copy	249	on Standard toolbar	Edit | Copy	Right-click selected text, Copy	Ctrl+C
Create new folder (in Open, Save As, or Insert Picture dialog box)	128	within dialog box			
Cut	248	on Standard toolbar	Edit | Cut	Right-click selected text, Cut	Ctrl+X
Date Field	241		Insert | Date and Time		Alt+↑Shift+D
Delete, rest of word	166				Ctrl+Del
Delete, word on left side of insertion point	165				Ctrl+←Backspace

Typeface Conventions Used in This Book

Essentials Microsoft Office 2003 uses the following typeface conventions to make it easier for you to understand the material.

Key terms appear in ***italic and bold*** the first time they are defined in a project.

Monospace type appears frequently and **`looks like this`**. It is used to indicate text that you are instructed to key in.

Italic text indicates text that appears onscreen as (1) warnings, confirmation, or general information; (2) the name of a file to be used in a lesson or exercise; and (3) text from a menu or dialog box that is referenced within a sentence, when that sentence might appear awkward if it were not set off.

Hotkeys are indicated by underline. Hotkeys are the underlined letters in menus, toolbars, and dialog boxes that activate commands and options, and are a quick way to choose frequently used commands and options. Hotkeys look like this: File, Save.

Student Resources

Companion Web Site (www.prenhall.com/essentials). This text-specific Web site provides students with additional information and exercises to reinforce their learning. Features include: additional end-of-project reinforcement material; online Study Guide; easy access to *all* project data files; and much, much more!

Accessing Student Data Files. The data files that students need to work through the projects can be downloaded from the Companion Web site (www.prenhall.com/essentials). Data files are provided for each project. The filenames correspond to the filenames called for in this book. The files are named in the following manner: The first character indicates the book series (E = *Essentials*), the second character denotes the application (W = Word, E = Excel, etc.), and the third character indicates the level (1 = Level 1, 2 = Level 2, and 3 = Level 3). The last four digits indicate the project number and the file number within the project. For example, the first file used in Project 3 would be 0301. Therefore, the complete name for the first file in Project 3 in the *Word Level 1* book is *EW1_0301*. The complete name for the third file in Project 7 in the *Excel Level 2* book is *EE2_0703*.

Instructor's Resources

Customize Your Book (www.prenhall.com/customphit). The Prentice Hall Information Technology Custom PHIT Program gives professors the power to control and customize their books to suit their course needs. The best part is that it is done completely online using a simple interface.

Professors choose exactly what projects they need in the *Essentials Microsoft Office 2003* series, and in what order they appear. The program also enables professors to add their own material anywhere in the text's presentation, and the final product will arrive at each professor's bookstore as a professionally formatted text.

To learn more about this new system for creating the perfect textbook, go to www.prenhall.com/customphit, where the online walk-through demonstrates how to create a book.

Instructor's Resource CD-ROM.

This CD-ROM includes the entire Instructor's Manual for each application in Microsoft Word format. Student data files and completed solutions files are also on this CD-ROM. The Instructor's Manual contains a reference guide of these files for the instructor's convenience. PowerPoint slides, which give more information about each project, are also available for classroom use.

Companion Web Site (www.prenhall.com/essentials).

Instructors will find all of the resources available on the Instructor's Resource CD-ROM available for download from the Companion Web site.

TestGen Software.

TestGen is a test generator program that lets you view and easily edit test bank questions, transfer them to tests, and print the tests in a variety of formats suitable to your teaching situation. The program also offers many options for organizing and displaying test banks and tests. A built-in random number and text generator makes it ideal for creating multiple versions of tests. Powerful search and sort functions let you easily locate questions and arrange them in the order you prefer.

QuizMaster, also included in this package, enables students to take tests created with TestGen on a local area network. The QuizMaster utility built into TestGen lets instructors view student records and print a variety of reports. Building tests is easy with TestGen, and exams can be easily uploaded into WebCT, Blackboard, and CourseCompass.

Prentice Hall has formed close alliances with each of the leading online platform providers: WebCT, Blackboard, and our own Pearson CourseCompass.

WebCT and Blackboard.

Each of these custom-built distance-learning course features exercises, sample quizzes, and tests in a course management system that provides class administration tools as well as the ability to customize this material at the instructor's discretion.

Blackboard
www.blackboard.com

CourseCompass.   CourseCompass is a dynamic, interactive online course management tool powered by Blackboard. It lets professors create their own courses in 15 minutes or less with preloaded quality content that can include quizzes, tests, lecture materials, and interactive exercises.

Performance-Based Training and Assessment: Train & Assess IT.   Prentice Hall offers performance-based training and assessment in one product—Train & Assess IT.

The Training component offers computer-based instruction that a student can use to preview, learn, and review Microsoft Office application skills. Delivered via Web or CD-ROM, Train IT offers interactive multimedia, computer-based training to augment classroom learning. Built-in prescriptive testing suggests a study path based not only on student test results but also on the specific textbook chosen for the course.

The Assessment component offers computer-based testing that shares the same user interface as Train IT and is used to evaluate a student's knowledge about specific topics in Word, Excel, Access, PowerPoint, Windows, Outlook, and the Internet. It does this in a task-oriented, performance-based environment to demonstrate students' proficiency and comprehension of the topics. More extensive than the testing in Train IT, Assess IT offers more administrative features for the instructor and additional questions for the student. Assess IT also enables professors to test students out of a course, place students in appropriate courses, and evaluate skill sets.

CREATING SPECIAL EFFECTS IN A WORKSHEET

OBJECTIVES

IN THIS PROJECT, YOU LEARN HOW TO

- Create WordArt

- Insert and rotate an AutoShape

- Create a text box

- Group objects

- Add emphasis with lines and arrows

- Add emphasis with callouts

- Insert and modify clips

- Insert a predefined diagram

WHY WOULD I DO THIS?

When you design worksheets for others to view, it is essential that they be aesthetically pleasing. Excel provides a variety of tools to help make worksheets look professional, yet be easy to use. Using Excel's special effects tools to enhance your worksheets is as fun as it is essential.

 VISUAL SUMMARY

Excel's toolbox of special effects includes AutoShapes—such as lines, arrows, basic shapes, and callouts—and text boxes, WordArt, pictures, clip art, and predefined diagrams. You can glimpse the power of Excel's special effects tools by viewing Figure 1.1.

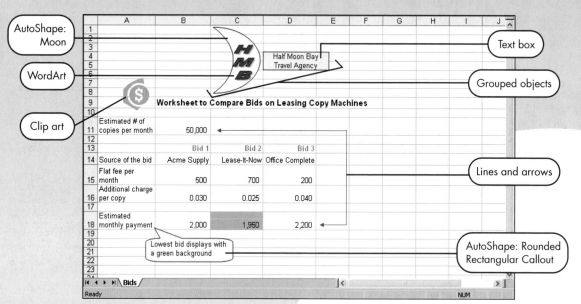

FIGURE 1.1

In the first seven lessons in this project, you add the special effects shown in Figure 1.1 to a worksheet for the Half Moon Bay Travel Agency. The worksheet computes the expected cost per month of leasing a copy machine—a cost that varies with the expected number of copies made. Consistent with company policy, three bids are being evaluated, each with a different fixed monthly fee and charge per copy. In the last lesson, you create and edit an organizational chart for the Half Moon Bay Travel Agency.

LESSON 1:   Creating WordArt

WordArt displays user-specified text in one of 30 predefined styles (refer to the WordArt Gallery in Figure 1.2). The styles include curved, slanted, and vertical text. Each style has a predefined color scheme.

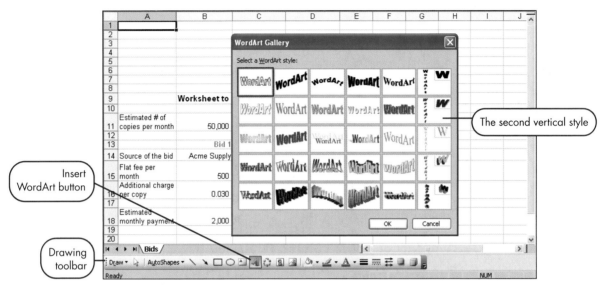

FIGURE 1.2

WordArt is not entered in a cell. It is a separate object placed on the worksheet that can be moved, sized, and edited. For example, you can select a WordArt object and change its color scheme, apply a shadow or 3-D effect, and edit its text.

In this lesson you select a vertical WordArt style, sizing it appropriately and applying it to the Half Moon Bay Travel Agency's initials, HMB. This begins the process of creating the three-object logo displayed at the top of the worksheet shown in Figure 1.1. You assemble the logo over the course of Lessons 1–4.

To Create WordArt

1 Open the *EE2_0101* file, and save it as **LeaseOptions**.
The file contains a single worksheet named Bids.

2 If the Drawing toolbar does not appear on your screen, select **View**, **Toolbars** and click Drawing.

3 Click the Insert WordArt button on the Drawing toolbar.

4 Click the second vertical style (refer to Figure 1.2), and click OK.
The Edit WordArt Text dialog box opens. You can also double-click a style to select it.

5 Replace *Your Text Here* by typing **HMB** (see Figure 1.3).

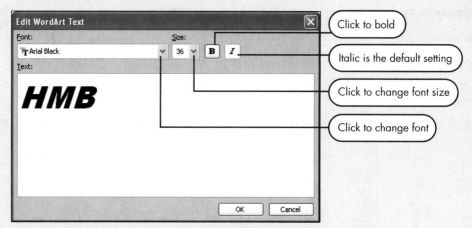

FIGURE 1.3

6 | **Click OK.**

The initials *HMB* display in the selected WordArt style in the middle of the screen. The white round sizing handles at the midpoints and corners indicate that the object is selected. The WordArt toolbar displays.

7 | **Drag the WordArt object to column B, above row 9.**

8 | **Make sure that the WordArt object is still selected; then drag one or more handles to resize the object within the range B2:B6 as shown in Figure 1.4.**

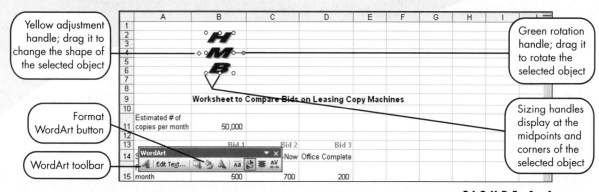

FIGURE 1.4

This is a temporary adjustment. In Lesson 2, you resize the object to fit within a moon shape.

9 | **Make sure that the WordArt object is still selected, and click the Format WordArt button on the WordArt toolbar (refer to Figure 1.4).**

The Format WordArt dialog box opens.

10 | **Locate the Fill section near the top of the Colors and Lines tab; then select Blue from the fill color drop-down list, and click OK.**

11 | **Click outside the WordArt object to deselect it, and save your changes to the *LeaseOptions* workbook.**

Keep the *LeaseOptions* workbook open for the next lesson, or close the workbook and exit Excel.

TO EXTEND YOUR KNOWLEDGE . . .

RESIZING AN OBJECT PROPORTIONATELY

If you press and hold down (⬆Shift) while dragging a corner handle, the height of a selected object changes in proportion to the change in width. You can also select *Lock aspect ratio* on the Size tab of the Format WordArt dialog box to maintain the proportions during resizing.

DELETING AN OBJECT

To delete WordArt or any other object, click within the object to select it, and press (Del).

FORMATTING WORDART

Use the Format WordArt dialog box to format a shape. You can display this dialog box by right-clicking the WordArt object and selecting Format WordArt from the shortcut menu, or you can click within the WordArt object to select it and choose Format, WordArt. You can then work with one or more of the following five tabs:

Colors and Lines	To add fill color, set the percentage of the fill transparency, and choose line or arrow color, style, and weight (thickness).
Size	To set height, width, rotation, and scale; also to specify whether to lock the aspect ratio when resizing the object.
Protection	To lock or unlock the object before setting protection; takes effect when the worksheet is protected.
Properties	To specify if an object is to move or resize when the cells under the object change, and to enable or disable printing of the object when the worksheet is printed.
Web	To add alternative text to an object that appears when the worksheet is loading as a Web page or if the object is missing from the Web page; Web search engines use alternative text to locate Web pages.

LESSON 2:   Inserting and Rotating an AutoShape

An *AutoShape* is a predefined shape that you create using the AutoShapes menu from the Drawing toolbar (see Figure 1.5). Categories of AutoShapes include Lines, Connectors, Basic Shapes, Block Arrows, Flowchart, Stars and Banners, and Callouts. More AutoShapes are available in the Clip Art collection.

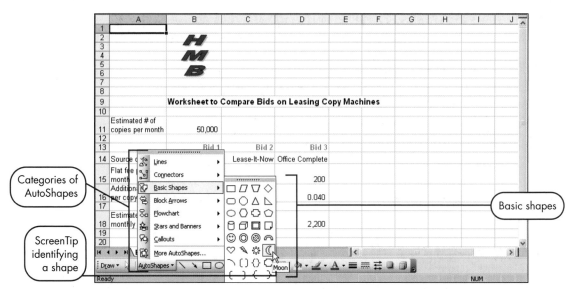

FIGURE 1.5

To create a shape, select it from the AutoShapes menu, and draw it on the worksheet with the mouse; alternatively, you can click a cell and let Excel draw it for you. You can then move, size, rotate, or flip the shape, and then apply a variety of formats.

If you select a shape with some open space inside of it—a banner, circle, star, block arrow, and so forth—you can insert text. Lines and connectors, on the other hand, show relationships and do not allow messages to be attached.

In this lesson, you create Half Moon Bay's corporate symbol, a half-moon. You select the basic Moon shape and flip it.

To Insert and Rotate an AutoShape

1 **Open the *LeaseOptions* workbook and display the Drawing toolbar, if necessary.**

2 **Click the A̲utoShapes button on the Drawing toolbar, and position the mouse pointer on *Basic Shapes*.**
A display of shapes, four in each row, appears to the right of the A̲utoShapes menu (refer to Figure 1.5).

3 **Click the Moon shape (the last option in the sixth row).**
The shape is a crescent moon curved in the direction of the letter C, or a left parenthesis. The mouse pointer changes to a thin black cross.

4 **Click cell A1.**
Excel inserts the shape and displays it with sizing handles, indicating the shape is selected.

5 **Click the D̲raw button at the left end of the Drawing toolbar, and position the mouse pointer on *Rotate or Flip*.**

Excel displays the flip options that can be applied to the selected object (see Figure 1.6).

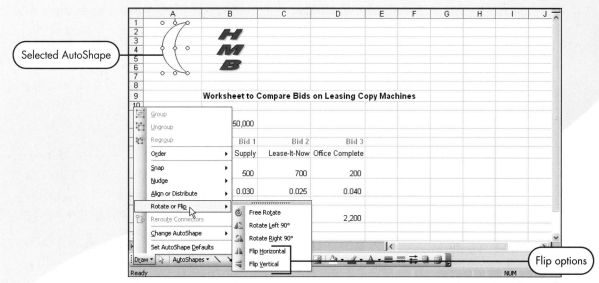

Selected AutoShape

Flip options

FIGURE 1.6

6 | Click *Flip Horizontal.*
The crescent moon flips to the opposite direction—that is, now it curves similar to a right parenthesis.

7 | **Click outside the object to deselect it, and save your changes to the *LeaseOptions* workbook.**
Keep the *LeaseOptions* workbook open for the next lesson, or close the workbook and exit Excel.

TO EXTEND YOUR KNOWLEDGE . . .

FORMATTING AUTOSHAPES
Use the Format AutoShape dialog box to format a shape. You can display this dialog box by right-clicking a shape and then selecting Format AutoShape from the shortcut menu. You can also click within an AutoShape to select it, and choose Format, AutoShape. The tabs available in the Format AutoShape dialog box are the same as those in the Format WordArt dialog box: Colors and Lines, Size, Protection, Properties, and Web.

ADDING TEXT TO AN AUTOSHAPE
To add text to an AutoShape, right-click the object and select Add Text from the shortcut menu. Type the text and then select the text. You can use the buttons on the Formatting toolbar to change the font style or size, and apply other enhancements such as color, if desired; then click outside the object to deselect it. If some of the text does not display, select the object and increase its size.

APPLYING A FILL COLOR TO AN AUTOSHAPE

You can apply a fill (background) color to an AutoShape without using the Format AutoShape dialog box. Select the shape, click the down arrow attached to the Fill Color button in the toolbar, click the desired color, and click outside the object to deselect it.

If a flashing cursor displays when you select an AutoShape, the object includes text, and text edit mode is active. Before you can apply a fill color, you must exit text edit mode by clicking the border of the selected object.

REPLACING ONE AUTOSHAPE WITH ANOTHER

You can easily change an AutoShape from one style to another. Click the AutoShape to select it and then click Draw on the Drawing toolbar. Select Change AutoShape, pick a general category, and click the desired style. Any modifications you made to the original AutoShape apply to the new AutoShape.

LESSON 3: Creating a Text Box

A **text box** is an object shaped like a square or rectangle that contains words. Text automatically wraps to fit within the boundaries of the box. You can change the dimensions of the box by dragging a sizing handle.

 Clicking Text Box on the Drawing toolbar starts the process of creating a text box. Specify the location by drawing a box on the worksheet or clicking a cell. If you create a text box by dragging the mouse pointer, it displays with a solid border. If you click the worksheet to add the box and then resize it or begin typing, the text box does not have a border.

You edit the words in a text box the same way that you would edit text in a word processing document—select the text to be changed and then type the correction. Some formatting can be done using the Fill Color, Line Color, Font Color, and Line Style toolbar buttons (see Figure 1.7). For other formatting options, you can choose Format, Text Box, and make selections within the Format Text Box dialog box.

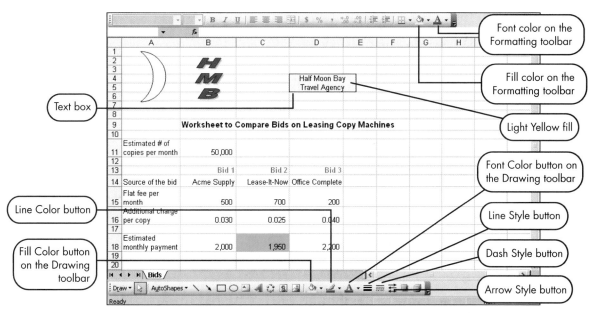

In this lesson, you create a text box containing the name of the Half Moon Bay Travel Agency. You draw the box using the mouse, enter the text using the default font, and apply a Light Yellow fill (background) to the box (refer to Figure 1.7).

To Create a Text Box

1 Open the *LeaseOptions* workbook, if necessary.

2 Click the Text Box button on the Drawing toolbar.
The pointer changes to a short horizontal bar intersecting a longer vertical bar. When this mouse pointer shape is active, you can draw a text box on a worksheet or click a cell to have Excel create it for you.

3 Beginning in cell D4, drag open a text box similar in size and position to the box shown in Figure 1.7.
The text box is selected. A flashing insertion point displays in the upper-left corner of the text box.

4 Click the Center button on the Formatting toolbar; then type `Half Moon Bay Travel Agency` in the text box (see Figure 1.8).

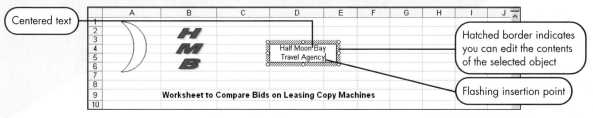

FIGURE 1.8

5 Click any point on the border of the text box.

The flashing insertion point disappears. Edit mode is no longer active. The dotted border indicates you can apply an action to the text box itself, rather than to the contents of the text box (see Figure 1.9). For example, when a dotted border surrounds an object, you can move, copy, resize, format, and delete the selected object.

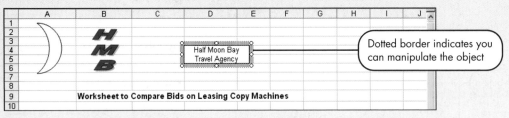

FIGURE 1.9

6 Click the down arrow to the right of the Fill Color button on the Formatting or Drawing toolbar (refer to Figure 1.7).

The Fill Color palette displays.

If you have problems . . .

If the Fill Color palette is dim, you did not select the text box border. Text boxes have two selection modes, both of which cause sizing handles to display. A flashing insertion point, which indicates text editing mode, displays if you click within a text box. Clicking the border of a text box enables you to edit the text box properties, including fill, border color, and line style.

7 Select Light Yellow from the Fill Color palette.

8 Click outside the text box to deselect it.

9 Make sure that your text box resembles the one shown in Figure 1.7, and save your changes to the *LeaseOptions* workbook.

Keep the *LeaseOptions* workbook open for the next lesson, or close the workbook and exit Excel.

TO EXTEND YOUR KNOWLEDGE . . .

FORMATTING A TEXT BOX

Use the Format Text Box dialog box to format a text box. You can display this dialog box by clicking within the text box, clicking a border of the box, and choosing Format, Text Box or by clicking within the text box, right-clicking a border of the box, and then selecting Format Text Box from the shortcut menu.

Five of the tabs in the Format Text Box dialog box are the same as those found in the WordArt and AutoShape dialog boxes: Colors and Lines, Size, Protection, Properties, and Web. There are also three additional tabs, as follows:

Font	To change font, font style, font size, and color of text; also to underline and apply special effects such as superscript or subscript.
Alignment	To set vertical and horizontal alignment, change text orientation, set automatic sizing of text to fit the box, and change text direction.
Margins	To change the distance between the borders of the text box and the contents within the text box; to choose an automatic setting or specify left, right, top, and bottom margins individually.

USING COLOR CONTRAST TO IMPROVE READABILITY

As you add text color and background fill, be mindful of a reader's ability to see the text. Strive for sharp color contrast. For example, yellow text on a white background is nearly impossible to read, and red on green is a problem for color-blind people.

LINKING TO TEXT

If the text you want to enter in a text box or AutoShape already exists in a cell, you can set a link to that cell instead of typing the text. This is an excellent way to focus attention on variable information. Click within the text box or shape, click the formula bar, type an equal sign, click the cell containing the desired text, and then press ↵Enter.

LESSON 4:   Grouping Objects

Grouped objects consist of two or more objects that can be manipulated as a single object. Prior to grouping, each object has its own set of sizing handles (see Figure 1.10). After grouping, a single set of sizing handles surrounds the objects.

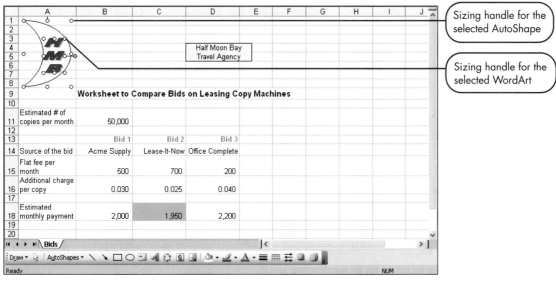

FIGURE 1.10

When objects are grouped, any action applied to the group impacts each object in the group. You can, for example, resize all the objects in a group, rotate and flip them, drag them to a different location, and apply attributes such as text, fill, and line color. If you want to change only one object in the group, you can ungroup the objects, make the change, and then regroup the objects.

Stacked objects, such as the moon and the *HMB* WordArt shown in Figure 1.10, display in layers. You can change the order in which objects display by using the Order option accessed through the Drawing toolbar, or by right-clicking any object in the group and selecting Order from the shortcut menu. Four options are available on the Order menu. *Send to Back* or *Bring to Front* places the selected object at the bottom or top of the stack, respectively. If there are three or more layers, use the *Bring Forward* and *Send Backward* options to move an object one layer at a time.

In this lesson, you group the moon and the *HMB* WordArt as one object and then add a third object to the group—the text box containing the company name. You start by adjusting size and order of the individual objects—the WordArt initials must fit within the moon shape, and the initials must display on top of the moon.

To Group Objects

1 **Open the *LeaseOptions* workbook, if necessary.**

2 **Drag the WordArt object on top of the moon.**
The moon obscures the WordArt object. Now reverse the two objects to get the effect of text inside the moon.

3 **Right-click the moon shape, position the mouse pointer on O_rder, and select *Send to Back*.**

4 **Resize the moon so that it extends from cell A1 to cell A8.**

5 **Click within the WordArt object, and resize it so that the initials *HMB* fit inside the moon.**

6 **Hold down ⇧Shift), and select both the moon and the WordArt objects.**
Each object displays its own set of sizing handles (refer to Figure 1.10).

7 **Click D_raw on the Drawing toolbar (see Figure 1.11).**

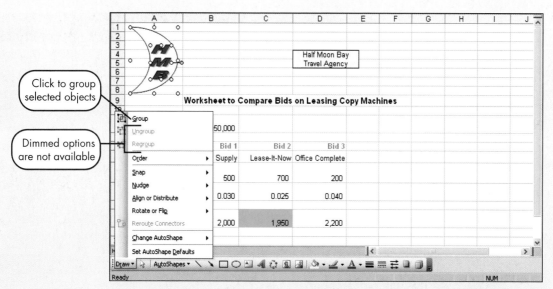

FIGURE 1.11

8 **Select _Group_.**

Now only one set of sizing handles appears because grouped objects take on the characteristics of a single object.

9 **Drag the grouped objects from column A to column C (see Figure 1.12).**

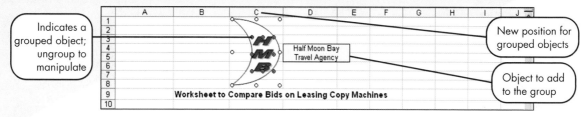

FIGURE 1.12

10 **Repeat the procedures described in steps 6–8 to include the text box in a grouping of three objects (see Figure 1.13).**

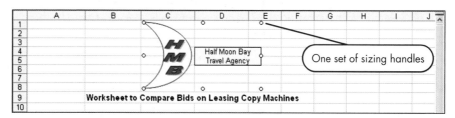

FIGURE 1.13

11 **Click outside the grouped objects, and save your changes to the _LeaseOptions_ workbook.**

Your logo design for the Half Moon Bay Travel Agency is now complete. Keep the _LeaseOptions_ workbook open for the next lesson, or close the workbook and exit Excel.

TO EXTEND YOUR KNOWLEDGE . . .

VIEWING STACKED OBJECTS
Sometimes an object in a stack is hidden by another object. You can select an object and then press ⟨Tab⟩ or ⟨Shift⟩+⟨Tab⟩ to move forward or backward through the objects on a worksheet.

UNGROUPING AND REGROUPING DRAWING OBJECTS
To ungroup drawing objects, click within any object in the group, display the Draw menu on the Drawing toolbar, and select Ungroup.

To regroup drawing objects, select any one of the objects previously grouped, display the Draw menu on the Drawing toolbar, and select Regroup.

LIMITATIONS OF GROUPING OBJECTS
Grouping works best on drawing objects. Including other objects, such as text boxes, limits what can be done with the group. You can rotate and flip an AutoShape, for example, but the same actions cannot be applied to a text box. Therefore, if one of the objects in a group is a text box, the group cannot be flipped and rotated. When this happens, the affected menu items or buttons appear dimmed.

LESSON 5: Adding Emphasis with Lines and Arrows

Use arrows to point to a specific location in a worksheet, or to show a connection between two or more related areas or objects on the worksheet. Lines can be used to frame an area, connect or separate areas and objects, or show relationships.

To create an arrow or line, select the object from the Drawing toolbar and then drag the line or arrow in the worksheet using the mouse. You can then apply line styles, such as color, thickness, pattern, and arrow. Figure 1.14 illustrates many of the tools for drawing lines and arrows.

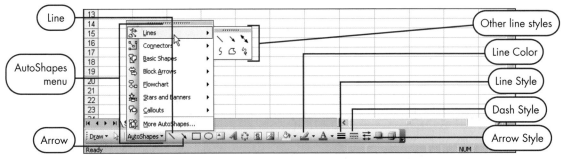

FIGURE 1.14

Lines and arrows are objects that can be moved, copied, resized, rotated, and formatted. Clicking anywhere on a line or arrow selects it and displays sizing handles at each end. To move the object to a new location, position the mouse pointer over it until you see the drag-

and-drop shape—a 4-headed arrow—and drag the line to its new location. To change the length, click a sizing handle, and drag the object longer or shorter, or pivot its angle.

In this lesson, you create objects to show a relationship in the Bids worksheet between the estimated number of copies per month and the estimated monthly payments. You create two left arrows connected with a vertical line (refer to Figure 1.1). You also apply a color to the lines and group them.

To Add Emphasis with Lines and Arrows

1 Open the *LeaseOptions* workbook, if necessary.

2 Make sure that row 18 displays; then click the Arrow button on the Drawing toolbar (refer to Figure 1.14).

3 Click near the right end of cell E18, and drag left to create a short arrow pointing to *2,200,* the contents of cell D18 (see Figure 1.15).

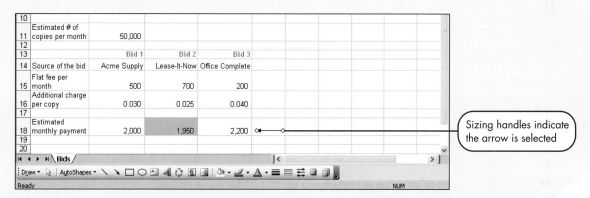

FIGURE 1.15

If you have problems . . .

If you can't make the arrow straight, press and hold down ⬆Shift before releasing the mouse button. If the object is still not drawn as you want, you can select it and press Del to start over, or you can move and size it as necessary.

---

4 Make sure that sizing handles display on the arrow, and click the Copy button on the Standard toolbar.

5 Click the Paste button.
The copied arrow displays below the original arrow.

6 Drag the copy of the arrow to cell E11, and lengthen the copied arrow by dragging its arrowhead end so that it points to *50,000* in cell B11 (see Figure 1.16).

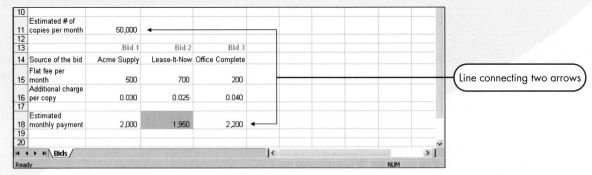

FIGURE 1.16

7 Click the Line button on the Drawing toolbar.

8 Drag a connecting line between the right ends of the arrows; then deselect the line.

A vertical line displays from cell E11 to cell E18. It connects the right ends of the two arrows (see Figure 1.17).

FIGURE 1.17

If you have problems . . .

You may find it difficult to drag an object the exact distance you need by using the mouse. You can move a selected object in very small increments by holding down Ctrl and clicking an arrow key that points to the direction you want to move the object—left, right, up, or down.

9 Hold down ⬆Shift and then click each of the three lines you just created.

Sizing handles at both ends of each line indicate that all three lines are selected.

10 Click the down arrow to the right of the Line Color button on the Drawing toolbar, and select Blue.

You applied a color to the lines. The three lines are still selected.

11 **Click the Draw button at the left end of the Drawing toolbar; then click Group.**

A single set of sizing handles surround the three objects that show the relationship between the input variable for the model (cell B11) and the calculated results (cells B18 through D18).

12 **Deselect the grouped lines, and save your changes to the *LeaseOptions* workbook.**

Keep the *LeaseOptions* workbook open for the next lesson, or close the workbook and exit Excel.

TO EXTEND YOUR KNOWLEDGE . . .

CREATING ARROWS AND LINES

An arrow is a line with an arrowhead symbol attached to either or both ends. You can use buttons and menu items to apply styles to lines and arrows (refer to Figure 1.14).

Use the Line Style button to specify the thickness of a solid line or arrow. Use the Dash Style button to change lines and arrows from solid to different patterns of lines.

Use the Arrow Style button to add or change the style of arrowhead attached to a line or arrow. You can also specify a diamond or circular shape at one or both ends instead of an arrowhead.

Use the Lines menu on the AutoShapes menu to select advanced line drawing tools such as curved, scribble, and freeform lines (refer to Figure 1.14). Use the Connectors menu on the AutoShapes menu to select a line style that connects two shapes and keeps them connected. After you select a connector style, blue connector sites appear on objects as you move the mouse pointer over them. The blue points indicate where you can attach a connector line.

USING THE FORMAT AUTOSHAPE DIALOG BOX
TO FORMAT LINES AND ARROWS

Two of the three sections on the Colors and Lines page of the Format AutoShape dialog box apply to lines and arrows. In the Line section, you can set line color, style, and weight (thickness). In the Arrows section, you can specify beginning and ending style and size.

LESSON 6: Adding Emphasis with Callouts

A *callout* is a text-filled object that points to other text or another object. Perhaps you have seen a callout as the balloon or cloud over a cartoon character's head showing what the character is thinking or saying.

You can select among predefined callout styles on the AutoShapes, Callouts menu (see Figure 1.18). Positioning the mouse pointer on a callout displays its name.

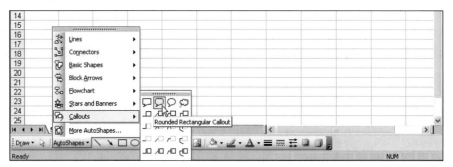

FIGURE 1.18

To create a callout, select the style you want to use and then begin drawing the callout or click a cell on the worksheet where you want to insert the object. Type the text that you want to display within the callout, and resize it as necessary. To change the area pointed to by a callout, drag the yellow adjustment handle (see Figure 1.19).

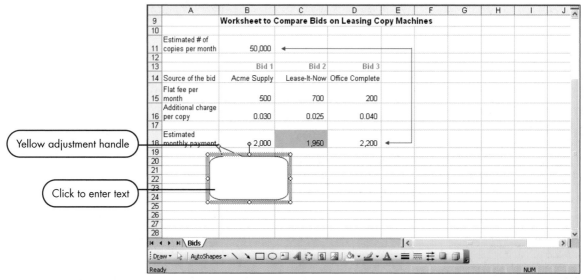

FIGURE 1.19

In this lesson, you create a rounded rectangular callout on the Bids worksheet. You select the callout style, draw it on the worksheet, type the appropriate message in the callout, and resize and position the callout.

To Add Emphasis with a Callout

1 Open the *LeaseOptions* workbook, if necessary.

2 Select <u>C</u>allouts from the A<u>u</u>toShapes menu on the Drawing toolbar (refer to Figure 1.18).

3 Choose *Rounded Rectangular Callout* (the second option in the first row).

4 Click cell B21, and drag sizing handles to increase the size of the callout. You can resize the callout again later.

5 Click the yellow adjustment handle, and drag to point the callout toward cell A18.

6 With the callout selected, type `Lowest bid displays with a green background`.

7 Make final adjustments to the size and position of the callout so that it is similar to the one shown in Figure 1.20.

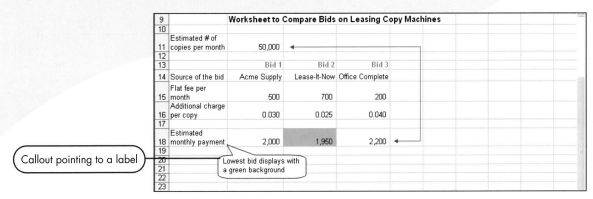

	Worksheet to Compare Bids on Leasing Copy Machines			
9				
10				
11	Estimated # of copies per month	50,000		
12				
13		Bid 1	Bid 2	Bid 3
14	Source of the bid	Acme Supply	Lease-It-Now	Office Complete
15	Flat fee per month	500	700	200
16	Additional charge per copy	0.030	0.025	0.040
17				
18	Estimated monthly payment	2,000	1,950	2,200
19				
20				
21				
22				
23				

Callout pointing to a label

Lowest bid displays with a green background

FIGURE 1.20

8 Click outside the callout, and then save your changes to the *LeaseOptions* workbook.
Keep the *LeaseOptions* workbook open for the next lesson, or close the workbook and exit Excel.

TO EXTEND YOUR KNOWLEDGE . . .

APPLYING SHADOWS AND 3-D EFFECTS TO SHAPES

You can add a shadow or a 3-D effect to most AutoShapes, including callouts. To add a shadow effect, select the shape, click the Shadow Style button in the Drawing toolbar, and click the desired style. Follow a similar process to apply a 3-D effect, substituting the 3-D Style button in place of the Shadow Style button.

LESSON 7: Inserting and Modifying Clips

When you add WordArt, a line, a callout, or another AutoShape in an Excel worksheet, you add a graphic that is available through buttons or menu selections. You can also insert a *clip*—a drawing, photograph, or other media type such as sound, animation, or movies.

Excel provides a Clip Art task pane that you can use to search for clips based on descriptive keywords, filename, or file format (see Figure 1.21). If you have an Internet connection open, search results automatically include content from additional clips provided online by Microsoft.

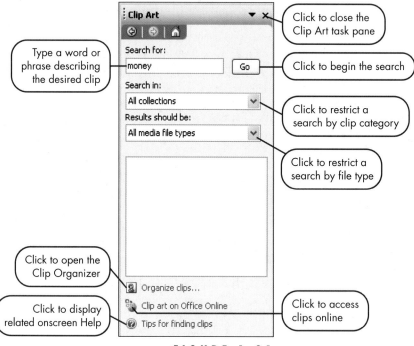

FIGURE 1.21

After you insert a clip, you can modify it using the Picture toolbar (see Figure 1.22). For example, clicking the Color button displays four options: Automatic, Grayscale, Black & White, and Washout. You might apply the fourth option so the clip can be used as a background for another object.

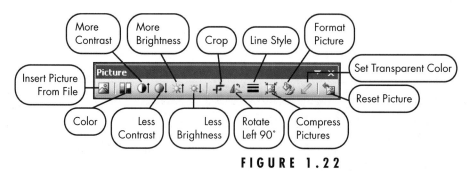

FIGURE 1.22

Four buttons enable you to increase or decrease contrast or brightness. Other buttons start the process to crop or rotate a clip, modify a line style, or apply formatting. If you do not like the changes you make to a clip, you can click Reset Picture on the Picture toolbar to restore the original settings.

In this lesson, you perform a keyword search of Microsoft Office clips, which include drawings—sometimes referred to as *clip art*—as well as photographs and sound files. You select an image among the search results, and insert the image in the Bids worksheet of the *LeaseOptions* workbook. After you change the size and position of the inserted image, you crop (cut off) a portion of the clip.

To Insert and Modify Clip Art

1 **Open the *LeaseOptions* workbook, if necessary; then click cell A3.**
Clicking cell A3 specifies the location for inserting clip art. The upper-left corner of the current cell becomes the upper-left corner of inserted clip art.

2 **Click the Insert Clip Art button on the Drawing toolbar.**
The Clip Art task pane opens at the right side of the screen.

3 **Type money in the *Search for* box (refer to Figure 1.21).**

4 **Click the Go button in the Clip Art task pane.**
Several thumbnails of money-related clips display in a scrollable list within the Clip Art task pane. A *thumbnail* is a miniature representation of an image. The results depend on whether an Internet connection is active when you begin a search.

If you have problems . . .

If no results are returned, your search conditions might be too restrictive. Make sure that *All collections* is the current setting in the *Search in* box and that *All media file types* is the current setting in the *Results should be* box (refer to Figure 1.21).

5 **Position the pointer on the thumbnail shown in Figure 1.23.**

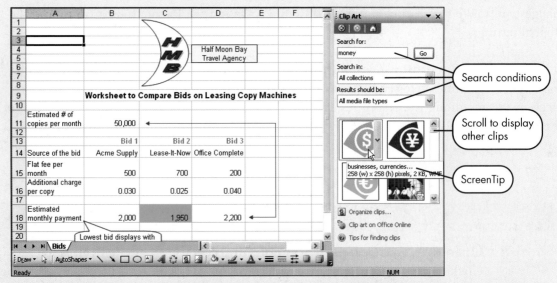

FIGURE 1.23

When you position the mouse pointer on a thumbnail, a ScreenTip shows related keywords, the width and height of the clip in pixels, the file size, and the file type (refer to Figure 1.23).

6 **Click the down arrow at the right side of the thumbnail, and click Insert in the drop-down list.**

Excel inserts the selected image and opens the Picture toolbar. Double-clicking the desired image would also insert it. The upper-left corner of the image is in cell A3, and sizing handles display at the corners and midpoints. Generally an inserted image is larger than you want.

7 **Drag the inserted clip to the approximate size and location shown in Figure 1.24.**

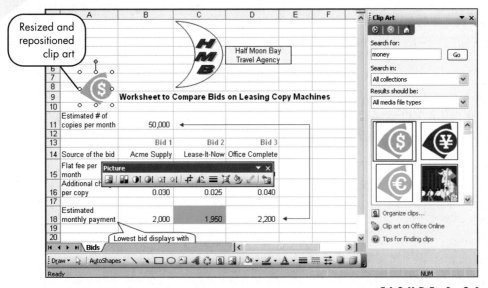

FIGURE 1.24

8 **Close the Clip Art task pane; then click Crop on the Picture toolbar.**
The long dash black border surrounding the clip indicates that crop mode is active.

9 **Position the mouse pointer on the middle of the left border of the clip.**
The pointer changes; it resembles the letter T turned on its side.

10 **Drag toward the right as shown in Figure 1.25.**

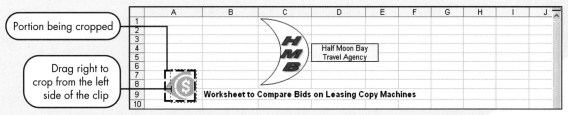

FIGURE 1.25

11 **Release the mouse button; then deselect the clip.**
You cropped the pointed left edge of the clip. This concludes your modifications to the worksheet, which should resemble those shown in the Visual Summary (see Figure 1.1).

 ## If you have problems . . .

To remove some or all cropping, select the clip if necessary, make sure that Crop is selected on the Picture toolbar, and drag the border away from the center of the figure. Clicking the Reset Picture button on the Picture toolbar removes all cropping. Use this button with caution because it also restores the original size of the clip and removes contrast, brightness, and color changes.

12 **Save your changes to the *LeaseOptions* workbook, and close the workbook.**

TO EXTEND YOUR KNOWLEDGE . . .

GRAPHICS FILE TYPES ACCEPTED BY EXCEL

You are not limited to using media files provided by Microsoft. Other sources of files include clip art that you can purchase, and images scanned from hardcopy or copied from the Web.

There are several graphics file types you can insert directly into a worksheet, including the following: Enhanced Metafile (.emf), Joint Photographic Experts Group (.jpg), Portable Network Graphics (.png), Microsoft Windows Bitmap (.bmp, .rle, .dib), Graphics Interchange Format (.gif) and Windows Metafile (.wmf).

You can also install graphics filters to insert other graphics file formats. The onscreen Help topic *Graphics file types Excel can use* provides a complete list.

ADDING BORDERS TO CLIPS
You can enhance a clip by adding a border around the object. Right-click the object, select Format Picture, and choose the Colors and Lines tab in the Format Picture dialog box; then select line thickness, style, and color for the border. Using the Lines button on the Picture toolbar enables you only to apply a line border and select the line thickness and style.

INSERTING A PICTURE
In this lesson, you added a clip art image to a worksheet. To insert a picture, use the Insert Picture dialog box, which you can open by clicking the Insert Picture From File button on the Picture toolbar (refer to Figure 1.22) or choosing Insert, Picture, From File on the menu bar.

LESSON 8: Inserting a Predefined Diagram

A ***diagram*** is a drawing that generally illustrates relationships. You can use the Diagram Gallery dialog box to insert one of six predefined diagram types—Organization Chart, Cycle, Radial, Pyramid, Venn, or Target—and enter text in the diagram.

When you add or change a diagram, the diagram is outlined by a nonprinting border and sizing handles. You can modify the original structure of a diagram—for instance, by removing a layer from a pyramid diagram or adding several circles to a target diagram. You can format the entire diagram with a preset style, or you can make formatting changes to selected portions of the diagram.

In this lesson, you create an organizational chart that illustrates the positions held by the employees of the Half Moon Bay Travel Agency. You add two layers to the original chart, enter employees' names and titles, adjust font sizing as necessary, and apply a predefined style. Your efforts produce an organizational chart similar to that shown in Figure 1.26.

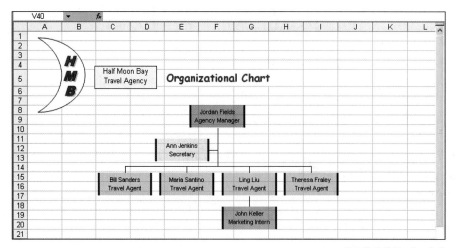

FIGURE 1.26

To Insert a Diagram

1 **Open the *EE2_0102* file, and save it as HMBstaff.**
The workbook contains a single worksheet named OrgChart. The Half Moon Bay Travel Agency logo, company name, and the phrase *Organizational Chart* display at the top of the worksheet.

2 **Click the Insert Diagram or Organization Chart button on the Drawing toolbar (or choose Insert, Diagram).**
The Diagram Gallery dialog box opens (see Figure 1.27). To select a diagram, click its picture.

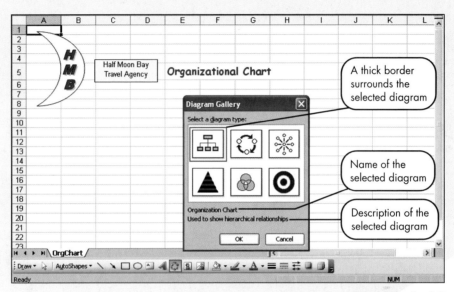

FIGURE 1.27

3 **Make sure that Organization Chart is the selected diagram, and click OK.**
The default organizational chart displays with drawing space around it, outlined by a nonprinting border and sizing handles (see Figure 1.28). The default chart includes three subordinate shapes below, and attached to, one superior shape. The Organization Chart toolbar also displays.

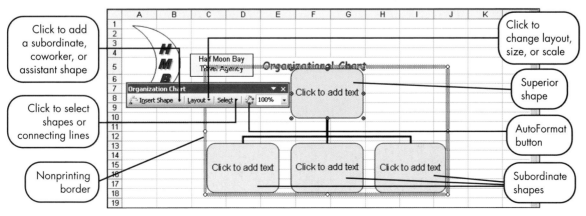

FIGURE 1.28

4 **If the default organizational chart overlaps existing cell contents, drag the nonprinting border to reposition the chart.**

5 **Select the superior shape (the top shape) by clicking its border, and click the down arrow at the right end of the Insert Shape button in the Organization Chart toolbar.**

A drop-down list displays with three options (see Figure 1.29). Select *Subordinate* to place the new shape below the selected shape and connect it to the selected shape. Select *Coworker* to place the new shape next to the selected shape and connect it to the same superior. Select *Assistant* to place the new shape below the selected shape with an elbow connector.

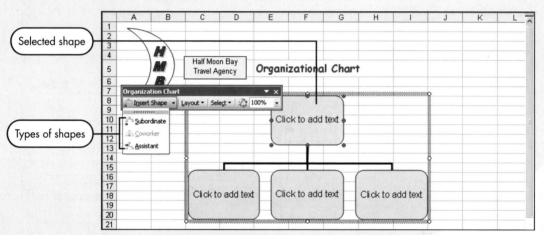

FIGURE 1.29

6 **Click *Assistant*.**

Excel places a new shape below the selected shape with an elbow connector.

7 **Click the border of the rightmost shape in the row of three shapes at the bottom of the chart.**

8 **Display the Insert Shape drop-down list, and click *Coworker*.**

Excel inserts a new shape to the right of the selected shape, and connects it to the selected shape (see Figure 1.30).

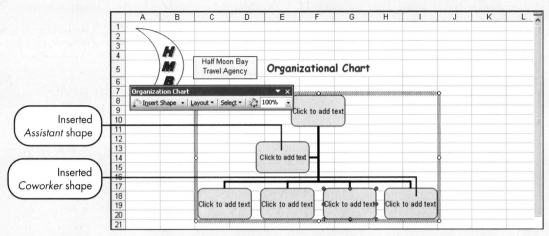

FIGURE 1.30

9 Be sure that the third of the four shapes is still selected, display the <u>I</u>nsert Shape drop-down list, and click <u>S</u>ubordinate.

Excel inserts a new shape below the selected shape, and connects it to the selected shape. Now enter the names and positions of employees.

10 Click within the top shape, type `Jordan Fields`, press ⏎Enter, and type `Agency Manager`.

11 Click within the next shape (the *Assistant* shape), type `Ann Jenkins`, press ⏎Enter, and type `Secretary`.

12 Follow the process described in the previous step, and enter the following names and positions in the four coworker shapes (refer to Figure 1.26):

Bill Sanders	Travel Agent
Maria Santino	Travel Agent
Ling Liu	Travel Agent
Theresa Fraley	Travel Agent

13 Click within the bottom (*Subordinate*) shape, type `John Keller`, press ⏎Enter, and type `Marketing Intern`.

14 Adjust font sizes if necessary (font is 8-point size in the Figure 1.26 sample).

15 Click the AutoFormat button in the Organization Chart toolbar, and select *Bookend Fills* in the Organization Chart Style Gallery dialog box (see Figure 1.31).

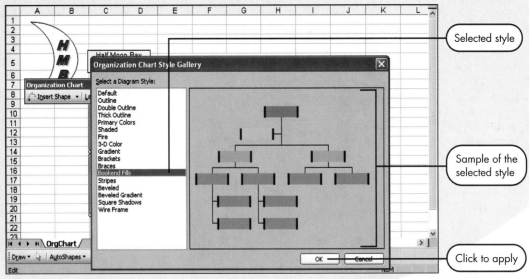

FIGURE 1.31

16 Click OK, and click outside the chart to deselect it; then check that your results resemble those shown in Figure 1.26. Make revisions as necessary.

If you have problems . . .

If text does not fit the organization chart shapes, select a smaller font size. Activate the organization chart and select Format, Organization Chart; then click the Font tab and choose a smaller font size.

17 Save your changes to the *HMBstaff* workbook, and close the workbook.
This concludes the lessons in Project 1. You can exit Excel, or continue with the end-of-project activities.

TO EXTEND YOUR KNOWLEDGE . . .

OTHER TYPES OF DIAGRAMS

Other diagram types include Cycle, Radial, Pyramid, Venn, and Target. (Refer to Figure 1.27 for examples of each.) You use a Cycle diagram to show a continuous cycle. A Radial diagram enables you to show relationships of elements to a core element. A Pyramid diagram shows relationships that build on a foundation. A Venn diagram illustrates areas of overlap between and among elements. The Target diagram is commonly used to show the steps toward a goal.

APPLYING A FILL COLOR TO THE BACKGROUND OF AN ORGANIZATION CHART

The organization chart is an object placed on the worksheet. By default, the background fill color is set to No Fill, thus allowing the worksheet grid lines to show through the chart. Adding a fill color to the background area of an organization chart can make the chart more readable. Activate the chart object, select F<u>o</u>rmat, <u>O</u>rganization Chart, and click the Colors and Lines tab. Next, select a light fill color such as White or Light Yellow. You might need to experiment to find a color that best enhances the chart. An alternative way to select and format the organization chart is to right-click the chart and select <u>F</u>ormat Organization Chart.

SUMMARY

In this project, you applied a variety of special effects to a worksheet. As an alternative to entering text in cells, you learned to create WordArt, text boxes, and selected AutoShapes—a basic moon shape and a rounded rectangular callout. You grouped objects to be manipulated as a unit. You also focused attention on specific areas of the worksheet using lines and arrows, added a picture, and created an organizational chart.

You can extend your learning by reviewing concepts and terms, and by practicing variations of skills presented in the lessons. Use the following table as a guide to the numbered questions and exercises in the end-of-project learning opportunities.

LESSON	MULTIPLE CHOICE	DISCUSSION	SKILL DRILL	CHALLENGE	DISCOVERY ZONE
Creating WordArt	2, 7, 10		2		2
Inserting and Rotating an AutoShape	1, 6, 9, 10		1, 3	1, 2	2
Creating a Text Box	3, 9		5	6	2
Grouping Objects	5, 10	2	5	4, 6	
Adding Emphasis with Lines and Arrows	6, 9			3	2
Adding Emphasis with Callouts	7, 9		4		
Inserting and Modifying Clips	8, 10	3	6	5	1, 2
Inserting a Predefined Diagram	4	1		6	3

KEY TERMS

AutoShape	**clip art**	**text box**
callout	**diagram**	**thumbnail**
clip	**grouped objects**	**WordArt**

CHECKING CONCEPTS AND TERMS

MULTIPLE CHOICE

Circle the letter of the correct answer for each of the following.

1. Which of the following is not an accurate statement about AutoShapes? [L2]

   a. AutoShapes include banners, flowchart symbols, and block arrows.

   b. You cannot change an AutoShape from one style to another; instead, you must delete the one you do not want and create another.

   c. You can add fill (background) color to an AutoShape by using the Format AutoShape dialog box or the Fill Color button on the Drawing toolbar.

   d. If you select an AutoShape and click a cell on the worksheet, Excel draws the selected AutoShape for you.

2. Which of the following is true? [L1]

   a. To delete WordArt, click within the object to select it, and choose <u>E</u>dit, <u>D</u>elete.

   b. WordArt is a separate object that can be moved, sized, and edited.

   c. Both a and b

   d. Neither a nor b

3. Which of the following would improve the readability of a text box? [L3]

   a. Use white text on a yellow background.

   b. Use green text on a red background.

   c. Use text and background with sharply contrasting colors.

   d. All of the above

4. Which of the following is not a predefined diagram style? [L8]

   a. Target

   b. Matrix

   c. Pyramid

   d. Radial

5. Which action cannot be applied to a group containing a callout and a text box? [L4]

   a. Adding fill color

   b. Changing line style

   c. Rotating and flipping

   d. Changing line color

6. Which of the following is not an accurate statement about AutoShapes, arrows, and lines? [L2, L5]

   a. The Format AutoShape dialog box includes an Alignment tab.

   b. An arrow is a line with an arrowhead on either or both ends.

   c. You can use buttons or menu items to apply styles to lines and arrows.

   d. You can use the <u>L</u>ines menu to select advanced line drawing tools such as curved, scribble, and freeform lines.

7. To change the shape of a selected object, but not its size, which of the following would you use? [L1, L6]

   a. The green dot handle

   b. The yellow diamond-shaped handle

   c. The hollow circle in a corner

   d. None of the above

8. Which of the following is not an accurate statement concerning clips? [L7]

    a. A clip can be a drawing, a photograph, or other media type such as sound, animation, or movies.

    b. After you insert a clip, you can modify it using the Picture toolbar.

    c. The Picture toolbar enables you to apply more or less contrast and more or less brightness.

    d. You can insert all graphics file types into a worksheet without installing graphics filters.

9. A text-filled object that points to other text or another object is a(n) _____. [L2, L3, L5, L6]

    a. text box

    b. flow chart

    c. callout

    d. arrow

10. Which of the following statements is not true? [L1, L2, L4, L7]

    a. If an object is selected, pressing ⬆Shift repeatedly selects the next object in the worksheet.

    b. WordArt displays user-specified text in one of 30 predefined styles.

    c. You can insert a picture in a worksheet using the Picture toolbar or an option on the Insert menu.

    d. You can move a selected object by clicking Draw on the Drawing toolbar, choosing Nudge, and clicking Up, Down, Left, or Right as desired.

DISCUSSION

1. Provide an example of how you might use each of the following diagram styles in an Excel worksheet: Cycle, Radial, Pyramid, Venn, and Target. [L8]

2. Explain why you would group objects, and what objects can be grouped. [L4]

3. Describe sources of clips and discuss how copyright laws impact your use of clips that you did not create. [L7]

SKILL DRILL

Skill Drill exercises reinforce project skills. Each skill that is reinforced is the same, or nearly the same, as a skill presented in the project. Detailed instructions are provided in a step-by-step format.

Before beginning your first Project 1 Skill Drill exercise, complete the following steps:

1. Open the file named *EE2_0103*, and immediately save it as **EE2_P1drill**.

   The *EE2_P1drill* workbook contains six sheets: an Overview, and sheets named #-1-Banner, #2-WordArt, #3-Block Arrow, #4-Callout, and #5-Text Box.

2. Click the Overview sheet to view the organization of the Project 1 Skill Drill Exercises workbook.

Each exercise is independent of the others, so you may complete them in any order. Be sure to save the workbook after completing each exercise. If you need a paper copy of the completed exercise, enter your name, centered in a header, before printing. Other print options have already been set to print compressed to one page and to display the filename, sheet name, and current date in a footer.

Be sure to save your changes and close the workbook if you need more than one work session to complete the desired exercises; then continue working on *EE2_P1drill* instead of starting over on the original *EE2_0103* file.

1. Creating a Banner

You decide to put the company name *Millennium Manufacturing* on a worksheet listing employees. To convey the name graphically, you decide to use one of the ribbons on the AutoShapes menu, type the name in the ribbon, and add a pink fill color. Also, you improve readability by making the text in the ribbon bold and centering it horizontally and vertically. Figure 1.32 illustrates the special effect you have in mind.

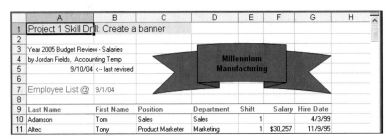

FIGURE 1.32

To add a banner to your worksheet, follow these steps:

1. Open the *EE2_P1drill* workbook, if necessary; then select the #1-Banner sheet.

2. Display the Drawing toolbar, if necessary; then select the Curved Up Ribbon style from the AutoShapes, Stars and Banners menu.

3. Click cell D2, and drag the lower-right sizing handle to cell H7.

4. Right-click the ribbon object and select *Add Text* from the shortcut menu.

5. Click Bold on the Formatting toolbar; then type `Millennium Manufacturing` within the shape.

6. Click the border of the shape to exit editing mode; then with the shape selected, choose Format, AutoShape, and select the Alignment tab.

7. In the Text alignment area of the Format AutoShape dialog box, select *Center* for the Horizontal and Vertical settings, and click OK.

8. While the ribbon object is selected, use the Fill Color button on the Drawing toolbar to apply the Pink fill color.

9. Move and resize the shape as necessary to display it between columns C and G above the list of employees; then save your changes to the *EE2_P1drill* workbook.

2. Creating WordArt

You decide to put the company name *Millennium Manufacturing* on a worksheet listing employees. To convey the name graphically, you decide to use WordArt, and rotate the image slightly to give it an upward slant from left to right. Figure 1.33 illustrates the special effect you have in mind.

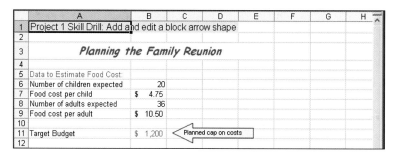

FIGURE 1.33

To add WordArt to your worksheet, follow these steps:

1. Open the *EE2_P1drill* workbook, if necessary; then select the #2-WordArt sheet.

2. Click Insert WordArt on the Drawing toolbar.

3. Select the WordArt style in the fourth column, third row, and click OK.

4. Type **Millennium Manufacturing** in the Edit WordArt Text dialog box, and click OK.

5. Move, size, and rotate the WordArt so that it displays above the data in row 9, from column C through column G, with its right end higher than the left.

   You can drag the green circle above the WordArt object, and rotate the right end up about three rows higher than the left end.

6. Make any final adjustments to size and position, and deselect the object.

7. Save your changes to the *EE2_P1drill* workbook.

3. Adding and Editing a Block Arrow Shape

You are planning the costs of a reunion, and you want to call attention to the target budget amount in cell B11 on the reunion worksheet. You decide to create a block arrow with a message. Figure 1.34 illustrates the special effect you have in mind.

FIGURE 1.34

To add a block arrow to your worksheet, follow these steps:

1. Open the *EE2_P1drill* workbook, if necessary; then select the #3-Block Arrow sheet.

2. Select the AutoShapes button on the Drawing toolbar and display the Block Arrows menu.

3. Select the Left Arrow style.

4. Click cell D10 to set the arrow object on the worksheet.

5. Right-click the arrow object, and select *Add Text*.

6. Type **Planned cap on costs** within the arrow; then apply an 8-point font size to the text, and center the message horizontally and vertically.

7. Resize the arrow so that the text fits within the arrow on one line; then position the arrow so that it points to the amount *$1,200* in cell B11.

If you have problems . . .

If either end of the arrow object keeps aligning with the edge of a cell, restricting your ability to position the object exactly where you want, choose Draw on the Drawing toolbar, point to Snap, and make sure the To Grid button is not active.

---

8. Add the Light Yellow fill color to the object.

You can use the Fill Color button on the Drawing toolbar or make your selections using the Colors and Lines tab on the Format AutoShape dialog box.

9. Deselect the arrow, and save your changes to the *EE2_P1drill* workbook.

4. Adding and Editing a Callout

You are planning the costs of a reunion, and you want to call attention to the target budget amount in cell B11. You think that the callout shown in Figure 1.35 can provide the desired focus.

1	Project 1 Skill Drill: Add and edit a callout						
2							
3	*Planning the Family Reunion*						
4							
5	Data to Estimate Food Cost:						
6	Number of children expected	20					
7	Food cost per child	$ 4.75					
8	Number of adults expected	36					
9	Food cost per adult	$ 10.50					
10			Planned cap				
11	Target Budget	$ 1,200	on costs				
12							

FIGURE 1.35

To add a callout to your worksheet, follow these steps:

1. Open the *EE2_P1drill* workbook, if necessary; then select the #4-Callout sheet.

2. Select the AutoShapes button on the Drawing toolbar, and display the Callouts menu.

3. Select the *Line Callout 2 (Accent Bar)* callout, the second option in row 3.

4. Position the mouse pointer near the left edge of cell C11, drag right and upward to open the callout, and release the mouse button.

   The hatched border indicates that editing mode is active.

5. Type **Planned cap on costs**; then click the border of the callout and apply a Light Green fill color.

6. Make adjustments as necessary to the size and position of the callout (refer to Figure 1.35).

7. Deselect the callout, and save your changes to the *EE2_P1drill* workbook.

5. Adding a Text Box and Grouping Objects

You are finalizing a monthly earnings report, and you want to add the company name *Music Mania* to a clip art image. You plan to use a text box without a border, and group the text box to the clip art (see Figure 1.36).

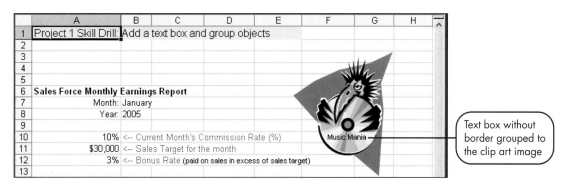

FIGURE 1.36

To add a text box to your worksheet and group two objects, follow these steps:

1. Open the *EE2_P1drill* workbook, if necessary; then select the #5-Text Box sheet.

2. Select Text Box on the Drawing toolbar.

3. Click any blank area and drag the box open; then resize as necessary to approximate the size shown in Figure 1.36.

   Remember, you click a location and then drag, because you want the text box to appear without a border. Dragging it open immediately creates an object with a border.

4. Click the text area, type **Music Mania**, and apply an 8-point font size.

5. Move the text box to the clip art image, and resize as necessary to reflect the size and position shown in Figure 1.36.

6. Hold down (⬆Shift), and select both the text box and the clip art.

7. Click D̲raw on the Drawing toolbar, and click *Group*.

8. Deselect the grouped objects, and save your changes to the *EE2_P1drill* workbook.

6. Getting Help on the Clip Organizer

You heard that Excel provides a Clip Organizer, and you want to learn about the feature. To view the related onscreen Help, follow these steps:

1. Type **Clip Organizer** in the *Type a question for help* box and press ⏎Enter.

2. Click *About the Clip Organizer* in the Search Results task pane; then read the general information in the Microsoft Excel Help window.

3. Click *Open Clip Organizer from an Office Program* in the Search Results task pane; then read the information in the Microsoft Excel Help window including the tip.

4. Click *Add a Clip to the Clip Organizer* in the Search Results task pane; then click *Add an object you created in a Microsoft Office program* in the Microsoft Excel Help window.

5. Close the Microsoft Excel Help window and close the Search Results task pane.

CHALLENGE

Challenge exercises expand on or are somewhat related to skills presented in the lessons. Each exercise provides a brief narrative introduction followed by instructions in a numbered-step format that are not as detailed as those in the Skill Drill section.

Before beginning your first Project 1 Challenge exercise, complete the following steps:

1. Open the file named *EE2_0104,* and immediately save it as **EE2_P1challenge**.

   The *EE2_P1challenge* workbook contains seven sheets: an Overview, and six exercise sheets named #1-StarText, #2-Oval, #3-Chart, #4-Ungroup, #5-Picture, and #6-Diagram.

2. Click the Overview sheet to view the organization of the Project 1 Challenge Exercises workbook.

Each exercise is independent of the others, so that you may complete the exercises in any order. Be sure to save the workbook after completing each exercise. If you need a paper copy of the completed exercise, enter your name centered in a header before printing. Other print options have already been set to print compressed to one page and to display the filename, sheet name, and current date in a footer.

Be sure to save your changes and close the workbook if you need more than one work session to complete the desired exercises; then continue working on *EE2_P1challenge* instead of starting over on the original *EE2_0104* file.

1. Adding Text to a Shape

You added a 16-point star to the worksheet showing budgeted revenues for the year 2005. Now you decide to enlarge the blank space in the center of the star and add text stating that 2005 is expected to be the best year yet.

To add text to the star shape, follow these steps:

1. Open the *EE2_P1challenge* workbook, if necessary; then select the #1-StarText sheet.

2. Click the star until you see the yellow adjustment handle.

3. Drag the yellow handle outward to enlarge the white space in the center (the space will hold the words *Best Year Yet!* with one word per line).

4. Add and center the phrase **Best Year Yet!** within the star, and apply a color fill of your choice.

5. Resize and reposition the object as desired.

6. Save your changes to the *EE2_P1challenge* workbook.

2. Circling Cell Contents Using an Oval Shape

The focus of the good news in budgeted revenues for the year 2005 is the Total Revenue in cell F17. You decide to emphasize this value by drawing a circle around it. The shape you draw covers the value, so you need to select the object and turn off the fill color.

To add and edit an oval shape around the cell, follow these steps:

1. Open the *EE2_P1challenge* workbook, if necessary; then select the #2-Oval sheet.

2. Select the Oval button on the Drawing toolbar, and drag it over cell F17.

   The shape covers the value in cell F17 so you can't see it. This happens because the fill color is White.

3. Change the fill color to No Fill.

4. Change the size and position of the oval as necessary so that it surrounds the value *1,949,100* in cell F17.

5. Save your changes to the *EE2_P1challenge* workbook.

3. Drawing a Line Between a Chart and Data

You created an embedded pie chart showing the expected greens fees for each quarter of the year 2005. Now, you want to draw a connection between the pie slice for the quarter with the highest expected revenue and the associated data cell in the worksheet. You don't want the connection to cross through the pie chart, so you decide to learn about curved lines before you start.

To draw the connection, follow these steps:

1. Open the *EE2_P1challenge* workbook, if necessary; then select the #3-Chart sheet.

2. Access onscreen Help; then search for and read information about your options to create curved lines.

3. Exit onscreen Help, and draw a curved line of your choice between the worksheet cell containing the highest expected greens fees for a quarter and the corresponding pie slice.

   The curved line should not cross through the plot area of the pie chart.

4. Apply a color of your choice to the curved line.

5. Save your changes to the *EE2_P1challenge* workbook.

4. Ungrouping, Editing, and Regrouping Objects

You created an eye-catching grouped object that includes clip art and a callout. You realize that some of the text in the callout does not display, and that an uppercase letter in the callout should be made lowercase. To make the changes, ungroup the objects, select only the callout, edit and resize as necessary, and then regroup the objects.

To ungroup, edit, and regroup the objects, follow these steps:

1. Open the *EE2_P1challenge* workbook, if necessary; then select the #4-Ungroup sheet.
2. Access onscreen Help; then search for and read information about ungrouping and regrouping objects.
3. Exit onscreen Help, and ungroup the cloud callout and the clip art.
4. Increase the size of only the cloud callout, so that all text displays.
5. Change the uppercase C in *Can't* to a lowercase c.
6. Regroup the two objects.
7. Save your changes to the *EE2_P1challenge* workbook.

5. Inserting and Modifying a Picture

You are using Excel to prepare the 2005 Glenn Lakes Golf Course revenue budget. To make it more appealing, you want to add a golf-related picture to the worksheet. You plan to search for suitable pictures on your computer and the Web. After you insert the selected image, you intend to move, size, and crop it as necessary.

To insert and modify the picture, follow these steps:

1. Open the *EE2_P1challenge* workbook, if necessary; then select the #5-Picture sheet.
2. Locate and insert an appropriate picture clip about golf.
3. Crop any unnecessary part of the graphic; then move it to a position to the right of the labels in rows 3 and 4, and resize as desired.
4. Open the Format Picture dialog box, and use the Color and Lines tab to add a 1.5-point colored border around the picture.
5. In cell A19, enter `Last revised by firstname lastname mm/dd/yy` (substitute your name and the current date).
6. Turn off the display of gridlines and row and column headings on printed output.
7. Use Print Preview to check your modified worksheet; then print (optional) the worksheet.
8. Save your changes to the *EE2_P1challenge* workbook.

6. Inserting and Modifying a Diagram

The Glenn Lakes Golf Course is conducting a new member drive in 2005, and you are developing a worksheet to keep current members informed about the recruiting project. To make the worksheet more informative and eye-catching, you decide to add a Target diagram to the worksheet that shows the recruiting goals for the year, and for each quarter within the year. Figure 1.37 illustrates the desired special effects.

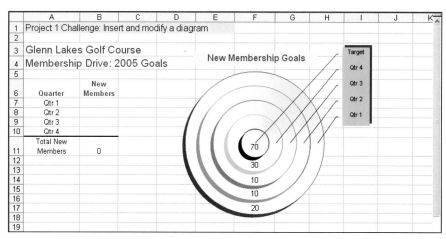

FIGURE 1.37

To insert and modify the diagram in your worksheet, follow these steps:

1. Open the *EE2_P1challenge* workbook, if necessary; then select the #6-Diagram sheet.

2. Insert a Target diagram on the worksheet; then resize and position it to the right of the Quarter and New Members labels in rows 6–11.

3. Click I̲nsert Shape on the Diagram toolbar until your diagram shows a bull's-eye and four circles.

4. Click AutoFormat on the Diagram toolbar, and choose *Square Shadows* from the Diagram Style Gallery.

5. Click the *Click to add text* object that points to the bull's-eye and type `Target`.

6. Repeat step 5 and type `Qtr 1`, `Qtr 2`, `Qtr 3`, and `Qtr 4` in each of the *Click to add text* boxes. Start with Qtr 1 in the outermost ring, Qtr 2 in the next ring, and so forth.

7. Hold down Ctrl, click each of the text boxes until all five are selected, release Ctrl, and click the Center button on the Formatting toolbar. Also apply an 8-point font size to the five text boxes.

8. Draw and fit a small text box in the Target diagram's bull's-eye and type `70` in the text box.

9. Draw and fit a small text box without a border at the bottom of each remaining ring, and enter the values `20`, `10`, `10`, and `30` beginning with the outermost ring (Qtr 1).

10. Make sure that the numbers are centered in each of the new text boxes.

11. Add a text box above the Target and type `New Membership Goals` within the box; then size, position, and format as shown in Figure 1.37.

12. Group all objects; then save your changes to the *EE2_P1challenge* workbook.

DISCOVERY ZONE

Discovery Zone exercises require advanced knowledge of topics presented in *Essentials* lessons, application of skills from multiple lessons, or self-directed learning of new skills.

Before beginning your first Project 1 Discovery Zone exercise, complete the following steps:

1. Open the file named *EE2_0105,* and immediately save it as **EE2_P1discovery**.

   The *EE2_P1discovery* workbook contains four sheets: an Overview, and three exercise sheets named #1-Distribute, #2-Apply, and #3-Diagram.

2. Select the Overview worksheet to view the organization of the Project 1 Discovery Zone Exercises workbook.

Each exercise is independent of the other, so you may complete them in any order. Be sure to save the workbook after completing each exercise. If you need a paper copy of the completed exercise, enter your name centered in a header before printing. Other print options have already been set to print compressed to one page and to display the filename, sheet name, and current date in a footer.

Be sure to save your changes and close the workbook if you need more than one work session to complete the desired exercises. Then, continue working on *EE2_P1discovery* instead of starting over on the original *EE2_0105* file.

1. Distributing Multiple Objects Horizontally

You noticed the *Align or Distribute* option when you clicked D<u>r</u>aw on the Drawing toolbar, and you think that you can use the feature in a worksheet tracking income for your travel agency. Use onscreen Help to learn about aligning and distributing multiple objects. Then distribute horizontally the four pictures in the #1-Distribute worksheet in the *EE2_P1discovery* workbook.

2. Applying Special Effects to a Worksheet

Assume that you decided on a number of special effects to apply to a worksheet. Open the *EE2_P1discovery* workbook, if necessary, and select the #2-Apply worksheet. Apply the special effects described in rows 4–8.

3. Creating a Radial Diagram

You completed a budget for Year 2005 Revenues for Glenn Lakes Golf Course. Now, you want to insert a diagram showing the types of revenue as they relate to total revenue. Open the *EE2_P1discovery* workbook, if necessary; then select the #3-Diagram worksheet and create a radial diagram above row 15 and to the right of the worksheet titles. Include appropriate labels; then apply formatting of your choice, including a different fill color for each circle.

2

DOCUMENTING AND PROTECTING WORKSHEETS AND WORKBOOKS

OBJECTIVES

IN THIS PROJECT, YOU LEARN HOW TO

- Create and use range names
- Attach comments to a cell
- Get help on protection features
- Protect cell contents and objects

- Unlock cells and objects
- View and set file properties
- Set a password for a worksheet range
- Set a password for a workbook

WHY WOULD I DO THIS?

Excel provides a variety of features that you can use to document and protect your work. For example, you can assign a name to a cell or range of cells and then use that name instead of a cell reference in a formula. User-specified comments can be added to any cell. You can unlock only the cells for which content might change, and prevent editing or deleting the contents of any other cells. You can also require a password to view a worksheet range or open a workbook.

VISUAL SUMMARY

In this project, you first work with creating and using English-like names for one or more cells. You enter a formula that includes the name *num_of_copies* instead of a reference to cell B6 (see Figure 2.1). In Lesson 2, you continue documenting a worksheet by attaching comments to cells.

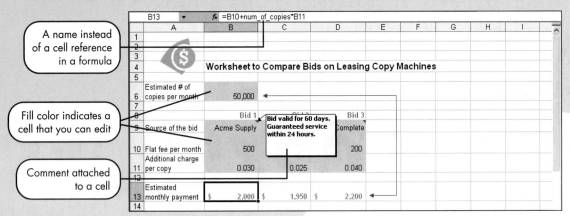

FIGURE 2.1

In Lessons 3–5, you learn to apply cell protection appropriately. You specify the cells that a user can edit (refer to the cells with color fill in Figure 2.1), and prevent changes to other cells. The remaining lessons include specifying workbook properties and setting passwords.

LESSON 1: Creating and Using Range Names

A ***range name*** is an English-like name applied to a cell or range of cells. The most common use for a range name is to make a formula easier to read and understand. You can also move the cell pointer to another section of a large worksheet by specifying the name assigned to that section instead of a cell reference.

A name must start with a letter or an underscore. The rest of the name can include numbers and letters up to a maximum of 255 characters. Spaces are not allowed, but you can use underscore characters and periods to separate words. You can use both uppercase and lowercase characters when you create a name, but Excel does not distinguish between them. For example, if you create a name *LowestBidder* and then later create a name *lowestbidder* with different cell assignments, the second range name overwrites the first without warning.

In this lesson, you specify two range names: one to use in a formula and the other to identify a section of the worksheet. You then include one defined name in a formula and use the other to go to the named location in the worksheet.

To Create and Use Range Names

1 Open the *EE2_0201* file and save it as `Protection`.
The file contains a single worksheet named Copy Bids.

2 Click cell B6, and click the Name box at the left end of the formula bar.

3 Type `num_of_copies` in the Name box, and press ↵Enter.
The name *num_of_copies* is assigned to cell B6 (see Figure 2.2).

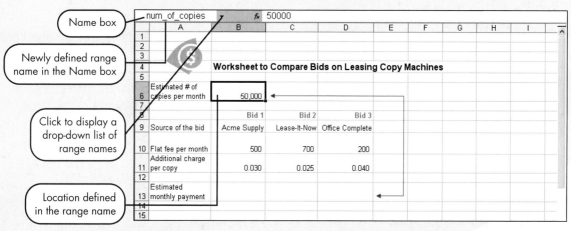

FIGURE 2.2

4 Select the range A20:A34, and click the Name box at the left end of the formula bar.

5 Type `ContactVendor` in the Name box, and press ↵Enter.
The name *ContactVendor* is assigned to the range A20:A34. Now enter a formula to calculate the first bid.

6 In cell B13, use the type-and-point method to enter the formula **=B10+B6*B11**, and make cell B13 the active cell.
When you click a cell reference instead of typing it as you create a formula, Excel displays its associated range name instead of the row-and-column reference (see the range name *num_of_copies* representing cell B6 in Figure 2.3).

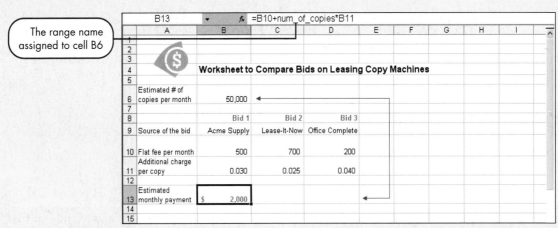

FIGURE 2.3

If you have problems . . .

If B6 displays in the formula instead of *num_of_copies,* you typed the reference to cell B6 instead of clicking cell B6.

7 **Copy the formula in cell B13 to the range C13:D13.**
The monthly payments for Bid 2 and Bid 3 are $1,950 and $2,200, respectively. The formula copies correctly because a range name uses absolute cell references.

8 **Choose Edit, Go To (or press F5).**
The Go To dialog box opens (see Figure 2.4).

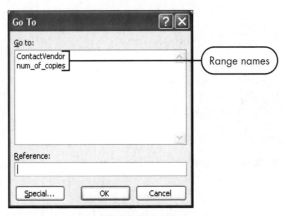

FIGURE 2.4

9 **Click ContactVendor, and click OK.**
The worksheet display shifts to the range containing vendor contact information.

10 **Click any cell to deselect the highlighted range A20:A34, and save your changes to the *Protection* workbook.**
Keep the *Protection* workbook open for the next lesson, or close the workbook and exit Excel.

TO EXTEND YOUR KNOWLEDGE . . .

USING THE DEFINE NAME DIALOG BOX TO CREATE A RANGE NAME

You know that you can apply a range name to a cell or range of cells by selecting the cell(s), clicking the Name box, typing the range name, and pressing ⏎Enter. You can also create a range name using the Define Name dialog box (see Figure 2.5). Choosing Insert, Name, Define opens the Define Name dialog box. Specify both the range name and the *Refers to* information, and click the Add button.

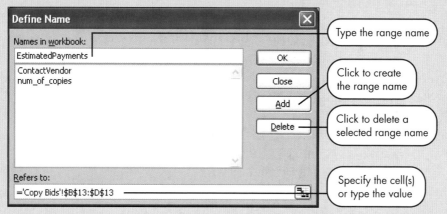

FIGURE 2.5

Usually range names refer to cells in the current workbook, as illustrated in Figure 2.5. You can also enter a specification in the *Refers to* text box that is not stored in the workbook. You can use this feature to create a shortcut for entering text, such as the full name of the person revising the workbook. For example, assume that the range name *LM* was defined by typing **LM** as the new range name and **="Lawrence Metzelaar"** in the *Refers to* box (start with an equal sign and enclose the text between quotation marks). After completing the process to create the range name, entering **=LM** in any cell in the workbook displays the full name *Lawrence Metzelaar*.

DELETING A RANGE NAME

You delete a range name using a three-step process. Select the command sequence Insert, Name, Define; select the name to delete from the list that appears in the Define Name dialog box; and click the Delete button in the dialog box (refer to Figure 2.5).

DOCUMENTING RANGE NAMES

If you want to find out what a name refers to, select the command sequence Insert, Name, Define, and select the name. Its range or value displays in the *Refers to* text box in the Define Name dialog box.

You can also create a two-column list of defined range names and the associated ranges or values. Select a cell to be the upper-left cell in a blank area large enough to hold the list; then select the command sequence Insert, Name, Paste. Complete the process by clicking the Paste List button in the lower-left corner of the Paste Name dialog box. Widen one or both columns as necessary to show all of the information in the two-column list.

LESSON 2:   Attaching Comments to a Cell

You can easily attach a comment to any cell in an Excel worksheet. A **comment** is an annotation attached to a cell that displays within a box whenever the mouse pointer rests on the cell. If a comment has been attached, you see the **comment indicator**—a small red triangle—in the cell's upper-right corner. Use the comment feature when you want supplementary information that is available, but not visible all the time.

You can alter the size of the comment box by dragging the handles on its sides and corners. You can also move a comment, change its text font or color, and hide or display comments and their indicators. The Page Setup dialog box includes options to print comments below the worksheet or where they are displayed on the worksheet.

In this lesson, you set a View option to display only comment indicators. You then create and view three comments, one for each vendor providing a bid for leasing copy machines.

To Attach Comments to a Cell

1 **Open the *Protection* workbook, if necessary; then choose Tools, Options.**
The Options dialog box opens.

2 **Select the View tab.**
The View tab includes four sections: Show, Comments, Objects, and Window options.

3 **Make sure that *Comment indicator only* is selected in the Comments section, and click OK.**

4 **Click cell B9.**
The cell containing *Acme Supply* is selected. Acme Supply is the provider of the first bid.

5 **Select Insert, Comment.**
Excel displays a comment box. An identifying name or other label generally displays bold in the upper-left corner of the box. An arrow extends from the upper-left corner of the box to the comment indicator in cell B9.

6 **Delete existing text in the box, if any, and type the following comment:**
`Bid valid for 60 days. Guaranteed service within 24 hours.`

7 **Click outside the box to deselect it.**

8 **Position the mouse pointer on cell B9.**
The newly created comment displays (see Figure 2.6).

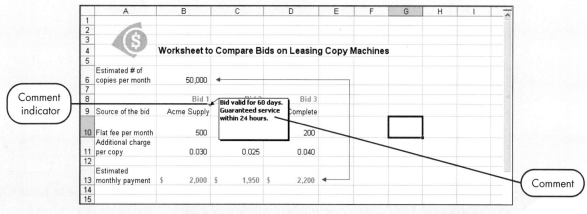

FIGURE 2.6

9 Click cell C9, and repeat steps 5–7 to create the following comment:
`Started business 6 months ago. Bid valid for 30 days. Same-day`
`service if call before noon.`

10 Click cell D9, and repeat steps 5–7 to create the following comment:
`Bid valid for 30 days. Promises service within 4 hours but has`
`not been reliable in the past.`

11 Select View, Comments.
The three comments display.

12 Select View, Comments again to remove display of the comments.

13 Save your changes to the *Protection* workbook.
Keep the *Protection* workbook open for the next lesson, or close the workbook and exit Excel.

TO EXTEND YOUR KNOWLEDGE . . .

FORMATTING, EDITING, AND DELETING COMMENTS

You can apply formats to a comment in a manner similar to that used in formatting a cell. With the comment box selected, choose Format, Comment to open the Format Comment dialog box. You can change the font, style, size, color, and other special effects for the comment.

Right-clicking a cell with an attached comment displays a shortcut menu. Select Edit Comment to revise the text in a comment. Select Delete Comment to remove the comment entirely.

If you want to remove all comments, select Go To on the Edit menu, click the Special button, click Comments, and click OK. This highlights all cells with attached comments; then select Edit, Clear, Comments.

PRINTING COMMENTS

You can print comments by selecting File, Page Setup and accessing the Sheet tab. In the Print section, select the Comments drop-down list, and select *At end of sheet* or *As displayed on sheet.* Click OK.

RESIZING AND MOVING COMMENTS

You can resize a comment by right-clicking the cell containing the comment, selecting Edit Comment from the shortcut menu, and dragging one or more of the sizing handles. To move a selected comment, click anywhere on the comment's border between sizing handles, and drag to the new location. The line and arrow pointing to the associated cell will adjust appropriately.

LESSON 3: Getting Help on Protection Features

Excel provides a variety of protection features that enable you to control accessing or editing worksheets and workbooks. Excel's Help feature provides extensive coverage of protection-related options.

In this lesson, you search for help on protection and view selected results. You also view security-related topics in Help's Table of Contents. The figures in this lesson reflect an active Internet connection. Your results are likely to vary if your system is not online.

To Get Help on Protection Features

1 **Open the *Protection* workbook, if necessary; then type protection in the *Type a question for help* box, and press ↵Enter.**
Help topics associated with the word *protection* display in the Search Results task pane (see Figure 2.7).

If you have problems . . .

The content of online Help is subject to change. If any Help topic listed in subsequent steps is not available, substitute another protection-related topic of your choice.

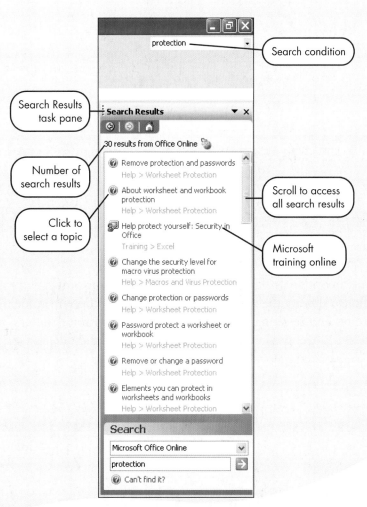

FIGURE 2.7

2 Select *About worksheet and workbook protection* (refer to Figure 2.7).
The Microsoft Excel Help window opens.

3 Read the short introductory paragraphs about *Worksheet protection* and *Workbook-level protection.*

4 Click the blue link titled *Protecting worksheet elements,* and scroll to view the related information.

5 Click the blue link titled *Protecting workbook elements and files,* and scroll to view the related information.

6 Close the Microsoft Excel Help window; then click the down arrow next to the title of the task pane and select **Help.**
The Excel Help task pane replaces the Search Results task pane.

7 Click **Table of Contents** and select the topic *Security and Privacy.*

8 Click the subtopic *Workbook and Worksheet Protection;* then view related information as desired.

9 | **Close the Microsoft Excel Help window; then close the Excel Help task pane.**
Keep the *Protection* workbook open for the next lesson, or close the workbook and exit Excel.

LESSON 4: Protecting Cell Contents and Objects

If you *protect* the contents of a worksheet, you cannot make changes to cell contents or objects unless you unlock them before activating protection. Excel also prevents viewing hidden rows or columns and making changes to items on chart sheets. You cannot add or edit comments, move or size objects, or make any changes in formatting to locked cells or objects.

Protection is an option on the Tools menu. In this lesson, you protect an entire worksheet and then attempt to modify the worksheet—changing cell contents, moving an object, applying a different color, and selecting another font style—all without success. In the next lesson, you remove the worksheet protection, unlock selected cells and objects, and restore worksheet protection of the remaining locked elements.

To Protect Cell Contents and Objects

1 | **Open the *Protection* workbook, if necessary; then select Tools, Protection, Protect Sheet.**
The Protect Sheet dialog box opens (see Figure 2.8).

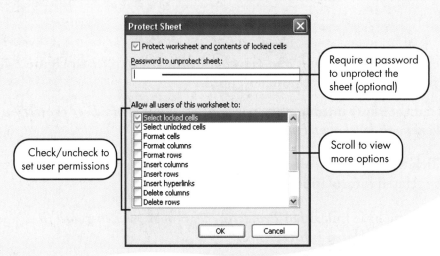

FIGURE 2.8

2 | **Click OK.**
All worksheet elements are protected. Now try to change the contents of cell B6.

3 | **Click cell B6, and start to type 40000.**
As soon as you type the **4**, a message states that the cell is protected. Now try moving an object.

4 | Click OK to close the message, and click within the $ sign image at the upper-left corner of the worksheet.
Sizing handles do not appear. You cannot select the object because it is protected.

5 | Select the range B8:D8, and display the Font Color drop-down list in the toolbar.
A grid of sample squares displays without any colors, indicating that you cannot apply a color change.

6 | Display the Font drop-down list and then select Times New Roman.
You are able to make the selection, but the new font style is not applied because the selected cells are protected.

7 | Deselect any selected items, and save your changes to the *Protection* workbook.
Keep the *Protection* workbook open for the next lesson, or close the workbook and exit Excel.

LESSON 5:   Unlocking Cells and Objects

In the previous lesson, you protected every worksheet element. That approach is suitable for data that are not subject to change, such as financial statements for the previous year that have already been audited and approved. In other worksheets, before you activate protection for the main body of the worksheet, you might prefer to unlock specific cells or objects that are likely to change. As a general guideline, all formulas, and most labels and objects, should remain locked. Cells containing numbers are generally unlocked.

When you **unlock** a cell or object, you remove the default locked setting that prevents change when worksheet protection is active. Unlocking a cell requires a four-step process—selecting the cell(s), opening the Format Cells dialog box, selecting the Protection tab, and clearing the *Locked* check box. The steps to unlock an object are similar; only the dialog box varies.

In this lesson, you disable worksheet protection, unlock several cells and an object, and restore worksheet protection.

To Unlock Cells and Objects

1 | Open the *Protection* workbook, if necessary; then select <u>T</u>ools, <u>P</u>rotection, Unprotect Sheet.
Worksheet protection is disabled. Now unlock the cells you want to be able to change—estimated number of copies in cell B6, and vendor data in the range B9:D11.

2 | Click cell B6, press and hold down Ctrl, select the range B9:D11, and release Ctrl.

3 | Select F<u>o</u>rmat, C<u>e</u>lls; then select the Protection tab (see Figure 2.9).

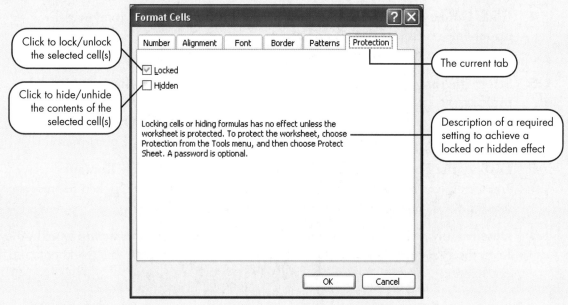

FIGURE 2.9

4 | **Click the box in front of _Locked_ to clear the check mark, and click OK.**
Cells B6 and B9 through D11 are unlocked; they remain selected.

5 | **Apply a Tan fill color to the selected cells.**
Shading unlocked cells before protecting a worksheet provides a visual means to identify cells that users can change. Now unlock the $ sign object just below cell A1.

6 | **Right-click the $ sign object, select Format Picture from the shortcut menu, and select the Protection tab in the Format Picture dialog box (see Figure 2.10).**

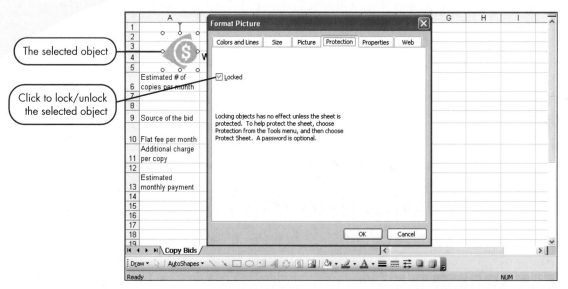

FIGURE 2.10

7 | **Click the box in front of _Locked_ to clear the check mark; then click OK, and click outside the object to deselect it.**
The $ sign object is unlocked. Now activate worksheet protection, and try again to make changes.

8 Select <u>T</u>ools, <u>P</u>rotection, <u>P</u>rotect Sheet; then leave the *Password to unprotect sheet* text box blank, and click OK.

Worksheet protection is active for all locked cells. Now make sure that you can access unlocked cells as well as the unlocked object.

9 Enter **40000** in cell B6.

Excel accepts the change because you unlocked cell B6 before enabling worksheet protection. The revised values for estimated monthly payments display in row 13—*$1,700* for bids 1 and 2, and *$1,800* for bid 3.

10 Press `Tab↹` repeatedly.

You can press `Tab↹` to move the cell pointer from one unlocked cell to the next in a protected worksheet.

11 Click the $ sign object.

Sizing handles indicate the object is selected. You can work with the object because you unlocked it before activating worksheet protection.

12 Deselect the object, and save your changes to the *Protection* workbook.

Keep the *Protection* workbook open for the next lesson, or close the workbook and exit Excel.

TO EXTEND YOUR KNOWLEDGE . . .

PROTECTING A WORKBOOK

Excel enables you to protect workbooks as well as worksheets within workbooks. After selecting the two-command sequence <u>T</u>ools, <u>P</u>rotection, select Protect <u>W</u>orkbook instead of <u>P</u>rotect Sheet.

Protection at this level applies to structure and windows. If you protect structure, users cannot view hidden worksheets. They also cannot insert, delete, move, hide, or rename worksheets. If you protect a workbook's windows, users cannot move, resize, or close the windows.

LESSON 6:   Viewing and Setting File Properties

The term *file property* describes a characteristic of a file such as file type, file size, storage location, author's name, and date last revised. You can view the properties of the active workbook by selecting <u>F</u>ile, Proper<u>t</u>ies and choosing one of five tabs in the Properties dialog box: General, Summary, Statistics, Contents, and Custom. You can also view the properties of any Microsoft Excel or Office file through the Open dialog box.

In this lesson, you display the Properties dialog box, view assorted information, and specify your name as the author of the current workbook.

To View and Set File Properties

1 **Open the *Protection* workbook, if necessary; then select File, Properties.**
The Properties dialog box opens.

2 **Select the General tab.**
Excel displays information about the current workbook's name, type, location, and size. You also see the equivalent MS-DOS name (restricted to eight characters) and the dates the workbook was created, modified, and accessed.

3 **Select the Summary tab, and delete any existing text (see Figure 2.11).**

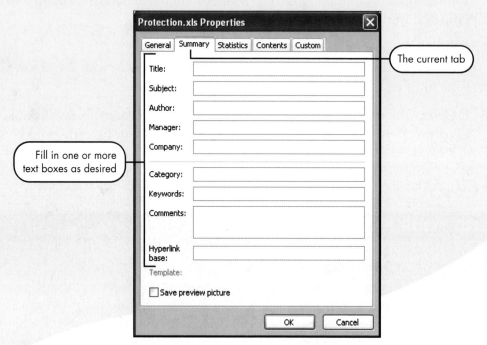

FIGURE 2.11

4 **Click within the *Author* text box, and type your name.**

5 **Click the Statistics tab.**
Excel displays information about key dates and editing time.

6 **Click the Contents tab.**
Excel lists the worksheets and named ranges in the workbook.

7 **Click the Custom tab.**
You can use the Custom tab to set up one or more information items in the *Name* box.

8 **Click OK.**
The Properties dialog box closes, and revised settings are in effect. If you click the Cancel button or the dialog box's Close button instead of OK, any revisions to settings are not saved.

9 **Save and close the *Protection* workbook.**
You can continue with the next lesson, or exit Excel.

TO EXTEND YOUR KNOWLEDGE . . .

VIEWING THE PROPERTIES OF ANY WORKBOOK

In this lesson, you viewed the properties of the active workbook. You can also view the properties of any workbook from the Open dialog box. Select <u>O</u>pen from the <u>F</u>ile menu, display the folder containing the file you want to review, and click the filename to select it (but do not click the <u>O</u>pen button yet). Click the Too<u>l</u>s button in the Open dialog box toolbar and select <u>P</u>roperties.

LESSON 7: Setting a Password for a Worksheet Range

A *password* is a set of case-sensitive characters that must be known to access a password-protected element, such as an Excel range, worksheet, or workbook. In Excel, a password is limited to 15 characters. It can contain a combination of letters, numbers, spaces, and symbols.

Make sure that you choose a password you can remember, because you cannot access a password-protected element without specifying it. You might want to keep a written list of passwords in a secure place.

You can require a password to open or edit a workbook, access a worksheet, or make changes to a range within a worksheet. In this lesson, you password-protect a range—the data that compare bids on providing copy machine service.

To Set a Password for a Worksheet Range

1 **Open the *EE2_0202* file and save it as RangeCode.**
The *RangeCode* file consists of a single worksheet named Copy Bids. The worksheet reflects the content and settings developed in Lessons 1–6 with one exception. In this worksheet, the cells containing vendor data in the range B9:D11 are locked. Cell B6 is the only unlocked cell, and worksheet protection is turned on.

2 **Select <u>T</u>ools, <u>P</u>rotection, <u>U</u>nprotect Sheet.**
Worksheet protection is disabled. Now select the range of locked cells that you want to be accessible if a password is supplied.

3 **Select the range B9:D11.**
The range containing bid-specific data is selected.

4 **Select <u>T</u>ools, <u>P</u>rotection, <u>A</u>llow Users to Edit Ranges.**
The Allow Users to Edit Ranges dialog box opens.

5 **Click the <u>N</u>ew button in the dialog box.**
The New Range dialog box opens.

6 **Type Bids in the _Title_ text box, and type 123change in the _Range password_ text box.**

Excel displays a large dot (or asterisk) for each character in the password you specify (see Figure 2.12). The dot is a security feature to prevent people from reading the password on the monitor as you type. You should also make sure that your keystrokes are not being observed as you type a password.

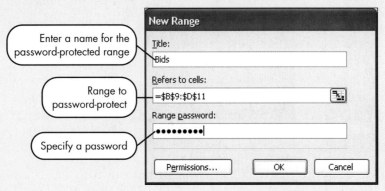

FIGURE 2.12

7 **Make sure that your specifications match those in Figure 2.12, and click OK.**
The Confirm Password dialog box opens.

8 **Type 123change in the _Reenter password to proceed_ text box, and click OK.**
The Allow Users to Edit Ranges dialog box displays the newly defined range (see Figure 2.13). Now restore worksheet protection from within the current dialog box.

FIGURE 2.13

9 **Click the Protect Sheet button in the lower-left corner of the dialog box.**
The Protect Sheet dialog box opens.

10 **Click OK to restore protection without setting a password at the worksheet level.**
Worksheet protection is enabled. Now try making a change to vendor data.

11 **Click cell B10, and start to type 600.**
The Unlock Range dialog box displays (see Figure 2.14). You must enter a password or you cannot continue with the edit.

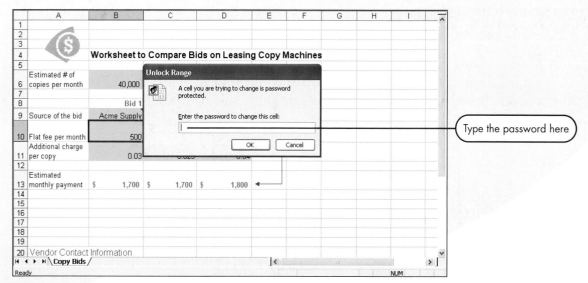

FIGURE 2.14

Type the password here

12 Type **123change** in the *Enter the password to change this cell* text box, and click OK.

13 Type **600** in cell B10, and press ⏎Enter.
Excel accepts the change because you supplied the correct password. The revised value for the Bid 1 estimated monthly payment is *$1,800*.

14 Save and close the *RangeCode* workbook.
Continue with the next lesson, or exit Excel.

TO EXTEND YOUR KNOWLEDGE . . .

GIVING SPECIFIC USERS ACCESS TO PROTECTED CELLS

If you are using the Windows 2000 (or later) operating system, you can enable specific users or groups to edit locked cells in a protected worksheet without specifying a password. Use the Permissions button in the Allow Users to Edit Ranges dialog box to identify the users or groups (refer to Figure 2.13).

LESSON 8:   Setting a Password for a Workbook

Excel supports password protection of a workbook at two levels: opening a workbook, and editing a workbook (see Figure 2.15). Each is independent of the other; you can set either one or both. Password protection is set up during execution of a Save As command.

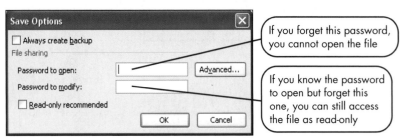

FIGURE 2.15

If a password is required to open a workbook but you don't know the password, you cannot access the file. If you can open a workbook but a password is required to modify it, and you don't know that password, you can at least open the file as read-only. A ***read-only*** file can be viewed but not changed if you save it under the same name. You can, however, modify it if you save it under a different name or save it to a different location.

In this lesson, you set up one password to open a workbook and another to modify that workbook. Because you are just learning this feature, you use a different file from the ones you used in previous lessons. That way, if you inadvertently set up a password that doesn't match the one in the instructions, and you can't remember what you typed, you can start the lesson over at step 1.

To Set a Password for a Workbook

1 **Open the *EE2_0203* file and save it as BookCode.**
The *BookCode* file consists of a single worksheet named Copy Bids. The worksheet reflects the content and settings developed in Lessons 1–6. Cell B6 and cells in the range B9:D11 are unlocked. Worksheet protection is turned on.

2 **Choose File, Save As; then click the drop-down arrow to the right of *Tools* near the upper-right corner of the Save As dialog box.**
The Tools drop-down list displays.

3 **Select General Options.**
The Save Options dialog box opens (refer to Figure 2.15).

4 **Type abc123 in the *Password to open* text box.**
Be sure to type in the first text box, and type the letters in the password in lowercase.

5 **Type xyz999 in the *Password to modify* text box.**
Be sure to type in the second text box, and type the letters in the password in lowercase.

6 | Click OK.

The Confirm Password dialog box opens, with a message to reenter the password to proceed (which is the same as the password to open).

7 | Type **abc123** in the text box, and click OK.

The Confirm Password dialog box opens again, with a message to reenter the password to modify.

8 | Type **xyz999** in the text box, and click OK.

9 | Click the <u>S</u>ave button and click Yes to confirm replacing the existing file; then close the workbook.

The workbook is saved with password protection at two levels. Now verify that the passwords work as intended.

10 | Open the *BookCode* workbook.

The Password dialog box opens with a message that the file is protected.

11 | Type **abc123** in the <u>*Password*</u> text box, and click OK.

The Password dialog box displays again with a message to enter the password for write access or open as read-only. ***Write access*** means you can modify a file.

If you have problems . . .

If you do not enter the correct password to open the file, which should be *abc123*, Excel displays a message that the password supplied is not correct. Repeat the process to open the password-protected file and supply the correct password (be sure to use the same capitalization as when you set up the password). If you still have problems, start the lesson over.

---

12 | Type **xyz999** as the password for write access, and click OK.

The Copy Bids worksheet in the *BookCode* file displays onscreen.

If you have problems . . .

If you enter text other than *xyz999*, Excel displays a message that the password supplied is not correct. If you cannot remember the password to modify, you can open the file as read-only and make changes as long as you save it under another name.

---

13 | Close the *BookCode* workbook.

This concludes the lessons in Project 2. You can continue with end-of-project exercises, or exit Excel.

TO EXTEND YOUR KNOWLEDGE . . .

CHANGING OR REMOVING A PASSWORD

To change or remove a password, start the process to set up a password—that is, select Save As from the File menu, display the Tools drop-down list, and select General Options. This displays current passwords in the Save Options dialog box. To change a password, select (highlight) the existing password and type a new one. To remove a password, select the existing password and press Del.

USING INFORMATION RIGHTS MANAGEMENT (IRM)

Microsoft Office 2003 (Professional Edition) includes new security options through its Information Rights Management (IRM) feature. It enables you to specify who can open, copy, print, or forward information created in selected Microsoft Office programs, including Word 2003, Excel 2003, and PowerPoint 2003.

Two actions must be taken to use IRM. First, a system administrator must install the Windows® Rights Management Client on the computers of everyone creating and accessing IRM-protected files and e-mail. Second, when creating an Office 2003 document, users must set the permissions for that document using File, Permission and choosing Unrestricted Access, Do Not Distribute, or Restrict Permission As. The default is Unrestricted Access.

 This feature can also be accessed using the Permission icon. Once applied, only the specified Office 2003 users can access restricted documents, and then only if their machine has Windows® Rights Management Client installed. For more information on IRM and permissions, search online Help.

SUMMARY

In this project, you worked with a variety of ways to document and protect worksheets and workbooks. To document your work, you assigned names to one or more cells, attached comments to cells, and entered summary information as part of the file's properties. You used two approaches to protect your work—one at the cell level and the other at the workbook level. At the cell level, you unlocked cells that you wanted to be able to change, and then enabled protection for all other cells in the worksheet. You also set up password protection for a range of cells. At the file level, you set up different passwords to open and to modify the workbook.

You can extend your learning by reviewing concepts and terms, and by practicing variations of skills presented in the lessons. Use the following table as a guide to the numbered questions and exercises in the end-of-project learning opportunities.

LESSON	MULTIPLE CHOICE	DISCUSSION	SKILL DRILL	CHALLENGE	DISCOVERY ZONE
Creating and Using Range Names	1, 9		1	3	4
Attaching Comments to a Cell	2		4	1, 2	1, 4
Getting Help on Protection Features		2		5	
Protecting Cell Contents and Objects	7	1	2, 3	4	1
Unlocking Cells and Objects	3, 7	3	2, 3		1, 2
Viewing and Setting File Properties	8		5		
Setting a Password for a Worksheet Range	4, 6				3
Setting a Password for a Workbook	5, 6, 10		6		

KEY TERMS

comment	password	unlock
comment indicator	range name	write access
file property	read-only	

CHECKING CONCEPTS AND TERMS

MULTIPLE CHOICE

Circle the letter of the correct answer for each of the following.

1. A range name _____. [L1]
   a. displays when you position the mouse pointer on a cell
   b. must start with a letter or underscore
   c. cannot include numbers
   d. None of the above

2. Which of the following is not a valid statement relating to comments? [L2]
   a. Right-clicking a cell with an attached comment displays a shortcut menu through which you can edit or delete the comment.
   b. A small red triangle in a cell's upper-right corner indicates that a comment is attached to the cell.
   c. You can alter the size of a comment box.
   d. You can view comments attached to cells, but you cannot print them.

3. What do you do to permit changing the contents of some cells, but prevent changing the contents of other cells? [L5]

   a. Enable worksheet protection; then unlock the cells subject to change

   b. Set a worksheet password

   c. Unlock the cells subject to change; then enable worksheet protection

   d. Either a or b

4. Which of the following is an accurate statement? [L7]

   a. An Excel password is case-sensitive.

   b. The set of characters *Ev2$aZ* comprises a valid Excel password.

   c. Both a and b

   d. Neither a nor b

5. Which of the following terms describes a file that can be viewed but not changed if you save it under the same name? [L8]

   a. Read-only

   b. Write access

   c. Locked

   d. None of the above

6. Which of the following is an accurate statement? [L7, L8]

   a. Assuming a Windows 2000 or later operating system, you can enable specific users to edit locked cells in a protected worksheet without specifying a password.

   b. Once you set up password protection for a workbook, you can change the password but you cannot remove the password protection.

   c. Both a and b

   d. Neither a nor b

7. Assume that a worksheet contains hidden rows, that all cells in the worksheet are locked, that all objects in the worksheet are not locked, and that worksheet protection is active. Which of the following is not an accurate statement? [L4, L5]

   a. You can move and size the objects.

   b. You can view the hidden rows.

   c. You cannot add or edit comments attached to the cells.

   d. You cannot apply formatting changes to the cells.

8. Which tab on the Properties dialog box enables you to enter a title, subject, and/or author? [L6]

   a. General

   b. Summary

   c. Statistics

   d. Comments

9. Which of the following is an accurate statement about range names? [L1]

   a. A defined range name must always refer to a cell or range of cells.

   b. To delete a range name, select it in the *Name* box and press `Del`.

   c. Both a and b

   d. Neither a nor b

10. Which of the following is an accurate statement about Information Rights Management (IRM)? [L8]

   a. Windows® Rights Management Client must be installed on the computers of everyone creating and accessing IRM-protected documents.

   b. Users must set the permissions for IRM-protected documents.

   c. Once applied, only specified Office 2003 users can access restricted Word, PowerPoint, and Excel documents.

   d. All of the above statements are true.

DISCUSSION

1. You can use the *Allow all users of this worksheet to* section in the Protect Sheet dialog box to turn on or off each listed modification in a protected worksheet. List at least 10 settings that you can turn on or off. [L4]

2. Use onscreen Help to learn about protecting charts. Describe how to protect an embedded chart versus a chart sheet. Explain the changes, if any, to a protected chart if you change the data on which the chart is based. [L3]

3. Review the worksheet shown in Figure 2.16. The worksheet is a planning tool for a party. The amounts for number of attendees and the costs of food per person, site rental, invitations, decorations, photographer, games, and prizes are all estimates and still subject to change. You feel confident, however, that you have set up the calculations correctly and that you have not forgotten any cost category. You want to protect the worksheet cells but still have the flexibility to change estimated costs. Which cells would you unlock and why? [L5]

	A	B	C	D	E	F
1		*Planning the Family Reunion*				
2						
3	Data to Estimate Food Cost:					
4	Number of children expected	20				
5	Food cost per child	$ 4.75				
6	Number of adults expected	36				
7	Food cost per adult	$ 10.50				
8						
9	Target Budget	$ 1,200				
10						
11	Budget allocations:					
12	Site rental	250.00				
13	Food	473.00				
14	Invitations/stamps	25.00				
15	Decorations/paper goods	175.00				
16	Photographer	300.00				
17	Games/prizes	120.00				
18	Total expected costs	1,343.00				
19						

FIGURE 2.16

SKILL DRILL

Skill Drill exercises reinforce project skills. Each skill that is reinforced is the same, or nearly the same, as a skill presented in the project. Detailed instructions are provided in a step-by-step format.

Before beginning your first Project 2 Skill Drill exercise, complete the following steps:

1. Open the file named *EE2_0204,* and immediately save it as **EE2_P2drill**.

    The workbook contains an Overview sheet and four exercise sheets labeled #1-Name, #2-Protect, #3-AutoShape, and #4-Comment.

2. Click the Overview sheet to view the organization and content of the Project 2 Skill Drill Exercises workbook.

There are six exercises, four of which use worksheets in the *EE2_P2drill* workbook; Skill Drill exercises 5 and 6 are not based on worksheet data. Each exercise is independent of the others, so you may complete the exercises in any order. However, once you complete exercise 6, which sets a password to open the workbook, you must supply that password whenever you open the workbook again. The password is **drill6**.

Be sure to save the workbook after completing each exercise. If you need a paper copy of the completed exercise, enter your name centered in a header before printing. Other print options have already been set to print compressed to one page and to display the filename, sheet name, and current date in a footer.

Be sure to save your changes and close the workbook if you need more than one work session to complete the desired exercises; then, continue working on *EE2_P2drill* instead of starting over on the original *EE2_0204* file.

1. Creating a Range Name and Using It in a Formula

One formula must still be entered in a worksheet that budgets quarterly revenue for the year 2005. The formula calculates the average quarterly revenue expected in a "best case" scenario. You decide to assign a name to the range of cells to average, and use the range name in the formula.

To create a range name and use it in a formula, follow these steps:

1. If necessary, open the *EE2_P2drill* workbook. If prompted for a password, enter **drill6**.

2. Select the worksheet named #1-Name.

3. Select the range B14:E14, and click the *Name* box at the left end of the formula bar.

4. Type **QtrRev** and press ↵Enter.

   The name *QtrRev* is assigned to the range B14:E14.

5. Enter **=average(QtrRev)** in cell A16, and make cell A16 the current cell.

   The amount *487,275* displays in cell A16, and *=AVERAGE(QtrRev)* displays in the formula bar.

6. Save your changes to the *EE2_P2drill* workbook.

2. Protecting Formulas and Labels

You completed a worksheet that budgets quarterly revenue for the year 2005. Now you want to apply worksheet protection appropriately. You decide that you want to be able to change only the numbers used as revenue projections.

To unlock the cells subject to change, and protect the rest of the worksheet—the labels, the formulas, and the AutoShape describing the scenario—follow these steps:

1. If necessary, open the *EE2_P2drill* workbook. If prompted for a password, enter **drill6**.

2. Select the #2-Protect worksheet.

3. Select the range B10:E12, and choose Format, Cells.

4. Select the Protection tab in the Format Cells dialog box.

5. Click the *Locked* check box to remove the check mark.

6. Click OK, apply a Light Yellow fill to the range B10:E12, and deselect the range.

    Applying a fill color is not required, but it does help to show a user which cells are unlocked.

7. Select Tools, Protection, Protect Sheet; then click OK without specifying a password.

8. Make sure that you can change any estimated quarterly revenue in the range B10:E12, and undo each change.

9. Make sure that you cannot select the AutoShape, change a label, or change a formula.

10. Save your changes to the *EE2_P2drill* workbook.

3. Unlocking an AutoShape

You unlocked cells containing numbers in a budget worksheet, and protected the rest of the worksheet. Now you decide that the AutoShape needs to be unlocked as well, so that you can edit its description (such as changing it from "Best Case" Scenario to "Worst Case" Scenario).

To turn protection off, unlock the AutoShape, and then turn protection back on, follow these steps:

1. If necessary, open the *EE2_P2drill* workbook. If prompted for a password, enter **drill6**.

2. Select the worksheet named #3-AutoShape.

3. Select Tools, Protection, Unprotect Sheet.

4. Click within the star-shaped AutoShape, and right-click the border that appears around the star-shaped AutoShape.

    The sizing handles display. You can select the object because protection is turned off.

5. Select Format AutoShape from the shortcut menu.

6. Select the Protection tab in the Format AutoShape dialog box, and click the *Locked* check box to remove the check mark.

7. Click the *Lock text* check box to remove the check mark, click OK, and deselect the AutoShape.

8. Select Tools, Protection, Protect Sheet; then click OK without specifying a password.

9. Make sure that you can select the AutoShape and change its text, even though protection is turned on again.

10. Save your changes to the *EE2_P2drill* workbook.

4. Adding, Editing, and Deleting a Comment

You decide to modify documentation for a budget worksheet by adding, editing, and deleting comments. Follow these steps:

1. If necessary, open the *EE2_P2drill* workbook. If prompted for a password, enter **drill6**.

2. Select the worksheet named #4-Comment.

3. Click cell B10, and select Insert, Comment.

4. Delete any existing text in the comment box, type **Net of seasonal discounts**, and click outside the comment box.

5. Right-click cell E12, and select *Edit Comment* from the shortcut menu.

6. Change *Christmas sales* to **Holiday sales** in the comment box, and click outside the box.

7. Right-click cell A16, and select *Delete Comment* from the shortcut menu.

8. Save your changes to the *EE2_P2drill* workbook.

5. Viewing the Properties of Unopened Excel Workbooks

You decide to view the properties of unopened workbooks while working in Excel. Follow these steps:

1. Choose File, Open.

2. Display the folder containing the student files for this project.

3. Click *EE2_0201* (but do not click the Open button).

4. Select Tools on the Open dialog box toolbar, and select Properties from the drop-down list.

5. View the information on the General, Summary, Statistics, and Contents tabs.

6. Close the Properties dialog box.

7. Click *EE2_0202* (but do not click the Open button).

8. Select Tools on the Open dialog box toolbar, and select Properties from the drop-down list.

9. View the information on the General, Summary, Statistics and Contents tabs.

10. Close the Properties dialog box.

11. View the properties for any other unopened file as desired, and close the Open dialog box.

6. Setting a Password to Open a Workbook

You want to set a password to open the *EE2_P2drill* workbook. Follow these steps:

1. Open the *EE2_P2drill* workbook, if necessary.

2. Choose File, Save As, and click the drop-down arrow to the right of *Tools* near the upper-right corner of the dialog box.

   The Tools drop-down list displays.

3. Select *General Options* to display the Save Options dialog box.

4. Type **drill6** in the *Password to open* text box.

   Be sure to type in the first text box, and type the letters in the password in lowercase.

5. Click OK.

   The Confirm Password dialog box opens with a message to reenter the password to proceed (which is the same as the password to open).

6. Type **drill6** and then click OK.

7. Click the <u>S</u>ave button in the Save As dialog box.

8. If the message displays that *EE2_P2drill* already exists, click Yes to replace the file.

9. Close the *EE2_P2drill* workbook; then open it again to make sure the password works as intended.

CHALLENGE

Challenge exercises expand on or are somewhat related to skills that are presented in the lessons. Each exercise provides a brief narrative introduction, followed by instructions in a numbered-step format that are not as detailed as those in the Skill Drill section.

Before beginning your first Project 2 Challenge exercise, complete the following steps:

1. Open the file named *EE2_0205,* and immediately save it as **EE2_P2challenge**.

   The *EE2_P2challenge* workbook contains five sheets: an Overview, and four exercise sheets named #1-DelComments, #2-EditComments, #3-DisplayNames, and #4-DelChart.

2. Click the Overview sheet to view the organization of the Project 2 Challenge Exercises workbook.

Each exercise is independent of the others, so you may complete the exercises in any order. Be sure to save the workbook after completing each exercise. If you need a paper copy of the completed exercise, enter your name centered in a header before printing. Other print options have already been set to print compressed to one page and to display the filename, sheet name, and current date in a footer.

If you need more than one work session to complete the desired exercises, continue working on *EE2_P2challenge* instead of starting over on the original *EE2_0205* file.

1. Deleting All Comments

You decide to delete the comments attached to cells in a worksheet. Follow these steps:

1. Open the *EE2_P2challenge* workbook, if necessary; then select the worksheet named #1-DelComments.

2. Right-click cell A15, and select Delete Comment from the shortcut menu.

   This technique is useful to delete a comment attached to one cell. Now you want to find out how to delete all comments.

3. Enter **delete comments** in the *Type a question for help* box, and select the topic *Delete comments.*

4. Read the information on removing all comments from a worksheet, and use the technique on the current worksheet.

5. Close the Microsoft Excel Help window and Search Results task pane; then save your changes to the *EE2_P2challenge* workbook.

2. Finding and Editing a Comment

You remember attaching a comment that includes the phrase "Expected loss." You decide this is not a comment you want users of the worksheet to see. To find and remove the comment, follow these steps:

1. Open the *EE2_P2challenge* workbook, if necessary; then select the worksheet named #2-EditComments.

2. Change the View setting so that you can see all comments and indicators instead of only the comment indicators.

3. Select the cell that includes the phrase *Expected loss* in its attached comment.

4. Edit that comment to remove the phrase *Expected loss.*

5. Restore the original display so that only the comment indicators appear (that is, a comment should not display unless you position the mouse pointer on a cell with an attached comment).

6. Save your changes to the *EE2_P2challenge* workbook.

3. Creating a List of Range Names

You would like to create a list of range names and their definitions in the current worksheet. Follow these steps:

1. Open the *EE2_P2challenge* workbook, if necessary; then select the worksheet named #3-DisplayNames.

2. Position the cell pointer on the upper-left cell of a two-column blank area below the other data on the worksheet; then enter and bold the phrase **List of Defined Names**.

   The blank area needs to be large enough to display all range names in one column and the associated cell references in the next column.

3. Start the process to insert a range name, and select Paste. (Use onscreen Help if you need assistance.)

4. Make the remaining selection(s) to create the list; then deselect the list.

   The worksheet contains five named ranges.

5. Save your changes to the *EE2_P2challenge* workbook.

4. Deleting an Embedded Chart in a Protected Worksheet

You decide to delete an embedded chart, but it is part of a protected worksheet. Follow these steps:

1. Open the *EE2_P2challenge* workbook, if necessary; then select the worksheet named #4-DelChart.

2. Disable worksheet protection.

3. Select the column chart below the monthly data, and delete it.

4. Restore worksheet protection.

5. Save your changes to the *EE2_P2challenge* workbook.

5. Getting Help on Information Rights Management

You know that Information Rights Management (IRM) is a new security feature in Microsoft Office Professional 2003. You want to learn more about it. To view related topics using the Excel Help system, follow these steps:

1. Search for help on Information Rights Management (IRM) using the *Type a question for help* box.

2. Locate information that describes the restrictions that can be set for an individual—view only, edit, print, copy, and so forth.

3. Determine whether IRM supports setting expiration dates for opening a file.

4. Determine whether IRM supports restricting the number of hard copies that can be printed.

5. Find out how you can view in Excel the permissions given to you.

6. Browse related topics of your choice; then close the Microsoft Excel Help window and Search Results task pane.

DISCOVERY ZONE

Discovery Zone exercises require advanced knowledge of topics presented in *Essentials* lessons, application of skills from multiple lessons, or self-directed learning of new skills.

Before beginning your first Project 2 Discovery Zone exercise, complete the following steps:

1. Open the file named *EE2_0206,* and immediately save it as **EE2_P2discovery**.

    The *EE2_P2discovery* workbook contains five sheets: an Overview, and four exercise sheets named #1-Protect, #2-Chart, #3-PasswordSheet, and #4-Document.

2. Select the Overview worksheet to view the organization of the Project 2 Discovery Zone Exercises workbook.

Each exercise is independent of the others, so you may complete the exercises in any order. Be sure to save the workbook after completing each exercise. If you need a paper copy of the completed exercise, enter your name centered in a header before printing. Other print options have already been set to print compressed to one page and to display the filename, sheet name, and current date in a footer.

Be sure to save your changes and close the workbook if you need more than one work session to complete the desired exercises. Then, continue working on *EE2_P2discovery* instead of starting over on the original *EE2_0206* file.

1. Deciding Which Cells to Unlock and Protecting the Rest

You completed a worksheet showing monthly and annual revenues, expenses, gross profit, net income, and gross profit percentages. Now you want to apply protection to the worksheet and properly document the cells that users can change using a light fill color and comments. Select the #1-Protect worksheet in the *EE2_P2discovery* workbook, and set up worksheet protection that allows only the appropriate cells to be changed. Apply a light fill color to the unprotected cells and add any comments that might improve a user's understanding of the worksheet.

2. Unlocking an Embedded Chart

You know how to unlock worksheet cells and objects before applying worksheet protection. Now you want to unlock a chart. Unlock the column chart in the #2-Chart sheet in the *EE2_P2discovery* workbook, and apply protection to the rest of the worksheet. (Hint: Select the chart before you select Format on the menu bar.)

3. Password-Protecting a Worksheet

You own and manage a small firm. You created a list of employees that includes a column for last name, a column for first name, and a hidden column with the related wage per hour data. You unlocked cells in the name columns so that your assistant can enter the full name of a new employee. Now you want to enable worksheet protection in the #3-PasswordSheet worksheet of the *EE2_P2discovery* workbook, but restrict turning that protection off unless a password is provided. Use the password **FWFwages**.

4. Documenting a Worksheet Using Range Names and Comments

You are finalizing a monthly earnings report. Assume that you already entered the complex formulas to calculate Bonus in the #4-Document sheet in the *EE2_P2discovery* workbook. Now you want to add the formulas for commission in column D (sales multiplied by the current month's commission rate) and monthly earnings in column F (commission plus bonus). Set up and use at least one defined name in a formula. Also attach comments to cells as needed to help document the worksheet.

MODIFYING CELLS AND WORKSHEET CONTENTS

OBJECTIVES

IN THIS PROJECT, YOU LEARN HOW TO

- Insert and delete cells

- Find and replace cell contents

- Find and replace cell formats

- Change contrast and brightness in clips

- Flip and rotate clips

- Use Paste Special

- Save a workbook in a different format

WHY WOULD I DO THIS?

Let's do a little math! Each Excel 2003 worksheet is comprised of 256 columns and 65,536 rows. That means you have 16,777,216 cells to use in every worksheet, and there can be as many as 255 worksheets within a workbook. With so many cells available, it makes sense to focus on modifying cells and worksheet contents as you continue developing your Excel skills.

Do you need just a few cells inserted or deleted within an existing worksheet? You can produce the desired result without adding or removing an entire row or column. Is there a word or phrase that you want to substitute for another? After applying the same format multiple times do you wish that you had used a different format? Excel supports replacing cell formats as well as cell contents. Are there minor adjustments you want to apply to clip art or pictures? A variety of edits are possible, such as fine-tuning contrast, controlling brightness, flipping the object, and changing its rotation.

Perhaps you want to modify cells by using Edit, Paste Special instead of Edit, Paste. For example, you can paste only the comments attached to copied cells instead of pasting cell contents, formats, and comments. Excel also supports saving the workbook itself in other formats.

👁 VISUAL SUMMARY

Figure 3.1 illustrates the changes to make in the first five lessons. After you insert and delete cells, you perform two replace operations: one replacing cell contents, and the other replacing cell formats. You also modify the appearance of both clips.

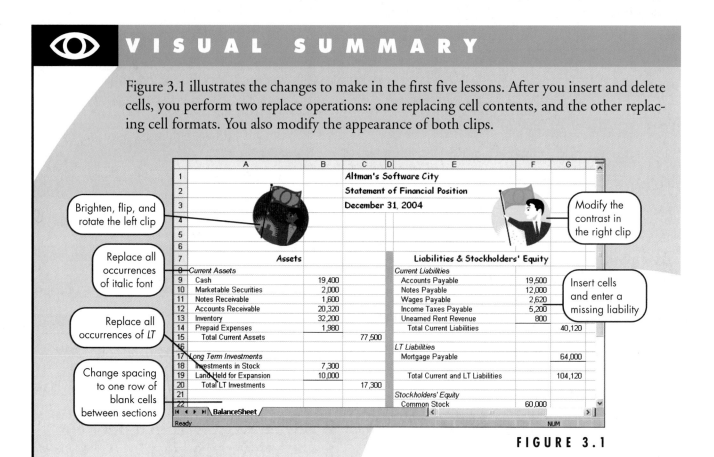

- Brighten, flip, and rotate the left clip
- Replace all occurrences of italic font
- Replace all occurrences of *LT*
- Change spacing to one row of blank cells between sections
- Modify the contrast in the right clip
- Insert cells and enter a missing liability

FIGURE 3.1

You continue by modifying the contents of another worksheet using the Paste Special dialog box (see Figure 3.2). In the last lesson, you save the workbook in a CSV (comma-separated values) format.

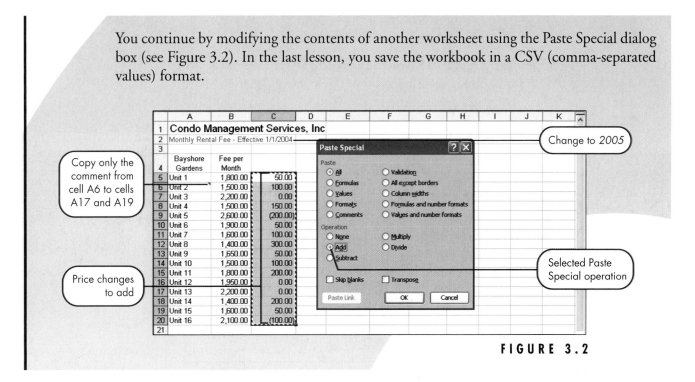

FIGURE 3.2

LESSON 1: Inserting and Deleting Cells

If you need blank cells within the existing cell content, you can insert columns or rows. You can also insert cells in a specified range and shift existing cell contents in that range right or down.

Make sure you understand the difference between deleting cell contents and deleting cells. You delete cell contents by selecting the range of cells and pressing Del. The result is a set of blank cells in the selected range because adjacent cell content does not move.

You delete cells by selecting the range of cells and choosing Edit, Delete. You also specify that adjacent cell content should move left or up. The results do not include a set of blank cells because adjacent cell content shifts in the specified direction.

In the following steps, you insert three cells in the Current Liabilities section of a Statement of Financial Position and enter a missing liability—Interest Payable of $300. You cannot insert a row to accommodate the missing liability because that action would cause unwanted blank cells in the Current Assets section to the left. You also delete three blank cells at the beginning of row 22 so that spacing between sections is consistent.

To Insert and Delete Cells

1 **Open the *EE2_0301* workbook and save it as SFP12_31_04.**
The workbook is comprised of a Statement of Financial Position on a single work-sheet named BalanceSheet (refer to Figure 3.1).

2 **Scroll down to view the bottom of the worksheet.**
Total Assets (242,500) should equal Total Liabilities & Stockholders' Equity (242,200). The imbalance is due to a missing current liability for $300.

3 **Select the range E12:G12. (That is, click cell E12, press and hold down the left mouse button, and drag the mouse pointer to cell G12. Release the left mouse button when the mouse pointer is in cell G12.)**

4 **Choose Insert, Cells on the menu bar.**
The Insert dialog box opens, and *Shift cells down* is the selected option (see Figure 3.3).

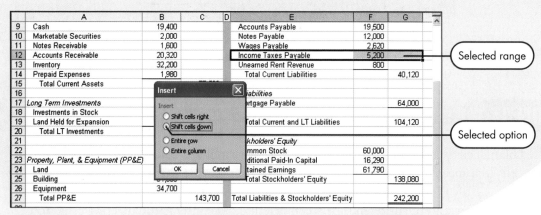

FIGURE 3.3

5 **Click the OK button in the Insert dialog box.**
Excel inserts cells in the selected range (see Figure 3.4). You can safely ignore the Insert Options button because you want the newly inserted cells to have the same formatting as above.

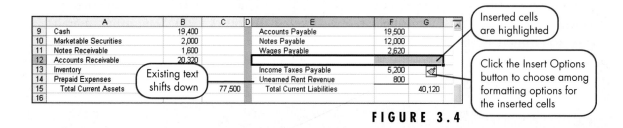

FIGURE 3.4

6 **Click the blank cell E12, type Interest Payable, and press →.**

7 **Enter 300 in cell F12.**
You inserted the missing liability. Total Assets (242,500) now equal Total Liabilities & Stockholders' Equity (242,500).

8   **Select the range A22:C22.**

The first three blank cells in row 22 are highlighted.

9   **Choose Edit, Delete from the menu bar.**

The Delete dialog box opens, and *Shift cells up* is the selected option (see Figure 3.5).

	A	B	C	D	E	F	G	
9	Cash	19,400			Accounts Payable	19,500		
10	Marketable Securities	2,000			Notes Payable	12,000		
11	Notes Receivable	1,600			Wages Payable	2,620		
12	Accounts Receivable	20,320			Interest Payable	300		
13	Inventory	32,200			Income Taxes Payable	5,200		
14	Prepaid Expenses	1,980			Unearned Rent Revenue	800		
15	Total Current Assets				Total Current Liabilities		40,420	
16								
17	Long Term Investments				Liabilities			
18	Investments in Stock				Mortgage Payable		64,000	
19	Land Held for Expansion							
20	Total LT Investments				Total Current and LT Liabilities		104,420	
21								
22					Stockholders' Equity			
23	Property, Plant, & Equipment (PP&E)				Common Stock	60,000		
24	Land				Additional Paid-In Capital	16,290		
25	Building				Retained Earnings	61,790		
26	Equipment	34,700			Total Stockholders' Equity		138,080	
27	Total PP&E		143,700					

Selected option — *Shift cells up*

Selected range

Delete dialog box:
- ○ Shift cells left
- ◉ Shift cells up
- ○ Entire row
- ○ Entire column

[OK] [Cancel]

FIGURE 3.5

10   **Click the OK button in the Delete dialog box.**

Excel deletes the three blank cells in the selected range. Text below the deleted range shifts up (see Figure 3.6).

	A	B	C	D	E	F	G
16							
17	Long Term Investments				LT Liabilities		
18	Investments in Stock	7,300			Mortgage Payable		64,000
19	Land Held for Expansion	10,000					
20	Total LT Investments		17,300		Total Current and LT Liabilities		104,420
21							
22	Property, Plant, & Equipment (PP&E)				Stockholders' Equity		
23	Land	45,000			Common Stock	60,000	
24	Building	64,000			Additional Paid-In Capital	16,290	
25	Equipment	34,700			Retained Earnings	61,790	
26	Total PP&E		143,700		Total Stockholders' Equity		138,080
27							

One row separates sections

FIGURE 3.6

11   **Click any cell to deselect the highlighted range and save your changes to the SFP12_31_04 workbook.**

Continue with the next lesson, or close the workbook and exit Excel.

TO EXTEND YOUR KNOWLEDGE . . .

IMPACT ON FORMULAS OF DELETING CELLS

When you delete cells, the references to adjacent shifted cells are automatically updated in formulas to reflect their new location. If a formula refers to a deleted cell, the error value *#REF!* displays.

LESSON 2: Finding and Replacing Cell Contents

Excel provides a variety of ways to manipulate both the content and appearance of text. Find and Replace are two options on the Edit menu that can substantially reduce editing time on large worksheets. Using the Find feature, you can search for the next occurrence of the word, number, phrase, or format you specify. Using the Replace feature, you can look for each occurrence of the word, number, phrase, or format you specify and replace any or all occurrences.

Selecting Find or Replace from the Edit drop-down menu opens the Find and Replace dialog box. The dialog box includes two tabs: Find and Replace (see Figure 3.7).

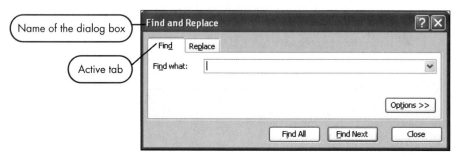

FIGURE 3.7

The Find tab displays a *Find what* text box in which you enter the word, number, phrase, or format you want to find. You then choose Find Next or Find All. Click the Find Next button repeatedly to jump from one occurrence to the next in the worksheet. If you click the Find All button, Excel displays a list of all the items that meet your specified criteria.

The Replace tab displays two text boxes: *Find what* and *Replace with*. After you enter your specifications in those boxes, you usually choose Replace All or Replace.

In the following steps, you use Excel's Replace feature to change all occurrences of an abbreviation to the full spelling.

To Find and Replace Cell Contents

1 **Open the *SFP12_31_04* workbook, if necessary; then locate three occurrences of the abbreviation *LT* on the BalanceSheet worksheet.**
The abbreviation displays in three cells: A20, E17, and E20. You want to replace all occurrences of the abbreviation *LT* with the phrase *Long Term*.

2 **Choose Edit, Replace.**
The Find and Replace dialog box opens.

3 **Make sure that the Replace tab is active; then enter LT in the *Find what* text box, and enter Long Term in the *Replace with* text box (see Figure 3.8).**

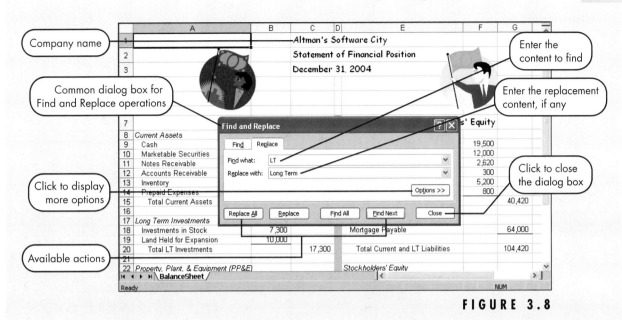

FIGURE 3.8

If you have problems . . .

Depending on the most recent Find or Replace operation, your Find and Replace dialog box might include additional settings above the buttons at the bottom of the box, including *Match case* and *Match entire cell contents*. To duplicate the display in Figure 3.8 and subsequent figures, make sure that the *Match case* and *Match entire cell contents* check boxes are not checked and then click the Options button to hide the extra options.

4 **Click the Replace All button in the lower-left corner of the dialog box (refer to Figure 3.8).**

Excel replaces all occurrences of the letters *LT* with the phrase *Long Term*. A message indicates that four replacements were made.

5 **Click OK to close the message box; then close the Find and Replace dialog box, and view the results.**

The results include an unintended replacement in cell C1. Because the Find condition was not case-sensitive, Excel replaced the lowercase letters *lt* in the company name so that it reads *ALong Termman's Software City* (see Figure 3.9).

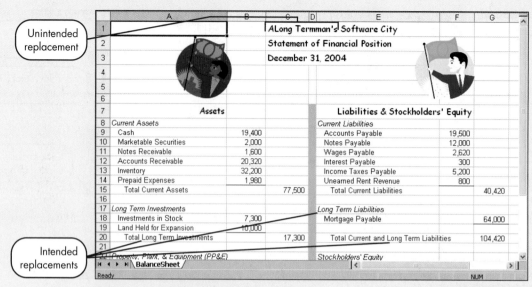

FIGURE 3.9

6 **Choose Edit, Undo Replace.**
Excels reverses the effects of the previous replace operation.

7 **Choose Edit, Replace; then click the Options button above the Close button.**
The dialog box expands. You can set search parameters using three drop-down lists and two check boxes.

8 **Check the Match case check box (see Figure 3.10).**

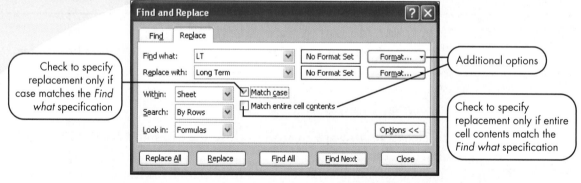

FIGURE 3.10

You specified that Excel should find and replace the two-letter combination LT only if the letters are uppercase.

9 **Click Replace All.**
Excel replaces all occurrences of the uppercase letters *LT* with the phrase *Long Term*. A message indicates that three replacements were made.

10 **Click OK to close the message box; then close the Find and Replace dialog box, and view the results.**
The phrase *Long Term* replaces *LT* in cells A20, E17, and E20.

11 **Save your changes to the SFP12_31_04 workbook.**
Continue with the next lesson, or close the workbook and exit Excel.

TO EXTEND YOUR KNOWLEDGE . . .

TIPS ON FINDING OR REPLACING CELL CONTENTS AND FORMATS

If you want to search an entire worksheet, click any cell in the worksheet and then select Edit, Find or Edit, Replace. If you only want to search part of a worksheet, select the range of cells you want to search before you select Edit, Find or Edit, Replace.

You can cancel a search in progress by pressing Esc.

You can use wildcard characters in your search criteria. A **wildcard character** is a symbol used in a filter, find, or replace operation. The question mark (?) wildcard character represents any single character in a search. For example, a search of local phone numbers using the search condition 7?7-32?? finds 727-3285 and 707-3299. The asterisk (*) wildcard character represents any number of characters in a search. For example, a search of cities using the search condition *ville finds Brookville and Steubenville.

LESSON 3:   Finding and Replacing Cell Formats

You can use Excel's Find and Replace feature to locate and change cell formats as well as cell contents. Click the Options button in the Find and Replace dialog box to display Format buttons and associated Preview text boxes to the right of the *Find what* and *Replace with* text boxes. Use the drop-down list for each Format button to specify the *Find what* and *Replace with* formatting.

In the following steps, you replace all occurrences of an italic format with a blue and bold format.

To Find and Replace Cell Formats

1 **Open the *SFP12_31_04* workbook, if necessary; then scroll to view the italic format applied to seven cells: A8, A17, A22, A28, E8, E17, and E22.**
You want to replace all occurrences of the italic format with blue and bold formats.

2 **Choose Edit, Replace.**
The Find and Replace dialog box opens. The Replace tab is active.

3 **If Format buttons do not display to the right of the *Find what* and *Replace with* boxes, click the Options button.**

4 **Delete existing *Find what* and *Replace with* specifications and uncheck *Match case* (see Figure 3.11).**

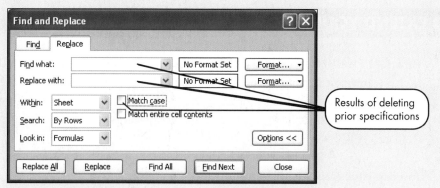

FIGURE 3.11

5 | Click the top Format button of the two Format buttons near the upper-right corner of the Find and Replace dialog box.

The Find Format dialog box opens.

6 | Select the Font tab, and click *Italic* in the *Font style* list (see Figure 3.12).

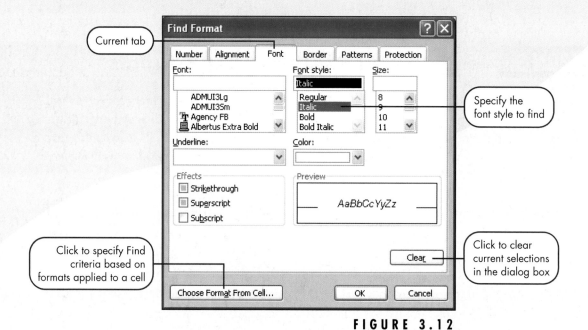

FIGURE 3.12

7 | Click OK.

The Find Format dialog box closes and Excel displays a sample of the *Find what* criteria—the italic font style (see Figure 3.13).

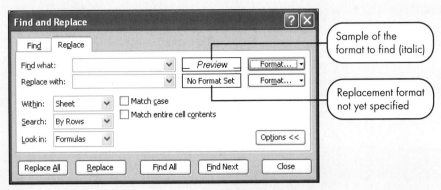

FIGURE 3.13

8 | Click the lower of the two For**m**at buttons near the upper-right corner of the Find and Replace dialog box.

The Replace Format dialog box opens.

9 | Select *Bold* in the *F**o**nt style* list, and select *Blue* from the *Color* drop-down list (see Figure 3.14).

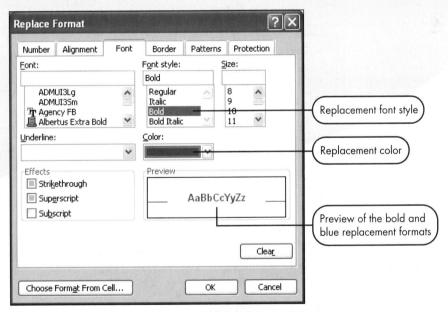

FIGURE 3.14

10 | Click OK.

The Replace Format dialog box closes and Excel displays a sample of the *Replace with* criteria—bold and blue (see Figure 3.15).

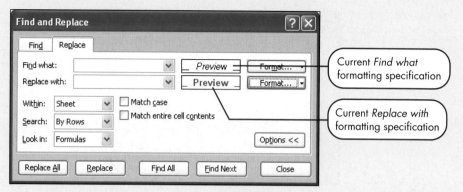

FIGURE 3.15

11 **Click the Replace All button in the Find and Replace dialog box.**
Excel replaces all occurrences of the italic formatting with bold and blue formatting. A message indicates that seven replacements were made.

12 **Click OK to close the message box; then close the Find and Replace dialog box, and view the results (see Figure 3.16).**

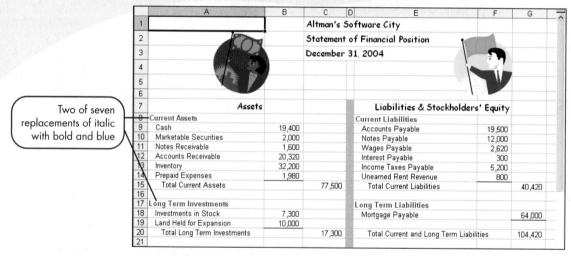

FIGURE 3.16

13 **Save your changes to the *SFP12_31_04* workbook.**
Continue with the next lesson, or close the workbook and exit Excel.

TO EXTEND YOUR KNOWLEDGE . . .

LISTING THE RESULTS OF A FIND OPERATION
If you choose Find All instead of Find Next in a Find operation, Excel displays information in a table layout about each occurrence found. Columns of information include Book, Sheet, Name, Cell, Value, and Formula.

ADDITIONAL FIND OPTIONS
Figure 3.17 illustrates additional options available for Find operations. For example, you can look for a specified word or phrase within comments attached to cells, or you can search for specified values within cells instead of their formulas.

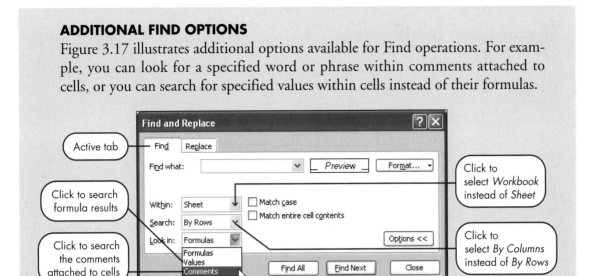

FIGURE 3.17

LESSON 4:   Changing Contrast and Brightness in Clips

When you create and revise a worksheet, the focus should be on ensuring that the labels, numbers, and formulas are accurate and complete. To improve the visual appeal of a well-designed worksheet, you can apply formatting and special effects.

If you decide to insert clip art or a picture, you might want to alter the contrast and/or brightness of the object. You can easily do so using buttons on the Picture toolbar (see Figure 3.18). The Picture toolbar provides, in button form, shortcuts to frequently used commands for changing the appearance of clips.

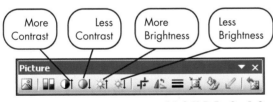

FIGURE 3.18

In this lesson, you modify two clips. You apply more brightness to one, and less contrast to the other.

To Change Contrast and Brightness in Clips

1 Open the *SFP12_31_04* workbook, if necessary; then click the clip to the left of the company name.
The Picture toolbar opens. The background of the selected clip is somewhat dark.

If you have problems . . .

If the Picture toolbar does not open, right-click the clip and select Show Picture Toolbar or select View, Toolbars, Picture from the menu bar.

2 | **Click the More Brightness button on the Picture toolbar six times (refer to Figure 3.18).**
The background of the selected clip continues to lighten with each click of the More Brightness button. Clicking the button six times changes the brightness as shown in Figure 3.19.

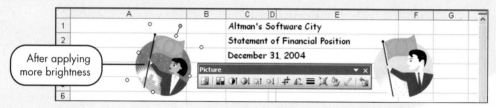

After applying more brightness

FIGURE 3.19

3 | **Now click the clip to the right of the company name.**
The building in the background of the selected clip is not visible.

4 | **Click the Less Contrast button on the Picture toolbar six times (refer to Figure 3.18).**
Applying less contrast makes the building in the background visible (see Figure 3.20).

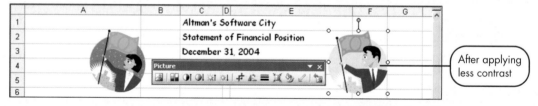

After applying less contrast

FIGURE 3.20

5 | **Deselect the clip, and save your changes to the *SFP12_31_04* workbook.**
Continue with the next lesson, or close the workbook and exit Excel.

TO EXTEND YOUR KNOWLEDGE . . .

USING THE COLOR BUTTON ON THE PICTURE TOOLBAR

In this lesson you learned to alter the appearance of a clip using buttons on the Picture toolbar. The Picture toolbar also includes a Color button that you can use to alter the appearance of a clip. Options include Automatic, Grayscale, Black &

White, and Washout. Choose Grayscale to replace color with gray tones or choose Black & White to replace color with black/white only. Applying Washout makes the selected clip appear dim. Clicking Automatic restores the colors in effect before you selected the alternative options.

LESSON 5: Flipping and Rotating Clips

In the previous lesson, you changed the brightness and contrast in clips. Excel provides additional means to change the appearance of clips. The Picture toolbar includes a Rotate Left 90° button, and the Drawing toolbar includes options to flip and rotate a selected object (see Figure 3.21).

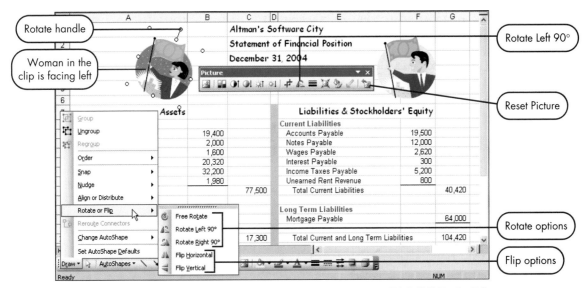

FIGURE 3.21

To flip an object, display the Draw menu on the Drawing toolbar and select one of the two flip options on the Rotate or Flip submenu. You can flip an object horizontally or vertically.

You can rotate a selected object to any angle without using a toolbar. Simply drag the green rotate handle (refer to Figure 3.21) in the direction you want to rotate the object and release it.

Clicking the Rotate Left 90° button on the Picture toolbar provides a quick means to turn an object on its left side. Clicking it again turns the original object upside down, and clicking it a third time turns the object on its right side. A fourth click restores the object to its original display. Similar rotation options are available on the Rotate or Flip submenu (refer to Figure 3.21).

In this lesson, you flip a clip horizontally. You also rotate the same clip by dragging its rotate handle.

To Flip and Rotate a Clip

1 Open the *SFP12_31_04* workbook, if necessary; then click the clip to the left of the company name.

The Picture toolbar opens, and a green handle indicates that you can rotate the selected object. The woman in the clip is facing left (refer to Figure 3.21).

2 Display the Drawing toolbar if it is not active.

3 Click D<u>r</u>aw at the left end of the Drawing toolbar, and point to Rotate or Fli<u>p</u> (refer to Figure 3.21).

4 Click *Flip <u>H</u>orizontal.*

Excel flips the selected clip so that the woman is facing right, and the image is still selected (see Figure 3.22). The persons in both clips appear to be looking toward the center of the financial statement. Now, you want to rotate the left clip a short distance to better match the alignment of the building and person in the other clip.

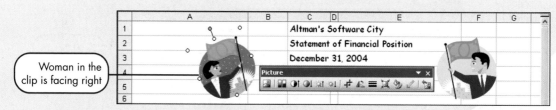

Woman in the clip is facing right

FIGURE 3.22

5 Drag the green rotate handle a short distance to the right until the dashed upper border is parallel with the gridline between rows 1 and 2 (see Figure 3.23).

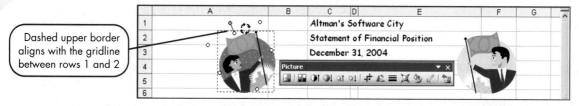

Dashed upper border aligns with the gridline between rows 1 and 2

FIGURE 3.23

6 Release the mouse pointer and click any cell to deselect the clip.

You rotated the left clip a short distance. Now the person and building in the left clip is in the same upright position as those same elements in the right clip.

7 Close the *SFP12_31_04* workbook, saving your changes.

Continue with the next lesson, or exit Excel.

TO EXTEND YOUR KNOWLEDGE . . .

ROTATING IN 15-DEGREE INCREMENTS
You can rotate a selected object in 15-degree increments by holding down ⬆Shift
while you drag the rotate handle.

LESSON 6:   Using Paste Special

You can easily modify a worksheet by copying cell contents from one location to another. The
process includes four steps: selecting the target range, executing a Copy command, specifying
the destination, and executing a Paste command.

This lesson focuses on pasting in special ways. For example, you can add the contents of existing cells to data already stored in the destination range. You can also copy only the formatting
applied to cells, or only the comments attached to cells. Figure 3.24 illustrates the options in
the Paste Special dialog box.

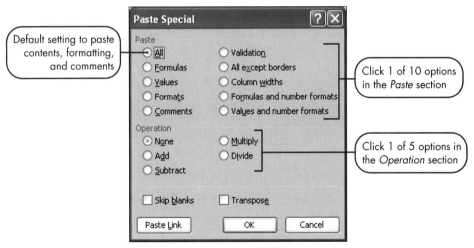

FIGURE 3.24

In this lesson, you use the *Add* option in the Paste Special dialog box to update a list of
monthly rental fees. You also use the *Comments* option to copy only the comment from one
cell to two other cells.

To Use Paste Special

1 **Open the *EE2_0302* workbook and save it as BayshoreFees.**
The workbook includes a single worksheet named Bayshore. The second column lists
the year 2004 monthly rent for each unit, and the third column temporarily holds
the year 2005 change in fee for each unit (see Figure 3.25).

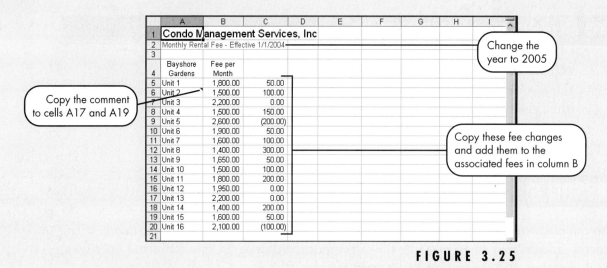

FIGURE 3.25

2 Edit the label in cell A2 so that it ends with `Effective 1/1/2005` instead of *Effective 1/1/2004.*

3 Note the fee and expected fee change for Unit 1 in row 5.

After you apply a Paste Special, Add command, the new monthly fee for Unit 1 should be 1,850—the original 1,800 plus the 50 increase.

4 Note the fee and expected fee change for Unit 16 in row 20.

After you apply a Paste Special, Add command, the new monthly fee for Unit 16 should be 2,000—the original 2,100 less the 100 decrease.

5 Select the range C5:C20 and choose Edit, Copy.

A moving border surrounds the range C5:C20. You can also copy a selected range by clicking the Copy button on the Standard toolbar or pressing the Ctrl+C key combination.

6 Click cell B5.

This selects the first cell in the destination range (see Figure 3.26).

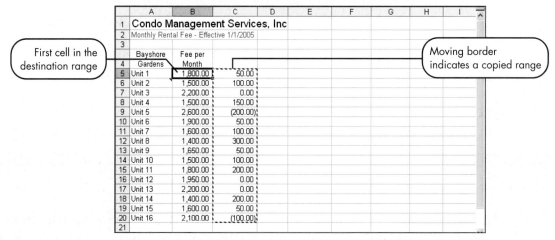

FIGURE 3.26

7 | **Choose Edit, Paste Special.**
The Paste Special dialog box opens.

8 | **Click *Add* in the *Operation* section (see Figure 3.27).**

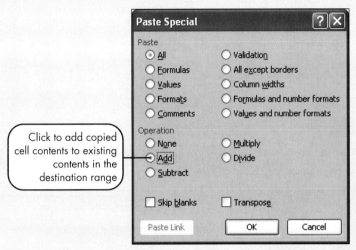

Click to add copied cell contents to existing contents in the destination range

FIGURE 3.27

9 | **Click OK.**
The Paste Special dialog box closes. Excel adds the copied cell contents to existing contents in the range B5:B20 (see Figure 3.28). The values in cells B9 and B20 are less than the original amounts. Adding a negative number has the effect of subtracting that number.

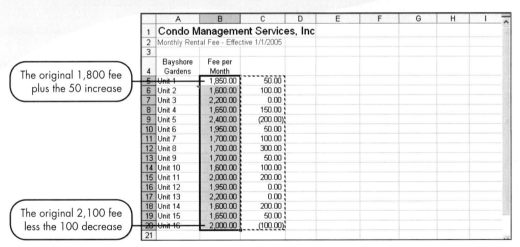

The original 1,800 fee plus the 50 increase

The original 2,100 fee less the 100 decrease

FIGURE 3.28

If you have problems . . .

If column B displays the same values as column C, you executed a Paste operation instead of a Paste Special operation. Choose Edit, Undo Paste and repeat steps 6–9.

10 Make sure that the values in your column B match those shown in Figure 3.28; then select the range C5:C20 and delete the fee changes.

11 Position the pointer on cell A6.

The comment *Minimum 2-year lease* displays. The comment indicator—a red triangle in the upper-right corner of the cell—indicates a comment is attached to the cell.

12 Click cell A6 and choose Edit, Copy.

A moving border surrounds cell A6.

13 Click cell A17, press and hold down Ctrl, click cell A19, and release Ctrl.

This selects the two destination cells A17 and A19.

14 Choose Edit, Paste Special; then click *Comments* in the *Paste* section of the Paste Special dialog box (see Figure 3.29).

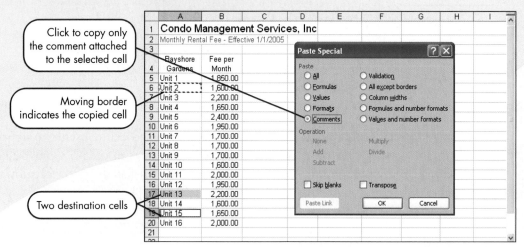

FIGURE 3.29

15 Click OK, press Esc to remove the moving border, and click cell A17.

The copied comment *Minimum 2-year lease* displays. The contents in cell A17 (Unit 13) remain unchanged.

If you have problems . . .

If Unit 2 instead of Unit 13 displays in cell A17, you executed a Paste operation instead of a Paste Special operation. Choose Edit, Undo Paste and repeat steps 14–15.

16 Make sure that the comment copied to cell A19 as well as cell A17; then save your changes to the *BayshoreFees* workbook.

Continue with the last lesson, or close the workbook and exit Excel.

TO EXTEND YOUR KNOWLEDGE . . .

ALTERNATIVE WAY TO ACCESS THE PASTE SPECIAL DIALOG BOX

If you want to execute a Paste Special operation, do not click the Paste button on the Standard toolbar. That action immediately pastes contents, formats, and comments applied to the copied range. You can, however, click the arrow to the right of the Paste button to initiate Paste Special operations (see Figure 3.30).

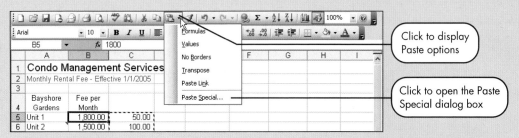

FIGURE 3.30

TRANSPOSING ROWS AND COLUMNS

Paste Special operations include transposing rows and columns. When you *transpose,* data from the top row of the copied range appear in the left column of the destination area, and data from the left column of the copied range appear in the top row. After you select and copy the area to transpose, you can click *Transpose* in the Paste Special dialog box (refer to Figure 3.29) or click *Transpose* on the Paste button drop-down list (refer to Figure 3.30).

LESSON 7:   Saving a Workbook in a Different Format

Clicking the Save button on the toolbar immediately resaves the current workbook under its current name and in its current storage location. If you want to change the name or storage location, or save the workbook as another file type, use the Save <u>A</u>s option on the <u>F</u>ile menu.

There is a *Save as type* text box near the bottom of the Save As dialog box. Clicking the arrow at the right end of the box displays predefined file types. For example, you can save as a Web page; save as a template; save as an earlier version of Excel, such as 5.0/95; and save as a (Lotus) 1-2-3, Quattro Pro, dBASE IV, or CSV (comma-separated values) file.

In the following steps, you save the *BayshoreFees* workbook in the CSV file format.

To Save a Workbook in Another File Format

1 Make sure that the *BayshoreFees* workbook is open; then choose <u>F</u>ile, Save <u>A</u>s. The folder in which you saved *BayshoreFees* displays in the *Save <u>i</u>n* drop-down list. You can use the same folder to save the workbook in another format.

2 In the *File <u>n</u>ame* text box, edit the filename to read **BayshoreFees2** instead of *BayshoreFees.*

3 Click the down arrow at the right end of the *Save as <u>t</u>ype* box; then scroll down and point to the CSV option (see Figure 3.31).

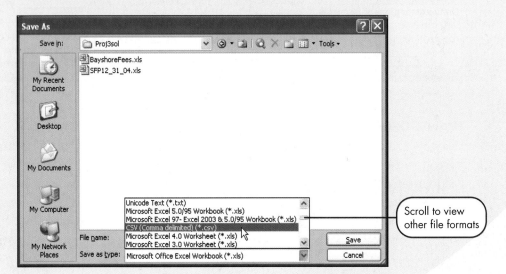

FIGURE 3.31

4 Click *CSV.*
You specified saving the current file as a comma-separated values file. *CSV (Comma delimited (*.csv)* displays in the *Save as <u>t</u>ype* box and the extension *.csv* displays in the *File <u>n</u>ame* box.

5 Click <u>S</u>ave.
A Microsoft Excel dialog box opens (see Figure 3.32).

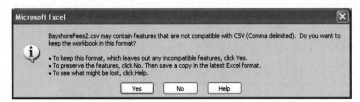

FIGURE 3.32

6 | Click the Yes button in the Microsoft Excel dialog box (refer to Figure 3.32).
Excel saves the file in the specified format.

7 | Close the *BayshoreFees2.csv* file.
This concludes the lessons in Project 3. Continue with end-of-project activities or exit Excel.

SUMMARY

This project illustrated a variety of ways to make changes in a worksheet. After you learned to insert and delete cells, you explored the ways to replace cell contents and cell formats. Two lessons focused on enhancing clips—changing brightness and contrast, flipping, and rotating. You also glimpsed the power of Paste Special commands by adding copied contents to existing data instead of overwriting the existing data, and by copying only the comment attached to a cell. In the final lesson, you learned to save a workbook in another format.

You can extend your learning by reviewing concepts and terms, and by practicing variations of skills presented in the lessons. Use the following table as a guide to the numbered questions and exercises in the end-of-project learning opportunities.

LESSON	MULTIPLE CHOICE	DISCUSSION	SKILL DRILL	CHALLENGE	DISCOVERY ZONE
Inserting and Deleting Cells	1, 2		2		
Finding and Replacing Cell Contents	3, 4, 5	3	1	2	
Finding and Replacing Cell Formats	5	3	3		
Changing Contrast and Brightness in Clips	6	1	4		1, 3
Flipping and Rotating Clips	7	1	4	1	3
Using Paste Special	8	2	5	3, 4, 5	2
Saving a Workbook in a Different Format	9, 10			1	

KEY TERMS

transpose

wildcard character

CHECKING CONCEPTS AND TERMS

MULTIPLE CHOICE

Circle the letter of the correct answer for each of the following.

1. Which action(s) can you take to delete the contents of a selected range of cells without shifting adjacent cells, rows, or columns? [L1]

   a. Choose Delete on the Edit menu

   b. Press Ctrl + Alt + Del

   c. Press Del

   d. Either a or c

2. Which is a true statement associated with deleting cells? [L1]

   a. The #REF! error value appears in place of a formula that refers to a deleted cell.

   b. The #REF! error value appears in place of a formula that refers to cells that shift as a result of deleting a cell.

   c. When you delete cells, formulas that reference adjacent shifted cells must be rewritten.

   d. Both a and c

3. Which is a correct statement about finding or replacing cell contents? [L2]

   a. Pressing Esc halts a Find or Replace action in progress.

   b. To search part of a worksheet, select the range of cells to be searched before selecting Find or Replace.

   c. In the search criteria 727-???? the question mark is a wildcard.

   d. All of the above

4. Which is a correct statement about the value 727-???? when used as the *Find what* criteria for finding and replacing cell contents? [L2]

   a. The results could include 727-9999 and 727-4215.

   b. The results could include all numbers that begin with 727-.

   c. The results could end with letters instead of numbers in the last four positions.

   d. All of the above

5. Find and Replace commands can locate cells based on which of the following criteria? [L2, L3]

   a. Contents or partial contents of a cell

   b. Formats applied to a cell

   c. Contents of cell comments

   d. All of the above

6. Which toolbar enables you to adjust the brightness and contrast of clip art? [L4]

   a. Drawing

   b. WordArt

   c. Picture

   d. Visual Basic

7. Which is not an option when rotating objects? [L5]

   a. Rotate an object right or left 90 degrees.

   b. Rotate an object right or left 45 degrees.

   c. Free-rotate an object.

   d. Both a and b are not options.

8. Which is a true statement about using Paste Special? [L6]

   a. You can click the Paste button on the Standard toolbar to access Paste Special operations.

   b. You can click the down arrow at the right side of the Paste button on the Standard toolbar to access Paste Special operations.

   c. To use Paste Special options accessible through the Paste button, check all that apply: Formulas, Values, No borders, Transpose.

   d. Both b and c

9. Which is an accurate statement about saving a workbook? [L7]

   a. You can click the Save button on the Standard toolbar to save a workbook under a new name and storage location.

   b. Excel enables you to save a workbook as a Lotus 1-2-3 workbook.

   c. Excel enables you to save a workbook as a dBASE IV database.

   d. Both b and c

10. Which is not a format in which you can save an Excel workbook? [L7]

   a. XML Spreadsheet (*.xml)

   b. Microsoft Access database (*.mdb)

   c. Web Page (*.htm, *.html)

   d. Template (*.xlt)

DISCUSSION

1. Sunset Art Auctions, Inc., is planning an art sale, and the current inventory is listed in an Excel worksheet (see Figure 3.33). Examine the objects between rows 4 and 16, and suggest improvements to the existing clips. [L4, L5]

FIGURE 3.33

2. Describe the general purpose of the Paste Special dialog box and explain the options in the *Paste* and *Operation* sections of that dialog box. Provide an example of applying an option in either the *Paste* or *Operation* section; your example should differ from those discussed in Lesson 6. Conclude your answer by explaining the *Transpose* option and providing an example of its use. [L6]

3. Discuss the difference between finding and replacing cell contents as opposed to finding and replacing cell formats. Provide an example of a Find and Replace operation that was not discussed in Lesson 2 or 3. [L2, L3]

SKILL DRILL

Skill Drill exercises reinforce project skills. Each skill that is reinforced is the same, or nearly the same, as a skill presented in the project. Detailed instructions are provided in a step-by-step format.

Before beginning your first Project 3 Skill Drill exercise, complete the following steps:

1. Open the file named *EE2_0303*, and immediately save it as **EE2_P3drill**.

   The workbook contains an overview sheet and six exercise sheets labeled #1-FindEdit, #2-Delete, #3-Replace, #4-ChangeClip, #5-PasteAdd, and Oct.

2. Click the Overview sheet to view the organization and content of the Project 3 Skill Drill Exercises workbook.

There are five exercises; you use the Oct worksheet in the fifth exercise. Each exercise is independent of the others, so you may complete them in any order.

Be sure to save the workbook after completing each exercise. If you need a paper copy of the completed exercise, enter your name centered in a header before printing. Other print options have already been set to display the filename, sheet name, and current date in a footer. With the exception of the large worksheet #3-Replace, worksheets are set to print compressed to one page.

Be sure to save your changes and close the workbook if you need more than one work session to complete the desired exercises; then, continue working on *EE2_P3drill* instead of starting over on the original *EE2_0303* file.

1. Finding and Editing a Record

You operate a lawn mowing service, and you use an Excel worksheet to list the locations you are currently servicing. You want to change the mowing day from Tuesday to Wednesday for a customer named Sandy Bell.

To use Excel's Find command to locate the customer's record, and make the change, follow these steps:

1. Open the *EE2_P3drill* workbook, if necessary; then select the #1-FindEdit sheet.

   The worksheet title *Mowing Schedule* displays in cell A3.

2. Choose Edit, Find.

    The Find and Replace dialog box opens.

3. Make sure that the Find tab is active and that any prior search conditions are deleted; then enter **Bell** in the *Find what* text box, and click Find All.

    The Find and Replace dialog box expands to include the locations of four cells that contain *Bell.* Three of the occurrences are the last names *Bellwood, Bellingham,* and *Bell;* the other is an address on *Bellflower Circle.*

4. Click the Options button to display two check boxes; then click the *Match entire cell contents* check box, and click Find Next.

    The first cell containing only the letters *Bell* becomes the active cell (cell B18). You can achieve the same result by clicking *$B$18* in the Cell column or *Bell* in the Value column at the bottom of the Find and Replace dialog box.

5. Close the Find and Replace dialog box, and change the day to mow from *Tues* to **Weds** for customer Sandy Bell.

6. Save your changes to the *EE2_P3drill* workbook.

2. Deleting Cells

You maintain a worksheet that provides a five-year trend analysis of sales. Before you enter 2004 data, you want to remove 1999 data. Deleting the column containing 1999 data would also remove labels that are needed in the worksheet. You decide to delete the cells containing 1999 data in a way that shifts data for remaining years to the left.

To delete cells, follow these steps:

1. Open the *EE2_P3drill* workbook, if necessary; then select the #2-Delete sheet.

    The worksheet includes a five-year trend analysis of sales for Flowers Your Way.

2. Select the range B9:B25.

    This selects the 1999 column heading and data.

3. Choose Edit, Delete.

    The Delete dialog box opens, and *Shift cells left* is the selected option.

4. Click OK in the Delete dialog box.

    Excel deletes cells in the selected range. Text to the right of the deleted range shifts left.

5. Click any cell to deselect the highlighted range B9:B25.

6. Save your changes to the *EE2_P3drill* workbook.

3. Replacing Cell Formats

You finished entering text, numbers, and formulas in a worksheet that generates financial reports. There are four sections in the large worksheet: a Trial Balance, an Income Statement, a Statement of Retained Earnings, and a Statement of Financial Position. Now you want to move around the large worksheet using Excel's Go To feature. After you view several occurrences of blue text applied to cells containing the firm's name, you decide to reformat the name using a different font and color.

To go to specific cells, and then replace cell formats, follow these steps:

1. Open the *EE2_P3drill* workbook, if necessary; then select the #3-Replace sheet.

   The organization's name, *Altman's Software City, Inc.,* displays blue in cell A3.

2. Choose <u>E</u>dit, <u>G</u>o To (or press F5).

   The Go To dialog box opens.

3. Type **D53** in the *Reference* text box, and click OK.

   The company name displays in blue in cell D53, the current cell.

4. Scroll down and to the right to view the rest of the Income Statement and the next occurrence of the company name in blue—cell G87.

5. Choose <u>E</u>dit, <u>G</u>o To (or press F5).

6. Type **L115** in the *Reference* text box, and click OK.

   Cell L115 becomes the active cell. You see another occurrence of the company name in blue in cell I96.

7. Press Ctrl+Home to make cell A1 the current cell.

8. Choose <u>E</u>dit, Rep<u>l</u>ace; if For<u>m</u>at buttons do not display to the right of the *Fi<u>n</u>d what* and *Replace with* boxes, click the Op<u>t</u>ions button.

9. Delete existing *Fi<u>n</u>d what* and *Replace with* specifications, if any.

10. Click the top For<u>m</u>at button of the two For<u>m</u>at buttons in the upper-right corner of the Find and Replace dialog box.

    The Find Format dialog box opens.

11. Click the *Choose Format From Cell* button in the lower-left corner of the dialog box; then click cell A3.

    Excel displays a sample of the *Fi<u>n</u>d what* criteria—the blue font color.

12. Click the lower of the two For<u>m</u>at buttons in the upper-right corner of the Find and Replace dialog box.

    The Replace Format dialog box opens.

13. Select the Font tab; then specify Comic Sans MS font and 12-point size.

14. Click the <u>C</u>olor drop-down list and select Automatic; then click OK.

    Excel displays a sample of the *Re<u>p</u>lace with* criteria in the Find and Replace dialog box.

15. Click the Replace <u>A</u>ll button.

    Excel replaces all occurrences of blue applied to cell contents with 12-point black Comic Sans MS. A message indicates that four replacements were made.

16. Click OK to close the message box; close the Find and Replace dialog box, and view the results.

17. Save your changes to the *EE2_P3drill* workbook.

4. Modifying Clips

You've added two clips to enhance the appearance of a worksheet that tracks revenues for your golf course. Now you want to flip the clips and make minor adjustments to contrast and brightness.

To modify the clips, follow these steps:

1. Open the *EE2_P3drill* workbook, if necessary; then select the #4-ChangeClip sheet.

   The worksheet includes two images: a female golfer facing left, and a view of a hole on a golf course in which the flag displays near the left side of the green and clouds are visible in the background.

2. Click within the clip of the female golfer; then display the Drawing toolbar if it is not active.

3. Click Draw at the left end of the Drawing toolbar, point to Rotate or Flip, and click Flip Horizontal.

   Excel flips the selected clip so that the woman is facing right.

4. Click within the image of the hole on a golf course.

5. Repeat the process described in step 3 to flip the selected image horizontally.

   The flag displays near the right side of the green, instead of near the left side. The clip is still selected.

6. Display the Picture toolbar if it is not active; then click the More Brightness button several times.

   The background of the selected clip continues to lighten with each click of the More Brightness button. The clouds are no longer visible in the background.

7. Click the Less Brightness, More Brightness, Less Contrast, and More Contrast buttons on the Picture toolbar until you are satisfied with the appearance of the golf course clip.

8. Deselect the clip and save your changes to the *EE2_P3drill* workbook.

5. Using the Add Option in the Paste Special Dialog Box

You manage a small business selling assorted "care packages" throughout the year. Sales are made to students by a group of 20 students, and you keep a running total of individual unit sales on an Excel worksheet. Now it's time to update the year-to-date (YTD) unit sales, and you want to use Excel's Paste Special feature to add the October values to the YTD values.

To add values to existing values using a Paste Special command, follow these steps:

1. Open the *EE2_P3drill* workbook, if necessary; then select the #5-PasteAdd sheet.

   The year-to-date unit sales display in the range B9:B28.

2. Click the Oct sheet tab to the right of the #5-PasteAdd sheet.

   The individual unit sales for October display in the range B6:B25.

3. Select the range B6:B25 in the Oct sheet, and click Copy on the Standard toolbar.

4. Click the #5-PasteAdd sheet tab, and click cell B9.

   The value 149 displays in cell B9 and in the formula bar. After you add Abby's October unit sales (14) to her current YTD sales (149), the value 163 should display in cell B9. After you add Amy's October unit sales (10) to her current YTD sales (140), the value 150 should display in cell B10.

5. Choose Edit, Paste Special; then click Add in the Operation section of the Paste Special dialog box, and click OK.

   The values for all students are updated to reflect the units sold in October.

6. Make sure that the values from the range B6:B25 on the Oct sheet are added to values in the range B9:B28 on the #5-PasteAdd sheet.

 If you have problems . . .

If the values 14 and 10 display in cells B9 and B10 of the #5-PasteAdd worksheet—instead of the values 163 and 150, respectively—you selected Paste instead of Paste Special. Choose Edit, Undo Paste and repeat the steps using Paste Special.

---

7. Enter **October** in place of September in cell B6, and save your changes to the *EE2_P3drill* workbook.

CHALLENGE

Challenge exercises expand on or are somewhat related to skills that are presented in the lessons. Each exercise provides a brief narrative introduction, followed by instructions in a numbered-step format that are not as detailed as those in the Skill Drill section.

Before beginning your first Project 3 Challenge exercise, complete the following steps:

1. Open the file named *EE2_0304,* and immediately save it as **EE2_P3challenge**.

   The *EE2_P3challenge* workbook contains six sheets: an overview, and five exercise sheets named #1-FlipClip, #2-ReplaceWord, #3-Comment, #4-Divide, and #5-Transpose.

2. Click the Overview sheet to view the organization of the Project 3 Challenge Exercises workbook.

Each exercise is independent of the others, so you may complete them in any order. Be sure to save the workbook after completing each exercise. If you need a paper copy of the completed exercise, enter your name centered in a header before printing. Other print options have already been set to print compressed to one page and to display the filename, sheet name, and current date in a footer.

If you need more than one work session to complete the desired exercises, continue working on *EE2_P3challenge* instead of starting over on the original *EE2_0304* file.

1. Flipping a Clip and Saving a Worksheet as a Web Page

You are compiling some statistics on the sale of two products. You want to flip the related image upside down, and then set up the worksheet to display as a Web page for others to review. To produce the desired effects, follow these steps:

1. Open the *EE2_P3challenge* workbook, if necessary; then select the #1-FlipClip sheet.

2. Select the clip, and use an option on the Drawing toolbar to flip the clip vertically.

3. Apply the Sand texture as background fill for the clip.

4. Save your changes to the *EE2_P3challenge* workbook.

5. Copy the #1-FlipClip worksheet to a new workbook.

6. Save that new workbook as a Single File Web Page using the name **Baseball.mht**; then close the file.

7. View *Baseball.mht* in your Web browser; then close the browser.

2. Replacing the Entire Contents of a Cell

Your firm is changing the name of the Sales department to the Distribution department. The name of the Sales Rep position won't change. To use Excel's Replace feature to edit an employee list, follow these steps:

1. Open the *EE2_P3challenge* workbook, if necessary; then select the #2-ReplaceWord sheet.

2. Open the Find and Replace dialog box.

3. Specify the settings to replace **Sales** with **Distribution** as intended.

4. Execute the Replace operation, and check that the replacement produced the desired results (15 replacements). Make sure that *Sales Rep* in the Position column did not change to *Distribution Rep*.

5. Save your changes to the *EE2_P3challenge* workbook.

3. Using Paste Special to Copy a Comment

You are developing a list of state parks that you would like to visit. At this point, the list is limited to parks in Indiana and Ohio. Temporarily the state parks in Ohio are identified with a blue font, and an identifying comment is attached to the first cell for an Ohio park. You want to copy the comment to other cells that contain the name of an Ohio park, and remove the blue font color. To make the desired changes, follow these steps:

1. Open the *EE2_P3challenge* workbook, if necessary; then select the #3-Comment sheet.

2. Copy the cell containing the attached comment.

3. Select the remaining cells formatted with a blue font.

4. Open the Paste Special dialog box, and select the setting to paste only comments.

5. Execute the Paste Special operation, and check that the paste produced the desired results.

6. Remove the blue font from four cells, and save your changes to the *EE2_P3challenge* workbook.

4. Using Paste Special to Convert Whole Numbers to Percentages

You entered scores earned on a first aid exam as numbers, and now wish that you had entered them as percentages. You want to convert the numbers to percentages by applying a Divide operation using Paste Special. Follow these steps:

1. Open the *EE2_P3challenge* workbook, if necessary; then select the #4-Divide sheet.

2. Enter **100** in cell C7, and then copy the number 100 to the range C8:C26.

3. Copy the range C7:C26; then click cell B7.

4. Open the Paste Special dialog box, specify a Divide operation, and execute the paste.

5. Deselect the destination range and press (Esc) to remove the moving border from copied cells; then format the range B7:B26 to display percentages (zero decimal places).

6. Erase the 100s you entered in the range C7:C26.

7. Save your changes to the *EE2_P3challenge* workbook.

5. Using Paste Special to Transpose Text

You play golf with the same foursome once a week. You set up a worksheet for tracking the scores, and have been using it for six weeks. You designed the worksheet so that each new score would be entered in the next column. Now you wish that you had designed the worksheet to show each week's score in the next row. That way, you could still print results on one page after 24 weeks of golf.

To use Paste Special to transpose the text, follow these steps:

1. Open the *EE2_P3challenge* workbook, if necessary; then select the #5-Transpose sheet.

   The worksheet tracks the golf scores of four people for six weeks. For example, Jordan's Week 2 score is 85 for 18 holes of golf.

2. Search for online Help on transposing, and read the related topic(s); then close the Microsoft Excel Help window and the Search Results task pane.

3. Copy the range A10:G14.

4. Click a blank cell in column A below the copied range.

5. Open the Paste Special dialog box and specify a Transpose operation; then execute the paste, deselect the destination range, and clear the moving border around the copied cells.

6. Make sure that the golfers' names display in columns instead of rows, that each week's scores display in a row instead of a column, and that golf scores are correct.

   For example, Jordan's score should still be 85 for Week 2.

7. Delete the original data, and remove extra blank rows, if any, between the WordArt and the golf scores.

8. Right-align the names of the players, and save your changes to the *EE2_P3challenge* workbook.

DISCOVERY ZONE

Discovery Zone exercises require advanced knowledge of topics presented in *Essentials* lessons, application of skills from multiple lessons, or self-directed learning of new skills.

Before beginning your first Project 3 Discovery Zone exercise, complete the following steps:

1. Open the file named *EE2_0305* and immediately save it as **EE2_P3discovery**.

   The *EE2_P3discovery* workbook contains four sheets: an overview, and three exercise sheets named #1-Washout, #2-Values, and #3-WebClip.

2. Select the Overview worksheet to view the organization of the Project 3 Discovery Zone Exercises workbook.

Each exercise is independent of the others, so you may complete them in any order. Be sure to save the workbook after completing each exercise. If you need a paper copy of the completed exercise, enter your name centered in a header before printing. Other print options have already been set to print compressed to one page and to display the filename, sheet name, and current date in a footer.

Be sure to save your changes and close the workbook if you need more than one work session to complete the desired exercises. Then, continue working on *EE2_P3discovery* instead of starting over on the original *EE2_0305* file.

1. Applying Washout to an Inserted Clip

You frequently revise worksheets, and you want a unique way to make it clear that a worksheet is not yet final. You decide to position a washed out "Coming Soon" clip across the initial draft of the #1-Washout sheet in the *EE2_P3discovery* workbook (see Figure 3.34). Insert *EE2_0306.gif* (if necessary, use onscreen Help to review the process to insert a picture from a file). Move, size, and rotate the clip as necessary, and apply the washed-out effect.

		Qtr 1	Qtr 2	Qtr 3	Qtr 4	Annual
1	Project 3 Discovery Zone: Apply washout to an inserted clip					
2						
3	Budget: Year 2005 Revenues					
4	Glenn Lakes Golf Course					
5						
6		Qtr 1	Qtr 2	Qtr 3	Qtr 4	Annual
7	Greens Fees	420,000	385,000	227,000	362,000	1,394,000
8	Golf Lessons	98,000	14,800	5,930	78,200	292,900
9	Pro Shop Sales	55,000	43,200	5,200	123,400	262,200
10						
11	Total Revenue	573,000	488,400	324,100	563,600	1,949,100
12						
13						
14						

FIGURE 3.34

2. Using Paste Special to Convert Formulas to Values

You want to revise a price list by applying the same percentage increase to all items. You are ready to compute the new selling prices for 20 items using the #2-Values sheet in the *EE2_P3discovery* workbook. Figure 3.35 illustrates the upper portion of that worksheet).

	A	B	C	D	E	F	G	H
1	Project 3 Discovery Zone: Use Paste Special to convert formulas to values							
2								
3	Bayshore Bargains Price List							
4								
5		10%	<-- price increase					
6								
7		Current Selling Price	New Selling Price					
8	Item #1	10.00						
9	Item #2	56.00						
10	Item #3	75.00						

FIGURE 3.35

After you compute the new selling prices, you want to convert the formula results to values, and remove all traces of the old prices and your calculations. Figure 3.36 shows the upper portion of the modified worksheet you have in mind.

	A	B	C	D	E	F	G	H
1	Project 3 Discovery Zone: Use Paste Special to convert formulas to values							
2								
3	Bayshore Bargains Price List							
4	Item #1	11.00						
5	Item #2	61.60						
6	Item #3	82.50						

Revised values, not formulas, in column B

FIGURE 3.36

Begin by selecting the #2-Values sheet in the *EE2_P3discovery* workbook. Use formulas to compute the new selling prices, convert the formula results to values, and make other changes as needed to reflect the desired content and organization (refer to Figure 3.36).

3. Inserting and Modifying a Clip from a Web Site

The #3-WebClip sheet within the *EE2_P3discovery* workbook is nearly complete. You want to add a company name of your choice using formatted text or WordArt. You also want to insert a clip from the Web that is representative of the product or service you provide; make sure that you do not select an image protected by copyright or trademark. Move, size, crop, rotate, and enhance the clip as desired. (Use onscreen Help if you do not know how to copy an image from the Web.) Enter the date you revised the worksheet and your name in the appropriate cells at the bottom of the worksheet.

FORMATTING AND DISPLAYING WORKSHEETS

OBJECTIVES

IN THIS PROJECT, YOU LEARN HOW TO

- Rotate text and change row height
- Create a custom number format
- Apply an AutoFormat
- Create and use styles

- Create a custom template
- Use a built-in template
- Hide and unhide worksheets
- Hide, unhide, and arrange workbooks

WHY WOULD I DO THIS?

Even small changes can add visual appeal to a worksheet and improve its readability. For example, you might decide to rotate text in cells or change the row height automatically applied by Excel. Perhaps there is a combination of formats that you frequently apply to a cell or group of cells. Excel makes it easy to apply those formats as a set, instead of one at a time.

Excel provides other features to promote consistency in worksheet content and formatting with a minimum of effort. These features include defining your own custom formats, creating and storing a worksheet model for repeated use, and applying a predefined combination of formats to an entire worksheet.

As you work with multiple worksheets and workbooks, you have substantial control over the onscreen view. For example, you are not limited to switching from a full screen view of a worksheet in one workbook to a full screen view of a worksheet in another workbook. Instead there are several ways that you can arrange open workbooks so that you can see at least a portion of each. You can also hide and unhide worksheets and workbooks for an extra level of security.

 VISUAL SUMMARY

You begin this project by rotating text, changing row height, and creating your own custom format. You also define and apply a user-defined combination of formats, and apply a predefined combination of formats, as shown in Figure 4.1.

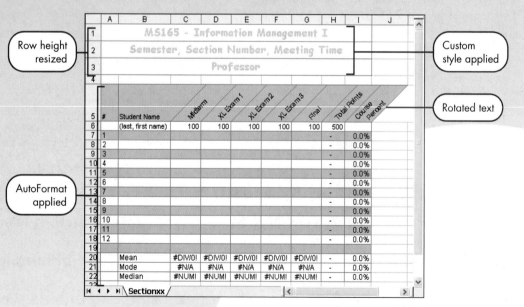

FIGURE 4.1

You continue by creating a workbook model of your own, and using a built-in worksheet model. The remaining lessons focus on hiding and unhiding worksheets and workbooks, and arranging workbooks.

LESSON 1: Rotating Text and Changing Row Height

Excel provides a variety of ways to manipulate the appearance of text. Changing the appearance of worksheet text not only makes a worksheet aesthetically pleasing, it enhances the readability of the document and contributes to a better understanding of its contents.

If the column labels in a worksheet are longer than the data they describe, you might want to rotate the column headings. Changing the orientation of text in a cell can enhance visual appeal and focus the reader's attention on specific information. Text can be rotated up to 90 degrees upward or downward.

Generally, Excel adjusts row height automatically if you apply a larger or smaller font size. You might prefer to change the height of a row as you develop a worksheet—perhaps to increase the spacing between the current cell's contents and contents in the cell above.

In this lesson, you work with a classroom grade book. You begin by changing the row height of headings at the top of the grade book by dragging within the worksheet frame. After you rotate a range of labels 45 degrees upward, you adjust row height using the Row Height dialog box.

To Rotate Text and Change Row Height

1 **Open the *EE2_0401* workbook, and save it as MS165grades.**
The workbook includes one sheet that is a model for entering grades for one course (see Figure 4.2). You see *#DIV/0!*, *#N/A*, or *#NUM!* within the range C20:G22. This range contains formulas, and calculated results display as soon as data are entered within the range C7:G18.

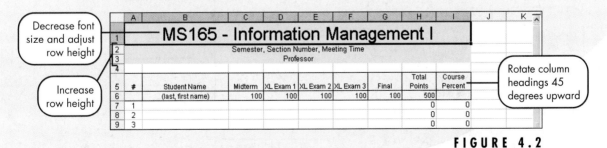

FIGURE 4.2

2 **Make sure that cell A1 is the current cell; then change the font size to 14 points.**
The row automatically resizes to fit the smaller font size. Now, you decide to increase the row height slightly for readability.

3 Position the pointer within the worksheet frame between rows 1 and 2.

4 Hold down the left mouse button and drag the pointer down to the size shown in the ScreenTip in Figure 4.3.

Pointer shape indicates you can change row height by dragging

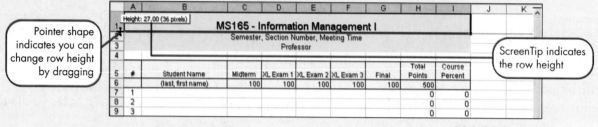

ScreenTip indicates the row height

FIGURE 4.3

5 Release the mouse button.
Row 1 is resized. Now, resize two more rows and rotate most of the column headings in row 5.

6 Repeat the process described in steps 3–5 to resize rows 2 and 3 to a height of 15.00 (20 pixels).

7 Select the range C5:I5.

8 Choose Format, Cells; then click the Alignment tab in the Format Cells dialog box.

9 Type 45 in the *Degrees* text box (see Figure 4.4).

Current tab

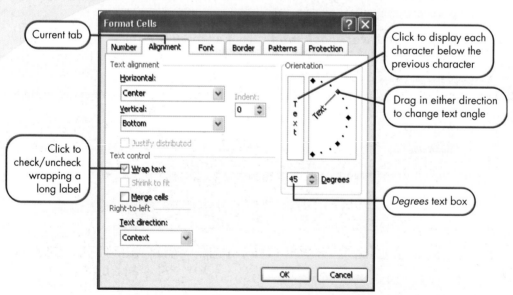

Click to display each character below the previous character

Drag in either direction to change text angle

Click to check/uncheck wrapping a long label

Degrees text box

FIGURE 4.4

10 Click OK, and click any cell to deselect the rotated range.
Rotated text does not display well within the cells (see Figure 4.5).

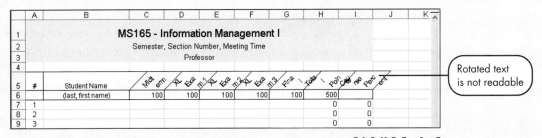

FIGURE 4.5

11 **Click any cell in row 5, and choose F̲ormat, R̲ow, Height.**
The Row Height dialog box opens.

12 **Type 55 in the _Row height_ text box, and click OK.**
All rotated text displays properly after you increase the height of row 5 (see Figure 4.6).

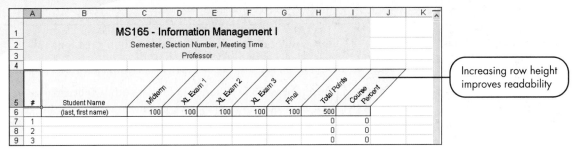

FIGURE 4.6

13 **Save your changes to the _MS165grades_ workbook.**
Keep the _MS165grades_ workbook open for the next lesson, or close the workbook and exit Excel.

TO EXTEND YOUR KNOWLEDGE . . .

AN ALTERNATIVE WAY TO RESIZE ROW HEIGHT

In this lesson, you resized row height by dragging the mouse pointer in the worksheet frame and by entering a specific height in the Row Height dialog box. You can also double-click in the worksheet frame to resize to fit the largest font in the row. Pick a spot on the frame between the row you want to resize and the row below.

LESSON 2: Creating a Custom Number Format

Formats are masks that, when applied to a cell, change the display of the content without changing the value in the cell. For a unique situation in which a predefined number format does not meet your needs, you can create a **custom number format** that Excel saves with the current workbook. The process includes displaying the Number tab in the Format Cells dialog box, selecting the Custom category, and typing the appropriate codes in the _T̲ype_ text box.

You can enter a variety of codes including codes for currency, percentage, scientific notation, days, months, years, hours, minutes, seconds, text, repeating characters, spaces, thousands separators, decimal places, colors, and conditions. Table 4.1 shows several custom number format examples found in Excel's onscreen Help.

TABLE 4.1

CUSTOM NUMBER FORMAT	EXAMPLE
#.000	Displays 8.9 as 8.900
#,	Displays 12000 as 12
???.???	Displays 44.398, 102.65, and 2.8 vertically aligned on the decimals
[Red][<=100]; [Blue][>100]	Displays numbers less than or equal to 100 in a red font and numbers greater than 100 in a blue font
$0.00 "Surplus";$0.00 "Shortage"	Displays the value in a Currency format with two decimal places; the word *Surplus* follows a positive number and the word *Shortage* follows a negative number

In this lesson, you create a custom format to display a grade in red if the value is less than 70, and to display a grade in blue if it is 70 or greater. You then apply the format to all cells in which grades are reported. Such formatting makes it easy to distinguish between grades equal to or higher than a C (blue) and those lower than a C (red). You create the custom format using the Format Cells dialog box.

To Create a Custom Format

1 Open the *MS165grades* workbook, if necessary; then click cell C7 in the Sectionxx worksheet.

2 Choose F**o**rmat, C**e**lls; then select the Number tab.

3 Click *Custom* in the **C**ategory list (see Figure 4.7).

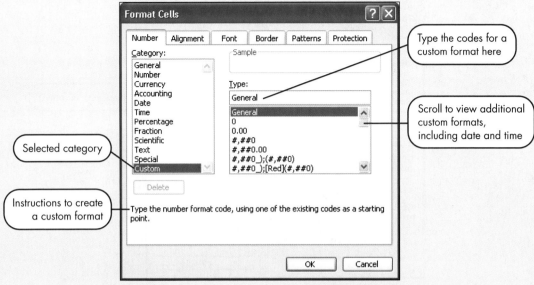

FIGURE 4.7

4 Delete any contents currently in the *Type* text box.

5 Type `[Red][<70];[Blue][>=70]` in the *Type* text box, and click OK.
Excel saves the custom format in addition to applying it to cell C7. This custom format enables you to quickly apply conditional formatting without specifying the criteria and font attributes required when using the F<u>o</u>rmat, Con<u>d</u>itional Formatting command. Now, apply the format to all cells that contain grades and summary statistics.

6 Select cells in the range C7:G18.

7 Choose F<u>o</u>rmat, C<u>e</u>lls; then select the Number tab in the Format Cells dialog box.

8 Click *Custom* in the <u>C</u>ategory list box.

9 Scroll down the list of custom formats and select the new custom format, the last one in the list (see Figure 4.8).

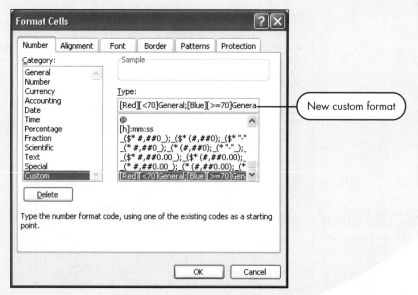

New custom format

FIGURE 4.8

Notice that Excel appended the word *General*—indicating the General format—after each condition.

10 **Click OK.**

The new custom format has been applied to the selected cells. Now test the custom format.

11 **Select cell C7, and enter the number 60.**

If the custom format was set up properly, the number *60* displays in red in cell C7.

12 **Enter the number 80 in cell C7.**

The number *80* displays in blue.

13 **Test other numbers in the range C7:G18 as desired; then delete the test entries, and save your changes to the *MS165grades* workbook.**

Keep the *MS165grades* workbook open for the next lesson, or close the workbook and exit Excel.

TO EXTEND YOUR KNOWLEDGE . . .

GETTING HELP ON NUMBER FORMAT CODES

You can use onscreen Help to view multiple examples of custom formats. Type the phrase **number format codes** in the *Type a question for help* box, and select a related topic.

APPLYING SPECIAL NUMBER FORMATS

Excel provides special number formats that are country-specific. For example, the options for the location *English (United States)* include Zip Code, Zip Code + 4,

Phone Number, and Social Security Number. If you apply the Phone Number format to a cell before or after you enter the number **1234567890**, Excel automatically displays *(123) 456-7890*. If you apply the Social Security Number format to a cell before or after you enter the number **123456789**, Excel automatically displays *123-45-6789*. If you enter a number and then select a special format for the cell, Excel provides a preview in the Sample area of how the number will look in your worksheet.

To apply a special number format, select the cell(s) and then choose Format, Cells. Select the Number tab, and click *Special* in the Category list; then select the language in the Locale (location) drop-down list, and select a special format in the Type list.

DELETING A CUSTOM NUMBER FORMAT

You can easily delete a custom number format stored in a workbook. Choose Format, Cells; then click the Number tab, and select *Custom* in the Category list. Scroll to the bottom of the list in the Type box; then click the custom format you want to remove, and click the Delete button.

LESSON 3:   Applying an AutoFormat

The *AutoFormat* command, located on the Format menu, enables you to apply one of 16 predefined formats to lists and cell ranges. Each predefined format combines color, line thickness, shading, and/or italics to give a distinctive look to a worksheet. Some AutoFormats also apply bold to text.

AutoFormats are grouped into six categories: Simple, Classic, Accounting, Colorful, List, and 3D Effects. Using the Options button, you can decide to apply or reject the AutoFormat's Number, Border, Font, Patterns, Alignment, and Width/Height formats.

In this lesson, you apply the List 1 AutoFormat to your grade book. To enhance the readability of the List 1 format, you deselect the Font option. After the AutoFormat has been applied, you add another enhancement—in this case, borders.

To Apply an AutoFormat

1 Open the *MS165grades* workbook, if necessary; then select the range A5:I22 in the Sectionxx worksheet.

2 Choose Format, AutoFormat; then click the Options button in the AutoFormat dialog box.
The AutoFormat dialog box opens. Six check boxes display at the bottom of the dialog box (see Figure 4.9).

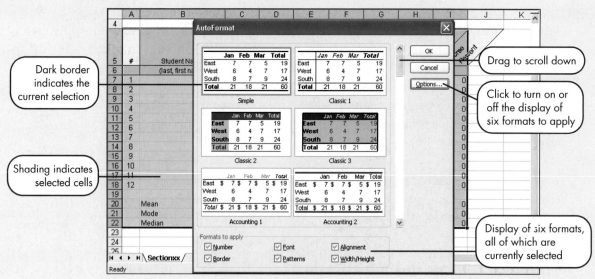

FIGURE 4.9

3 **Uncheck the _Font_ check box near the bottom of the dialog box.**
Deselecting this option retains your current font formatting.

4 **Scroll down and click the List 1 format when it appears (format descriptions display below the related format).**
The dark border surrounding the List 1 display indicates a selected AutoFormat.

5 **Click OK.**
You applied the List 1 format. Applying the AutoFormat removed the rotation applied to the column headings in row 5.

If you have problems . . .

If you apply the wrong AutoFormat and want to immediately reverse this action, you can use the Edit, Undo AutoFormat command, click Undo on the Standard toolbar, or press Ctrl+Z.

---

6 **Choose Format, Cells and then select the Border tab.**

7 **Click the Outline and Inside buttons in the Presets area.**
The border colors from the applied AutoFormat are maintained (see Figure 4.10).

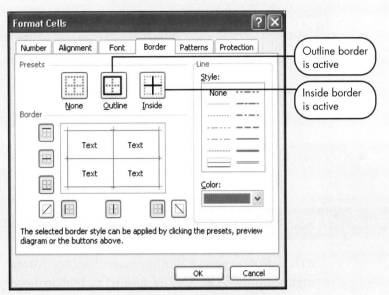

FIGURE 4.10

8   **Click OK, and click any cell to deselect the range.**
Borders surround the cells in the range A5:I22 (see Figure 4.11).

	A	B	C	D	E	F	G	H	I	J	K	L	M
4													
5	#	Student Name	Midterm	XL Exam 1	XL Exam 2	XL Exam 3	Final	Total Points	Course Percent				
6		(last, first name)	100	100	100	100	100	500					
7	1							0	0				
8	2							0	0				
9	3							0	0				
10	4							0	0				
11	5							0	0				
12	6							0	0				
13	7							0	0				
14	8							0	0				
15	9							0	0				
16	10							0	0				
17	11							0	0				
18	12							0	0				
19													
20		Mean	#DIV/0!	#DIV/0!	#DIV/0!	#DIV/0!	#DIV/0!	0	0				
21		Mode	#N/A	#N/A	#N/A	#N/A	#N/A	0	0				
22		Median	#NUM!	#NUM!	#NUM!	#NUM!	#NUM!	0	0				
23													

List 1 AutoFormat and cell borders applied

FIGURE 4.11

9   **Rotate the column headings 45 degrees in the range C5:I5, and adjust the height of row 5 as necessary.**

10   **Apply a Comma format with one decimal place to the range C7:H22, and apply a Percent format with one decimal place to the range I7:I22.**
Dashes display in the Total Points column, and *0.0%* displays in the Course Percent column.

11   **Save your changes to the *MS165grades* workbook.**
Keep the *MS165grades* workbook open for the next lesson, or close the workbook and exit Excel.

TO EXTEND YOUR KNOWLEDGE . . .

REMOVING AN AUTOFORMAT
To remove an AutoFormat, execute the steps to apply an AutoFormat, and select the last AutoFormat, named *None*. This action removes all formatting in the selected range unless you click the <u>O</u>ptions button and uncheck one or more of the formatting options.

LESSON 4:   Creating and Using Styles

A *style* is a means of combining more than one format, such as font type, size, and color, into a single definition that can be applied to one or more cells. Styles can include all of the properties available in the Format Cells dialog box.

Use styles to maintain a consistent look to a worksheet. If you want to change that look, you can change the style once and reapply it, rather than editing individual cell attributes in multiple locations.

You might be surprised to know that you already use styles. When you create a new workbook, each cell is formatted using the Normal style containing Excel's default formats.

The easiest way to create a style is to apply all of the desired formats to a cell and then open the Style dialog box and set up a name for the style. You can also define a new style by opening the Style dialog box and modifying one or more of the current formats as desired. You can apply a style by taking four actions: selecting the cell(s) to receive the new style, opening the Style dialog box, selecting the desired style from a drop-down list, and clicking OK.

In this lesson, you define a style named *Comic14boldgold*. The style includes settings for applying a 14-point bold Comic Sans MS font in a gold color. You create the style, apply it in another location, and remove the style from one location.

To Create and Use Styles

1 **Open the *MS165grades* workbook, if necessary; then select cell B20 in the Sectionxx worksheet.**
You are ready to create a style by first applying several formats to cell B20.

2 **Choose F<u>o</u>rmat, C<u>e</u>lls; then select the Font tab in the Format Cells dialog box.**

3 **Specify the Comic Sans MS font, Bold font style, 14-point size, and Gold color settings shown in Figure 4.12.**

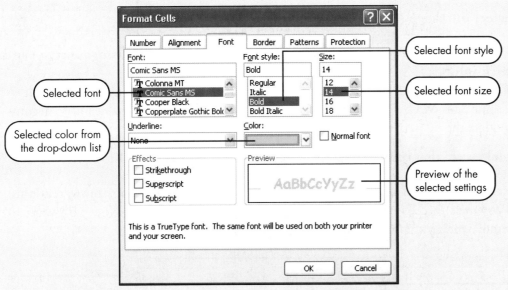

Selected font style

Selected font size

Preview of the selected settings

Selected font

Selected color from the drop-down list

FIGURE 4.12

You selected for cell B20 all of the settings you want to include in this style, which specifies only font-related attributes.

4 | **Click OK.**
Excel applies the four format changes to cell B20.

5 | **Make sure that cell B20 is the current cell, and choose Format, Style.**
The Style dialog box opens. *Normal* displays in the *Style name* text box. The font assigned to the Normal style—Arial 10—is listed in the *Style includes* section.

6 | **Type Comic14boldgold to replace *Normal* in the *Style name* text box.**
Excel automatically displays the newly applied font settings—Comic Sans MS 14, Bold Color 44—to the right of the *Font* check box (see Figure 4.13).

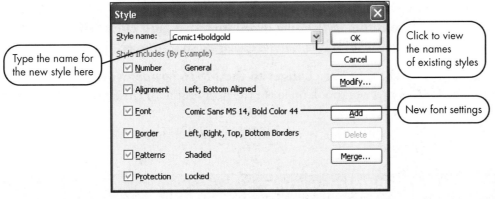

Type the name for the new style here

Click to view the names of existing styles

New font settings

FIGURE 4.13

7 | **Click the Add button, and click OK.**
Excel adds the *Comic14boldgold* style to other defined styles. Now apply the new style.

8 Select the range A1:A3, and choose F**o**rmat, **S**tyle.

9 Display the *Style name* drop-down list, select the *Comic14boldgold* style, and click OK.

The labels in A1:A3 display left-aligned with attributes defined in the selected style—Comic Sans MS bold 14-point font in a gold color. Adjust the row height to accommodate the new style and center the headings.

10 Make sure that cells A1:A3 are selected, and center the headings.

11 Resize the height of rows 1–3 as needed to make the headings more readable.

The labels in cells A1:A3 reflect the changes (see Figure 4.14). Now, you want to remove the style applied to cell B20.

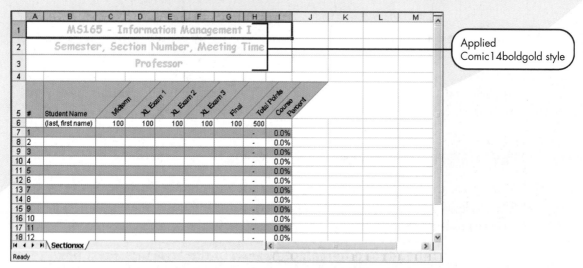

Applied
Comic14boldgold style

FIGURE 4.14

12 Click cell B20, and choose F**o**rmat, **S**tyle.

13 Select *Normal* from the *Style name* drop-down list, and click OK.

Excel removes the elements of the *Comic14boldgold* style from cell B20.

14 Click cell A1, and save your changes to the *MS165grades* workbook.

Keep the *MS165grades* workbook open for the next lesson, or close the workbook and exit Excel.

TO EXTEND YOUR KNOWLEDGE . . .

MODIFYING AND DELETING STYLES

You can easily modify or delete a style. Open the Style dialog box, select the style, and click the **M**odify or **D**elete button as needed. Selecting **M**odify opens the Format Cells dialog box. Revise the selections as needed and click OK. Selecting **D**elete immediately removes the selected style.

COPYING STYLES FROM ANOTHER WORKBOOK

You can copy styles from one workbook to another. Open both workbooks. In the workbook you want to copy the styles to, complete the following steps. Choose Format, Style and then click the Merge button to display the Merge Styles dialog box. In the *Merge styles from* list, double-click the name of the workbook that contains the styles you want to copy. If the two workbooks contain styles with the same name but different format settings, you must confirm whether or not you want to replace the styles.

LESSON 5:   Creating a Custom Template

A *template* is a workbook containing standardized content and/or formatting that you can use as the basis for other workbooks. A template has an .xlt extension, as compared to the .xls extension that indicates a workbook.

A *custom template* is a workbook that you create and save with your preferred content and/or formatting in one or more worksheets. For example, in the *MS165grades* workbook, only the students' names and grades change each semester. If you save the *MS165grades* workbook as a custom template, you can use it to create a new workbook each semester.

To save a workbook as a template, select the *Save As* option on the File menu, and select *Template* from the *Save as type* drop-down list. Excel automatically selects the Templates folder as the storage location (see Figure 4.15). You can, however, specify another location.

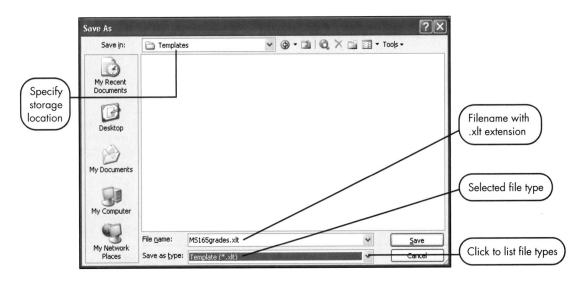

FIGURE 4.15

You can use a template as the basis for a new workbook by choosing File, New from the menu bar, clicking the On my computer link on the New Workbook task pane, locating and opening the template, modifying content as desired, and saving the file as a workbook. In this lesson, you save the *MS165grades* workbook as a template, and use the template to create a new workbook.

To Create and Use a Custom Template

1 | Open the *MS165grades* workbook, if necessary.

2 | Choose <u>F</u>ile, Save <u>A</u>s.

3 | Select *Template* from the *Save as type* drop-down list.
The settings in the Save As dialog box resemble those shown in Figure 4.15. If your system displays filename extensions, you see MS165grades.xlt in the File <u>n</u>ame text box. If you are working in a lab environment, the Templates folder might be on a different drive.

4 | If you are working in a lab environment that doesn't permit saving to the Microsoft Templates folder, specify your own folder location in the *Save <u>i</u>n* drop-down list.

5 | Click <u>S</u>ave.

6 | Choose <u>F</u>ile, <u>C</u>lose.
The *MS165grades* file now exists as both a workbook (.xls extension) and a template (.xlt extension). Now use the template to create a new workbook.

7 | Choose <u>F</u>ile, <u>N</u>ew from the menu bar.
The New Workbook task pane displays at the right side of the screen.

8 | Choose *On my computer* in the New Workbook task pane; then click the General tab in the Templates dialog box, if necessary.
The *MS165grades* template icon displays along with the blank workbook icon and others that might have been added to your General tab (see Figure 4.16).

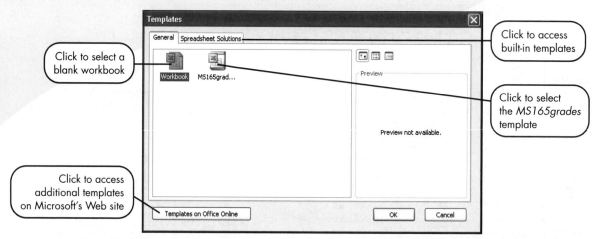

FIGURE 4.16

If you have problems . . .

If you specified a different folder for storing the template in step 4, close the Templates dialog box and choose <u>F</u>ile, <u>O</u>pen. In the *Look <u>i</u>n* box within the Open dialog box, specify the folder you used in step 4. In the *Files of type* box, select *Templates (*.xlt),* and continue with the next step.

9 Click the *MS165grades* template, and click OK.
Excel opens the template as a workbook named *MS165grades1.xls.*

10 Edit cells A2 and A3 as shown in Figure 4.17.

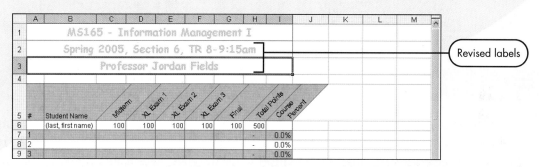

FIGURE 4.17

11 Choose <u>F</u>ile, Save <u>A</u>s; then specify the folder in which you are saving your lesson files in the *Save <u>in</u>* drop-down list.

12 Type `MS165grades_Spr05` in the *File <u>n</u>ame* text box.

13 Make sure that *Microsoft Office Excel Workbook* is selected in the *Save as type* drop-down list; then click the <u>S</u>ave button.

14 Close the *MS165grades_Spr05* workbook.
Keep Excel open and continue to the next lesson, or close Excel.

TO EXTEND YOUR KNOWLEDGE . . .

CREATING AND USING DEFAULT TEMPLATES

You can also create default workbook and worksheet templates to replace the blank ones with minimal formatting provided by Excel. The ***default workbook template*** creates the workbook that opens when you start Excel or open a new workbook without specifying a template. Excel uses the ***default worksheet template*** when you insert a worksheet in a workbook.

To create your own default worksheet template, create a workbook with one worksheet that contains the formatting, column widths, text, and so forth that you want to appear on all new sheets. Save the workbook as a template in the Microsoft Office XLSTART folder using the name **sheet**. The XLSTART folder is usually a subfolder within Program Files\Microsoft Office\OFFICE11.

To create your own default workbook template, create a workbook that contains the worksheets, text, formulas, and so forth that you want in new workbooks. Save the workbook as a template in the Microsoft Office XLSTART folder using the name **book**.

To restore the original default worksheet, delete *sheet.xlt* in the XLSTART folder. To restore the original default workbook, delete *book.xlt* in the XLSTART folder.

LESSON 6: Using a Built-In Template

A **built-in template** is a template provided by Excel that contains content and formatting designed to meet a common business need. Built-in templates include models for a balance sheet, expense statement, loan amortization schedule, sales invoice, and timecard. To open one of these templates as the basis for a new workbook, select the Spreadsheet Solutions tab in the Templates dialog box, and click the built-in template of choice.

In this lesson, you work with a template that generates an amortization schedule for a loan that requires equal payments at a fixed interest rate. At a minimum, an amortization schedule lists each payment across the life of the loan, shows the distribution of a payment between interest and debt reduction (principal), and displays the amount still owed at any point in time. You open the template, add user instructions, apply a fill color to emphasize the cells that a user can change, and save the file as a workbook. You also use the model by entering and changing loan terms.

To Use a Built-In Template

1 Choose <u>F</u>ile, <u>N</u>ew from the menu bar.
The New Workbook task pane displays at the right side of the screen.

2 Click *On my computer* under Templates in the New Workbook task pane.
The Templates dialog box opens.

3 Select the Spreadsheet Solutions tab, and click the *Loan Amortization* template (see Figure 4.18).

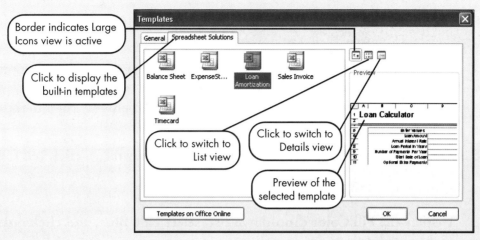

FIGURE 4.18

Excel displays the built-in templates and shows the selected template in the Preview area. A list may appear instead of the icons shown in Figure 4.18, depending on which view is active—Large Icons, List, or Details.

4 **Click OK.**

A workbook opens that contains one worksheet named Amortization Table. Loan Amortization1—the default name assigned by Excel—displays in the title bar.

5 **Reduce the zoom setting, if necessary, to display columns A–I (see Figure 4.19).**

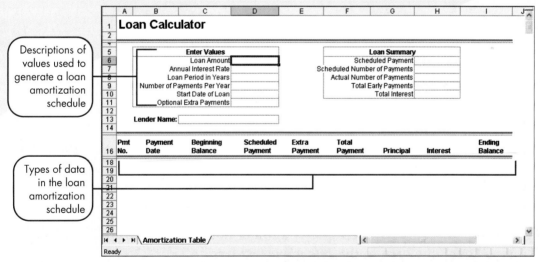

FIGURE 4.19

The model generates an amortization schedule, beginning in row 18, after the user enters values in the range D6:D11. Worksheet protection is enabled. You can change only the contents of cell C13 and cells in the range D6:D11. Now disable worksheet protection, and add user instructions.

6 Choose <u>T</u>ools, point to <u>P</u>rotection, and click Unprotect Sheet.

Previously protected cells can now be changed.

7 Click cell D1, and enter `To generate the amortization schedule, enter data in the blue cells.`

You added user instructions to the worksheet. Now, apply a fill color to the cells that a user can change.

8 Select the range D6:D11; then press and hold down Ctrl, click cell C13, and release Ctrl.

Cells C13 and D6:D11 are selected.

9 Display the Fill Color drop-down list, select Pale Blue, and click outside the highlighted cells to deselect them.

Color emphasizes the cells a user can change (see Figure 4.20). Now restore worksheet protection and save the workbook.

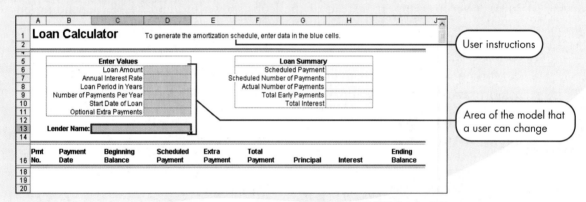

FIGURE 4.20

10 Choose <u>T</u>ools, point to <u>P</u>rotection, and click <u>P</u>rotect Sheet; then click OK to close the Protect Sheet dialog box without specifying a password or changing the user permissions.

Worksheet protection is restored. A user can change only the cells that have a blue background. Now save your changes to the model before using it to generate a schedule. You can save it as a template if you want to modify the loan amortization template provided by Excel. In this lesson, you save it as a workbook.

11 Choose <u>F</u>ile, Save <u>A</u>s; then specify a folder in the *Save <u>i</u>n* drop-down list, and type `LoanSchedule` in the *File <u>n</u>ame* text box.

12 Make sure that *Microsoft Office Excel Workbook* is selected in the *Save as <u>t</u>ype* drop-down list, and click the <u>S</u>ave button.

The revised template is saved as an Excel workbook. Now enter values to generate a loan amortization schedule.

13 Enter the following data in the cells indicated; then click cell C13.

In cell	Enter
D6	**150000**
D7	**6%**
D8	**30**
D9	**12**
D10	**1/1/2005**

Excels generates the loan amortization schedule starting with the first payment in row 18 (see Figure 4.21). Summary data displays in the range H6:H10. For a 30-year, 6%, $150,000 loan, the scheduled monthly payment is $899.33, and the total interest on the loan is $173,757.28.

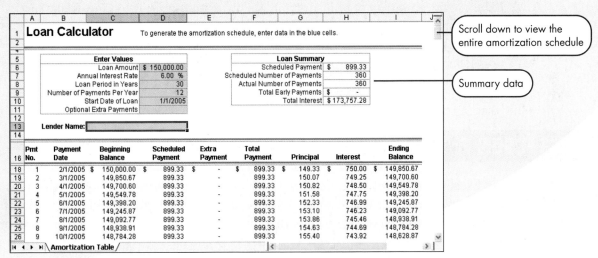

FIGURE 4.21

14 Scroll down to view row 377, the bottom of the amortization schedule.
The balance remaining in cell I377 is zero.

15 Scroll up and click cell D8; then change the number of years to 15.
Excels generates a new loan amortization schedule. Cutting the loan time in half raises the monthly payment to $1,265.79, an increase of $366.46 per month; however, the total interest is now only $77,841.34—$95,915.94 less than the interest on a 30-year loan.

16 Click cell D11, and enter **100** as the optional extra payment every month.
You can see in the Loan Summary area that paying $100 extra each month enables you to eliminate the last 20 payments—only 160 of the 180 scheduled payments are needed to pay off the loan.

17 Generate other loan amortization schedules of your choice by varying the amount borrowed, the annual interest rate, and/or the number of years that payments are due. When you finish, close the workbook without saving your changes.

In the *LoanSchedule* workbook you saved in step 12, the cells for loan terms are blank. By closing the file now without saving specific loan terms, you have a model stored on disk that you can open and use for any loan specifications. Continue with the next lesson, or exit Excel.

TO EXTEND YOUR KNOWLEDGE . . .

TEMPLATES ON OFFICE ONLINE
Excel provides a variety of built-in templates that you can access online. Make sure that you have a live Internet connection, display the New Workbook task pane, and click the *Templates on Office Online* link. Selections include business, educational, and personal templates.

LESSON 7:   Hiding and Unhiding Worksheets

If you use Excel where others might casually observe an open workbook, you might want to hide one or more worksheets that contain sensitive data. If a worksheet is hidden, its sheet tab does not display. It would not be obvious that all of the worksheets in the active workbook were not visible.

You can hide a worksheet by choosing *Sheet* on the Format menu, and selecting *Hide*. To unhide a worksheet, start with the same menu sequence that you used to hide it; then click *Unhide* and select the worksheet(s) that you want to redisplay.

In this lesson, you create a multiple-sheet workbook by making a copy of an existing worksheet. After you rename the two worksheets, you hide and unhide one of them.

To Hide and Unhide a Copied Worksheet

1 Open the *MS165grades_Spr05* workbook.

2 Choose Edit, Move or Copy Sheet.
The Move or Copy dialog box displays.

3 Click *(move to end)* in the *Before sheet* section.

4 Check the *Create a copy* check box.
You made selections to duplicate the worksheet Sectionxx in the *MS165grades_Spr05* workbook (see Figure 4.22).

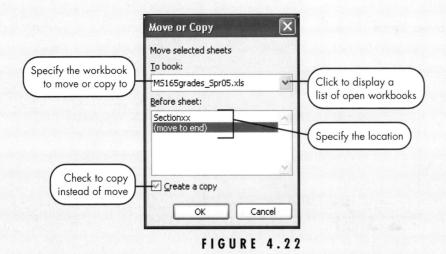

FIGURE 4.22

5 **Click OK.**
Excel makes a copy of the worksheet and names it Sectionxx (2).

6 **Double-click the Sectionxx sheet tab, type `Section06`, and press ⏎Enter.**

7 **Double-click the Sectionxx (2) sheet tab, type `Section07`, and press ⏎Enter.**

8 **In the Section07 sheet, change the section, days, and time in cell A2 to `Section 7, TR 9:30-10:45am`.**

9 **Save your changes to the *MS165grades_Spr05* workbook.**

10 **Make sure that Section07 is the current worksheet; then select F<u>o</u>rmat, S<u>h</u>eet, <u>H</u>ide.**
The *Section07* worksheet and sheet tab disappear (see Figure 4.23).

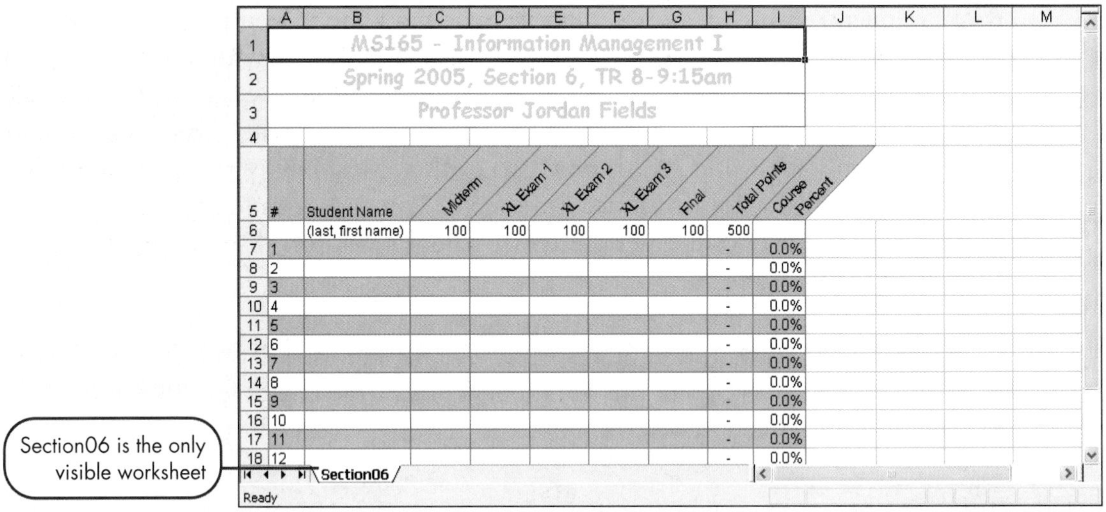

FIGURE 4.23

11 **Select F̲ormat, S̲heet, U̲nhide.**
The Unhide dialog box opens (see Figure 4.24).

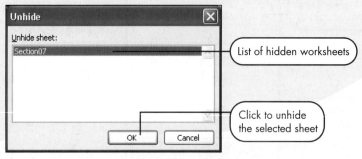

FIGURE 4.24

12 **Make sure that Section07 is selected, and click OK.**
The Section07 worksheet reappears and the sheet tab displays at the bottom of the screen.

13 **Close the *MS165grades_Spr05* workbook.**
You can exit Excel, or continue with the next lesson.

LESSON 8: Hiding, Unhiding, and Arranging Workbooks

In the previous lesson, you learned to hide and unhide a worksheet. You can also hide and unhide an open workbook. A hidden workbook does not display in a list of open workbooks.

If you frequently switch between multiple open workbooks, you might want to arrange them so that a portion of each open workbook is visible. Clicking within any portion of a visible workbook makes it the current workbook. Using the W̲indow, A̲rrange command, you can display multiple open workbooks on the screen at the same time. Arranging workbooks vertically or horizontally works well if only two or three workbooks are open. You might prefer a tiled arrangement for four or fewer workbooks. You can cascade any number of open workbooks. In a cascaded arrangement, each workbook's window displays slightly to the right of, and below, the previous one.

In this lesson, you hide and unhide a workbook containing Glenn Lakes 2004 Revenue data. After you create two copies of the workbook and edit the copies for 2005 and 2006 data, you arrange the three Glenn Lakes workbooks on the screen and edit two of them.

To Hide, Unhide, and Arrange Workbooks

1 **Open the *EE2_0402* workbook and save it as `GLrev2004`.**
The workbook includes a worksheet showing revenue data for 2004.

2 **Select <u>W</u>indow, <u>H</u>ide.**
The *GLrev2004* workbook disappears. The screen is blank and there is no filename in the title bar.

3 **Select <u>W</u>indow, <u>U</u>nhide; then make sure that *GLrev2004* is selected.**
The Unhide dialog box opens (see Figure 4.25).

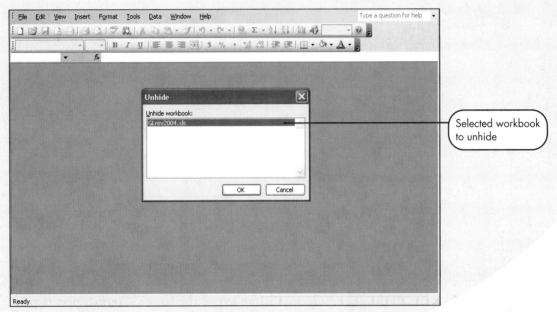

FIGURE 4.25

4 **Click OK.**
The hidden workbook reappears.

5 **Save the *GLrev2004* workbook as `GLrev2005`; then save the workbook again as `GLrev2006`.**
You created two workbooks based on the original workbook. *GLrev2006* is the open workbook.

6 **Leave the current *GLrev2006* workbook open, and open *GLrev2004* and *GLrev2005*.**
The three workbooks named *GLrev2004, GLrev2005,* and *GLrev2006* are open; one workbook is visible.

7 **Select <u>W</u>indow in the menu bar.**
The Window drop-down list displays (see Figure 4.26). The names of the open workbooks appear at the bottom of the list.

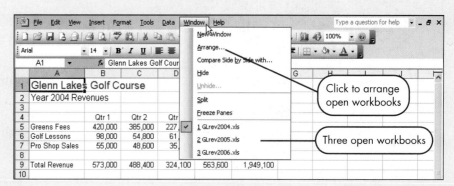

FIGURE 4.26

8 **Click *Arrange*.**

The Arrange Windows dialog box opens (see Figure 4.27).

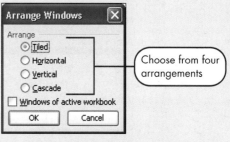

FIGURE 4.27

9 **Click *Tiled*, and click OK.**

Three workbooks display in a tiled arrangement (see Figure 4.28). The active workbook appears in the larger window at the left of the screen. Your display depends on which workbook was currently selected when you activated the arrangement feature.

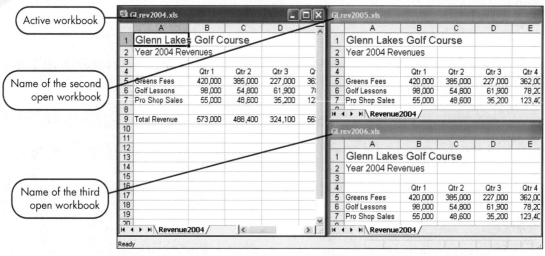

FIGURE 4.28

10 **Click within the *GLrev2005* workbook, and change the contents of cell A2 from *Year 2004 Revenues* to Year 2005 Revenues.**

11 Delete the contents in the range B5:E7; then rename the *Revenue2004* worksheet tab `Revenue2005`.

12 Click within the *GLrev2006* workbook, and change the contents of cell A2 from *Year 2004 Revenues* to `Year 2006 Revenues`.

13 Delete the contents in the range B5:E7; then rename the *Revenue2004* worksheet tab `Revenue2006`.

You made revisions in two open workbooks, as shown in Figure 4.29.

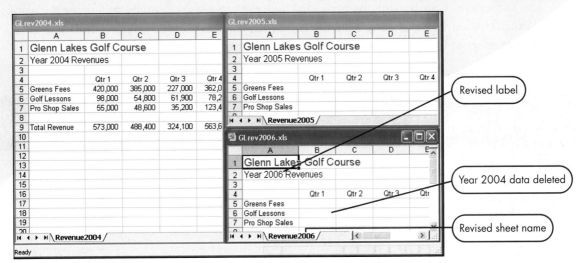

FIGURE 4.29

14 Close all workbooks, saving your changes.

This completes the lessons in Project 4. Continue with end-of-project activities or exit Excel.

TO EXTEND YOUR KNOWLEDGE . . .

REORDERING ARRANGED WORKBOOKS

You can easily change the order of arranged workbooks by making a different workbook the active workbook, and then repeating the desired Window, Arrange command. You can also drag the title bar of a workbook's window to a new location and release the mouse button.

SUMMARY

This project focused primarily on techniques to enhance worksheets with a minimum of effort for repetitive tasks. You created a custom format, applied a predefined AutoFormat, defined a style combining a number of font-related attributes, saved a workbook as a template that could serve as the starting point for creating similar workbooks, and modified a built-in template provided by Excel. You also learned to resize rows, rotate text, copy a worksheet, and hide and unhide worksheets and workbooks.

You can extend your learning by reviewing concepts and terms, and by practicing variations of skills presented in the lessons. Use the following table as a guide to the numbered questions and exercises in the end-of-project learning opportunities.

LESSON	MULTIPLE CHOICE	DISCUSSION	SKILL DRILL	CHALLENGE	DISCOVERY ZONE
Rotating Text and Changing Row Height	1,6	1	1	1	
Creating a Custom Number Format	7	2	3	3	1
Applying an AutoFormat	4		2	2	
Creating and Using Styles	2,3			2	
Creating a Custom Template	3,5		4	4	
Using a Built-In Template	8	3		4	3
Hiding and Unhiding Worksheets	9		5		
Hiding, Unhiding, and Arranging Workbooks	10				2

KEY TERMS

AutoFormat	custom template	style
built-in template	default workbook template	template
custom number format	default worksheet template	

CHECKING CONCEPTS AND TERMS

MULTIPLE CHOICE

Circle the letter of the correct answer for each of the following.

1. Which is a true statement about rotating text or resizing a row? [L1]

   a. Labels can only be rotated in 15-degree increments.

   b. Use the Alignment tab in the Format Cells dialog box to resize a row.

   c. Excel automatically resizes row height when you apply a larger or smaller font size.

   d. Both b and c

2. Which of the following is not an accurate statement about styles? [L4]

   a. You can copy styles from one workbook to another.

   b. You cannot edit a style; instead, delete it and create a new style with the desired changes.

   c. To remove the effects of applying a style, select the appropriate cell range, and apply a different style or the Normal style.

   d. The easiest way to define a style is to apply all of the desired formats to a cell before you create the style.

3. A _____ is a means of combining more than one format into a single definition that can be applied to one or more cells. [L4, L5]

   a. style

   b. template

   c. Both a and b

   d. Neither a nor b

4. Which of the following is a valid statement about AutoFormat? [L3]

   a. You can apply one of 16 AutoFormat styles to lists and cell ranges.

   b. You can remove an AutoFormat by applying the AutoFormat style named *None*.

   c. AutoFormats are grouped into six design groups: Simple, Classic, Colorful, Accounting, List, and 3D Effects.

   d. All of the above are valid statements.

5. Which of the following determines the workbook that opens when you start Excel? [L5]

   a. Built-in template

   b. Custom template

   c. Default workbook template

   d. Default worksheet template

6. What is the maximum number of degrees that you can rotate cell contents? [L1]

   a. 15

   b. 30

   c. 45

   d. 90

7. Which tab in the Format Cells dialog box enables you to create a custom format? [L2]

   a. Number

   b. Alignment

   c. Font

   d. Custom

8. Which is an accurate statement about built-in templates? [L6]

  a. Built-in templates contain content and formatting to meet common business needs.

  b. Built-in templates include Balance Sheet, Expense Statement, Loan Amortization, Sales Invoice, and Timecard.

  c. Built-in templates can be accessed when creating a new workbook.

  d. All of the above are correct.

9. Which of the following is the command sequence for hiding a worksheet? [L7]

  a. Edit, Sheet, Hide

  b. Format, Sheet, Hide

  c. Window, Hide

  d. Tools, Format, Hide

10. Which arrangement of open workbooks displays each additional workbook to the right of and below the previous one? [L8]

  a. Tiled

  b. Horizontal

  c. Vertical

  d. Cascade

DISCUSSION

1. Describe the usual reason(s) to rotate text and resize row height. Also, summarize the process for rotating cell contents. [L1]

2. Explain the purpose of a custom format. Also provide an example of a custom format that you can select from the Custom category on the Number tab within the Format Cells dialog box. [L2]

3. Open a built-in template of your choice that is stored on your computer. Pick a template other than the Loan Amortization template you worked with in this project. Explain the purpose of the template. Also describe modifications that you might make to the template. [L6]

SKILL DRILL

Skill Drill exercises reinforce project skills. Each skill that is reinforced is the same, or nearly the same, as a skill presented in the project. Detailed instructions are provided in a step-by-step format.

Before beginning your first Project 4 Skill Drill exercise, complete the following steps:

1. Open the file named *EE2_0403* and immediately save it as **EE2_P4drill**.

   The *EE2_P4drill* workbook contains six sheets: an overview, and five sheets named #1-Rotate, #2-Reapply, #3-ApplyFMT, #4-CustomTMP, and #5-HideSheet.

2. Click the Overview sheet to view the organization of the Project 4 Skill Drill Exercises workbook.

Each exercise is independent of the others, so you may complete the exercises in any order. Be sure to save the workbook after completing each exercise. If you need a paper copy of the completed exercise, enter your name, centered in a header, before printing. Other print options have already been set to print compressed to one page and to display the filename, sheet name, and current date in a footer.

Be sure to save your changes and close the workbook if you need more than one work session to complete the desired exercises. Then, continue working on *EE2_P4drill* instead of starting over on the original *EE2_0403* file.

1. Rotating Column Headings

You have a worksheet containing an inventory of used cars and you want to improve its readability. To do this, you plan to rotate the headings above the data so that they better fit over the data. To rotate text, follow these steps:

1. Open the *EE2_P4drill* workbook, if necessary; then click the #1-Rotate sheet tab.
2. Select A6:I6.
3. Select Format, Cells; then choose the Alignment tab in the Format Cells dialog box.
4. Type **60** in the *Degrees* box, and click OK.
5. Deselect the formatted range, and save your changes to the *EE2_P4drill* workbook.

2. Applying a Different AutoFormat

The Accounting 2 AutoFormat is applied to an inventory of used cars. Now you want to change that AutoFormat to one that has more color.

To apply a different AutoFormat, follow these steps:

1. Open the *EE2_P4drill* workbook, if necessary; then click the #2-Reapply sheet.
2. Select the range A6:I28, and choose Format, AutoFormat.
3. Scroll down to view AutoFormats with color settings.
4. Select the AutoFormat named List 2, and click OK.
5. Click any cell to deselect the highlighted AutoFormat range.
6. Save your changes to the *EE2_P4drill* workbook.

3. Inserting Cells and Applying a Custom Number Format

You are constructing a worksheet to display percent, decimal, and fraction equivalents for values between zero and 1. The decimal values are already in place. Shift those values to the right so you can present percentage values in the first column. Copy the decimal values twice, creating values in the percent column the first time, and values in the fraction column the second time. Use a toolbar button to change display in the first column to percents. Apply a custom format to change display in the third column to fractions.

To make the changes, including a custom number format to display fractions, follow these steps:

1. Open the *EE2_P4drill* workbook, if necessary; then click the #3-ApplyFMT sheet.
2. Select the range A5:A25, and choose Insert, Cells.

3. Ensure that *Shift cells right* is selected in the Insert dialog box, and click OK.

4. Type **Percent** in cell A5.

5. Copy the contents of B6:B25 to A6:A25, and again to C6:C25; then press Esc to remove the moving border around the copied cells.

6. Select A6:A25, and click the Percent Style button in the toolbar.

   Check that *5%, 10%, 15%,* and so forth display in the percent column A.

7. Select C6:C25, and choose F̲ormat, C̲ells.

8. Select the Number tab, and click Custom at the bottom of the C̲ategory list.

9. Scroll down to view other options in the T̲ype list; then select the custom format *# ??/??,* and click OK.

   Check that *1/20, 1/10, 3/20,* and so forth displays in the fraction column C.

10. Right-align the labels in A5:C5; then apply a Blue font to that range, and deselect it.

11. Adjust column widths to eliminate unnecessary white space.

12. Save your changes to the *EE2_P4drill* workbook.

4. Creating a Custom Template

As you expand your business, you want to distribute a standard worksheet model to other sales locations. To create a custom template, follow these steps:

1. Open the *EE2_P4drill* workbook, if necessary; then click the #4-CustomTMP sheet.

2. Select E̲dit, M̲ove or Copy Sheet, and check C̲reate a copy.

3. Display the T̲o book drop-down list, choose *(new book),* and click OK.

   You created a new workbook that includes only the worksheet #4-CustomTMP. Continue working in this new workbook.

4. Select B7:C28; then apply a Blue font color, and click Bold.

5. Select F7:F28; then use buttons on the Formatting toolbar to set a Currency format with zero decimal places.

6. Widen column F, if necessary, to display all numbers.

7. Select cells in the range B7:H28, and press Del.

   Be careful not to delete the formulas in cells I7:I28. Notice that *#DIV/0!* displays in the Payment column. You can safely ignore this error message; when the model is used, formula results will display.

8. Deselect the highlighted range; then select F̲ile, Save A̲s.

9. Type **ExperiencedCars** as the filename, and select *Template (*.xlt)* as the file type.

10. Select the folder in which you are saving your solutions for this project; then click S̲ave.

11. Close the template.

5. Hiding a Worksheet

As you work on a worksheet, you decide that you don't want it to be available for people to see when you are not around. To protect the worksheet, you hide it from view. Before you use this feature, you decide to try hiding and unhiding the worksheet a few times to become proficient using the process.

To hide and unhide a worksheet, complete the following steps:

1. Open the *EE2_P4drill* workbook, if necessary; then click the #5-HideSheet sheet.

2. Select Format, Sheet, Hide.

   The #5-HideSheet worksheet is no longer visible in the workbook. Now make sure that you can unhide the worksheet.

3. Select Format, Sheet, Unhide.

4. Select *#5-HideSheet* from the Unhide sheet list and click OK.

   The #5-HideSheet reappears in the workbook.

5. Hide the #5-HideSheet worksheet again, and save your changes to the *EE2_P4drill* workbook.

CHALLENGE

Challenge exercises expand on or are somewhat related to skills that are presented in the lessons. Each exercise provides a brief narrative introduction, followed by instructions in a numbered-step format that are not as detailed as those in the Skill Drill section.

Before beginning your first Project 4 Challenge exercise, complete the following steps:

1. Open the file named *EE2_0404* and immediately save it as **EE2_P4challenge**.

   The *EE2_P4challenge* workbook contains four sheets: an overview, and three exercise sheets named #1-RotateResize, #2-Remove2, and #3-SpecialFMT.

2. Click the Overview sheet to view the organization of the Project 4 Challenge Exercises workbook.

Each exercise is independent of the others, so you may complete them in any order. Be sure to save the workbook after completing each exercise. If you need a paper copy of the completed exercise, enter your name centered in a header before printing. Other print options have already been set to print compressed to one page and to display the filename, sheet name, and current date in a footer.

If you need more than one work session to complete the desired exercises, continue working on *EE2_P4challenge* instead of starting over on the original *EE2_0404* file.

1. Changing Rotation and Row Height

You work for Experienced Wheels, Inc., and currently you are trying out various enhancements in a worksheet that lists the inventory of used cars. You want to see if the column headings in row 9 would look better if they were centered vertically within the row, but not rotated. To change rotation and alignment, follow these steps:

1. Open the *EE2_P4challenge* workbook, if necessary; then select the #1-RotateResize sheet.

2. Set rotation in cells A9:I9 to zero degrees.

3. Set both vertical and horizontal alignment in cells A9:I9 to Center.

4. Apply bold and the color Blue to the column headings in row 9.

5. Resize the height of row 9 as desired, and save your changes to the *EE2_P4challenge* workbook.

2. Removing Enhancements

You are concerned that too many enhancements have been applied to a worksheet listing the inventory of used cars. You want to compare ways to remove enhancements. You decide to restore the Normal style to data in columns F–I, and to remove the AutoFormat effects that remain in other columns. To remove a style and an AutoFormat, follow these steps:

1. Open the *EE2_P4challenge* workbook, if necessary; then select the #2-Remove2 sheet.

2. Select the range F9:I31, and apply the Normal style.

    Applying the Normal style removes the AutoFormat effects from columns F–I. Previously set number styles no longer apply. Prices do not display a comma separator. Each APR—annual percentage rate—displays as a decimal instead of as a percent.

3. Select the range A9:E31, access the AutoFormat option, and select *None*.

    Excel automatically applies the Normal style to the selected range. Now apply predefined number styles to three columns.

4. Apply the Comma, zero decimal places format to the values in Column F.

5. Apply the Percent, one decimal place format to the values in Column G.

6. Apply the Currency, two decimal places format to the values in Column I.

7. Save your changes to the *EE2_P4challenge* workbook.

3. Applying a Special Number Format

You are planning a trip to France, and you created a list of French hotels and their corresponding phone numbers. You understand how formatting American phone numbers makes them easier to read. You decide to apply the French special format *Numéro de téléphone* to your list of French phone numbers. To apply a special number format, follow these steps:

1. Open the *EE2_P4challenge* workbook, if necessary; then select the #3-SpecialFMT sheet.

2. Select the list of French phone numbers in the range C5:C9.

3. Apply the French (France) special format *Numéro de téléphone.*

4. Save your changes to the *EE2_P4challenge* workbook.

4. Creating a Custom Template from a Built-In Template

CREATIVE SOLUTION

You discover that the built-in templates provided by Excel include a sales invoice. You want to modify that template for use by your company. To modify the *Sales Invoice* template, and save it as a custom template, follow these steps:

1. Use the New Workbook task pane to open the Templates dialog box.

2. Select the Spreadsheet Solutions tab, and select the *Sales Invoice* template.

   The built-in *Sales Invoice* template opens. Excel assigns the name *Sales Invoice1* in the title bar.

3. Double-click the italicized phrase *Insert Company Information Here* at the top of the Sales Invoice, and read the information in a text box that explains how to enter multiple lines of text.

4. Enter your choice of name for your company, and enter at least two lines of an assumed address.

5. Disable worksheet protection, and apply formatting of your choice to the company name and address.

6. Insert a suitable clip art or picture near the company name and address.

7. Enter the text of your choice in the *Insert Fine Print Here* section near the bottom of the invoice; then apply formatting of your choice.

8. Enter the text of your choice in the *Insert Farewell Statement Here* section at the bottom of the invoice; then apply formatting of your choice.

9. Restore worksheet protection.

10. Save the file as a template named **MySalesInvoice** (save to the folder in which you are saving your project files), and close the template.

    Make sure that you select Template in the *Save as type* drop-down list at the bottom of the Save As dialog box.

DISCOVERY ZONE

Discovery Zone exercises require advanced knowledge of topics presented in *Essentials* lessons, application of skills from multiple lessons, or self-directed learning of new skills. Each exercise is independent of the others, so you may complete them in any order.

1. Hiding the Contents of Cells

Open the *EE2_0405* workbook and save it as **EE2_P4discovery**. You are responsible for maintaining the HideCells sheet in the *EE2_P4discovery* workbook. The worksheet includes employees' hourly wage rates. You don't want the wage rates to be visible to others when the worksheet is active. Use onscreen Help to learn about hiding cell contents; then create a custom format to hide cell contents and apply it to the wage rates in column B of the HideCells sheet. After you successfully hide the wage rates, make sure that you can redisplay the rates in a Comma format with two decimal places. Apply the custom number format to hide cell contents again, and save your changes to the *EE2_P4discovery* workbook.

2. Save Workbooks in an Arranged Workspace

You frequently want to view three workbooks at the same time in a horizontal arrangement, and you wonder if there is a way to open all three of them in the arrangement you prefer. Use onscreen Help to learn how to save workbooks in an arranged workspace. Open the *GLrev2004, GLrev2005,* and *GLrev2006* workbooks, and arrange them vertically so that the workbooks display in order of year, with the earliest year at the left side of the screen. Save the arrangement as a workspace named **GLrev.xlw** in the folder you are using to store project files. Close all open workbooks, and then open the newly created workspace. After you have made sure that you achieved the desired effect, close all workbooks again.

3. Revising a Template from Office Online

You want to become familiar with accessing and using the templates that are available through Office Online. Display the New Workbook task pane and link to the templates on Office Online. Choose one to work with, and make changes as necessary to adapt the template to your needs. Below the original contents of the template, enter a list of the changes you made to the template. Save your work as an Excel workbook named **FromOnlineTemplate**.

INTEGRATING APPLICATIONS

OBJECTIVES

IN THIS PROJECT, YOU LEARN HOW TO

- Use the Research task pane

- Link Excel data to a Word document

- Embed Excel data in a Word document

- Link Excel data to a PowerPoint slide

- Link an Excel chart to a PowerPoint slide

- Import data from a text file

- Import data from an Access database

- Get data from the Web

WHY WOULD I DO THIS?

Sometimes your information needs can be met by entering labels, numbers, and formulas of your own in a blank Excel worksheet and printing the results. But what if the data you need already exist—in a Word table, in an Access database, on a Web site, or in some other format? Excel provides a variety of ways to bring data into a worksheet from other sources.

The reverse is also true. The data you've entered and verified in an Excel workbook can easily be used in other programs. For example, you can insert data from an Excel worksheet in a Word document, and continue to use Excel to edit and update the data. You can copy an Excel chart to a PowerPoint slide.

You are not limited to the transfer of existing data. Just imagine that you are working in Excel and want to learn the definition of a word, find an alternate word using a thesaurus, look up a stock quote, or translate a phrase to another language. You can quickly get the information you need without leaving Excel. Selected Microsoft Office 2003 applications—Word, Excel, PowerPoint, Outlook, Publisher, Visio, and OneNote—include a research service that you can use to access information online or stored on your computer system.

 VISUAL SUMMARY

In the first lesson of this project, you sample the resources available in the **Research task pane,** a tool for looking up words and phrases in more than a dozen resources. Your activities include displaying a Spanish translation of a phrase stored in a worksheet (see Figure 5.1). You also look up a term in an encyclopedia and dictionary, request a stock quote, and look for related articles from a news service.

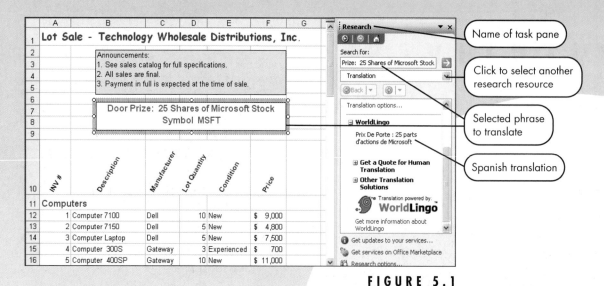

FIGURE 5.1

Lessons 2–7 enable you to sample the powerful integrating opportunities available with Excel. These lessons focus primarily on integrating Excel data with data from Word, PowerPoint, and Access. The procedures, however, are basically the same no matter what objects or programs you use. In the last lesson, you learn several ways to get data from the Web.

LESSON 1:   Using the Research Task Pane

Research can be done electronically from within Microsoft Excel using the Research task pane (see Figure 5.2). The process requires only a few steps—opening the task pane, entering a word or phrase in a *Search for* box, selecting the research resource, and clicking the *Start searching* button. When you execute the search, research results display in a scrollable section of the task pane.

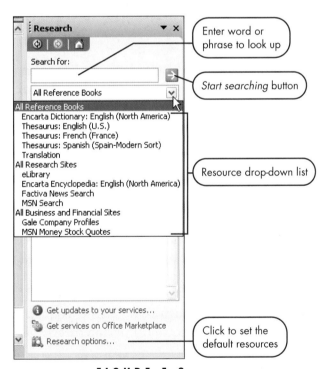

F I G U R E   5 . 2

In this lesson, your screens may not exactly match those shown in this book. The items you see in the resource drop-down list (refer to Figure 5.2) reflect the settings on your system. For example, you are likely to see at least one thesaurus. A ***thesaurus*** is a tool that enables you to look up alternative words—synonyms—for a specified word.

Clicking *Research options* at the bottom of the Research task pane opens the Research Options dialog box (see Figure 5.3). You can use this dialog box to check or uncheck individual items you want to see or hide each time you display the resource drop-down list.

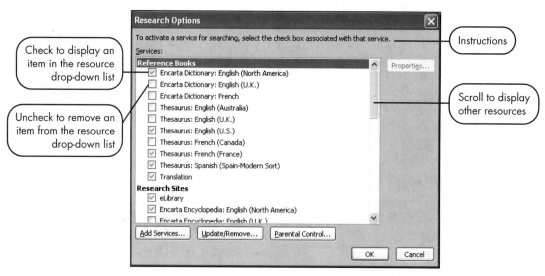

Check to display an item in the resource drop-down list

Uncheck to remove an item from the resource drop-down list

Instructions

Scroll to display other resources

FIGURE 5.3

A resource can be a service provided by a vendor other than Microsoft Corporation—sometimes referred to as a ***third-party service.*** For example, you can search for news (Factiva News Service), news and periodicals (eLibrary), company profiles (Gale), and translations (WorldLingo).

If the word or phrase you want to research is already entered in a cell, Excel provides a quick way to open the Research task pane and specify that term in the *Search for* box. Press and hold down (Alt), click the cell containing the search term, and release (Alt).

In this lesson, you complete three sets of hands-on steps. In the first set, you open an Excel workbook that lists items offered in an electronics sale and you look up several terms using the Encarta Dictionary, the Encarta Encyclopedia, and MSN Search. You also research a specific stock. In the second set of steps, you use eLibrary and Factiva News Service to research another term. Finally, you translate a phrase in a worksheet from English to Spanish.

A thesaurus and a bilingual dictionary are available if you are working *offline*—that is, not connected to the Internet. To access other resources, you need to work online.

The steps in this project are written as though your Internet connection is active. You might need to take additional actions to connect to your ISP (Internet Service Provider).

The results that you see are likely to vary from those illustrated in the figures. Web-based resources are updated frequently to provide you with the most current information.

To Use a Dictionary, an Encyclopedia, and MSN Search

1 | **Open the Excel workbook** *EE2_0501*, **and save it as** `LotSale`.
The workbook consists of one worksheet listing 50 items for a lot sale of electronics.

2 | **Scroll down to view the term** *Peripherals* **in cell A25.**
You want to look up information about this term using the Research task pane.

3 | **Hold down** Alt **and click cell A25.**
Excel opens the Research task pane and copies the contents of cell A25—*Peripherals*—to the *Search for* box in the task pane.

4 | **In the box below the** *Search for* **box, click the down arrow to display the resource drop-down list (refer to Figure 5.1); then select the dictionary for North America or U.S. English.**
Selecting an option from the resource drop-down list automatically executes the research operation. The results display in a scrollable area within the task pane (see Figure 5.4).

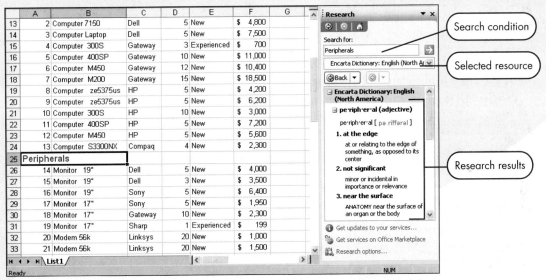

FIGURE 5.4

5 | **Click the resource list drop-down arrow below the** *Search for* **box; then select the encyclopedia for North America or U.S. English.**
The results display in a scrollable area within the task pane (see Figure 5.5).

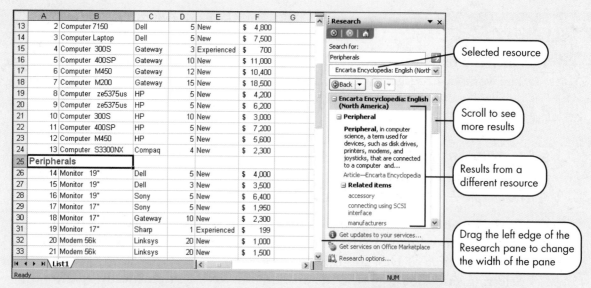

FIGURE 5.5

6 Press and hold down (Alt), click cell B40, and release (Alt).

Excel automatically researches the term *Router* using the currently selected resource—an encyclopedia.

7 Click the resource list drop-down arrow; then select *MSN Search*.

Figure 5.6 illustrates a large number of research results using the existing search condition (Router) and a new resource (MSN Search).

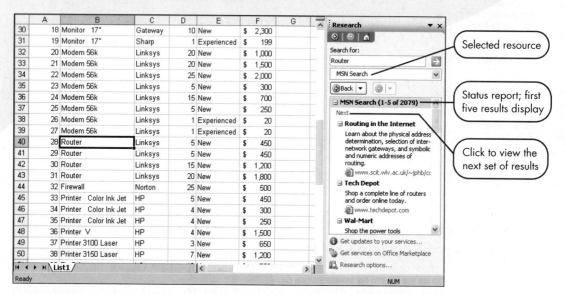

FIGURE 5.6

If you have problems . . .

Don't be concerned if your results vary from those shown in Figure 5.6; remember that Web resources are updated frequently to provide you with the most current information.

8 Type MSFT in the *Search for* box; then select the option for finding stock quotes from the drop-down list of resources.

You entered the ticker symbol for Microsoft Corporation's common stock as the research condition. Research results include information about the stock's price and volume traded (see a representative sample in Figure 5.7).

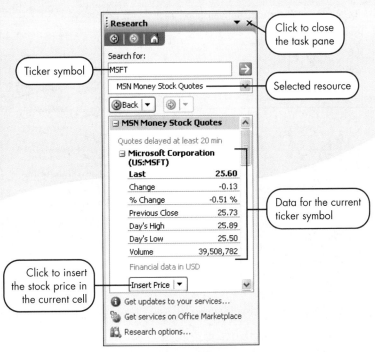

FIGURE 5.7

9 Click the Close button in the upper-right corner of the Research task pane (refer to Figure 5.7).

Keep the *LotSale* workbook open for the next set of steps.

Two other services—eLibrary and Factiva News Search—provide more in-depth coverage of key terms and phrases. If you do not have Internet access, you can learn the process to use these services by reading, rather than working through, the following hands-on steps.

To Use eLibrary and Factiva News Search

1 Make sure that the *LotSale* workbook is open.

2 Hold down Alt; then click any cell in column C containing the word *Dell*.

3 Select *eLibrary* from the drop-down resource list.

The first results appear in the results box on the Research task pane with more to be viewed by clicking Next.

4 **Select *Factiva News Search* from the resource drop-down list.**

The Factiva News Search generates a much higher volume of results (see the representative results in Figure 5.8). When results number in the hundreds or thousands, search again using more specific search criteria.

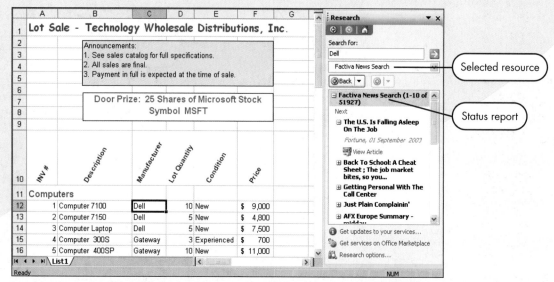

FIGURE 5.8

5 **Edit the contents of the *Search for* box to read Dell computers; then click the green *Start searching* button.**

The revised search condition produces fewer results. Keep the *LotSale* workbook open for the next set of steps.

You can use the Research task pane to ***translate*** text, changing a word or phrase from one language to a different language. For example, you can change a phrase in English to its Spanish equivalent or you can change a word in French to its English equivalent. In the final set of steps in this lesson, you display the Spanish equivalent of an English phrase.

To Translate a Word or Phrase

1 **Make sure that the *LotSale* workbook is open.**

2 **Display the resource drop-down list, and click *Translation*.**

3 **Click the *From* drop-down list and select *English (U.S.)*.**

4 **Click the *To* drop-down list and select *Spanish (Spain– Modern Sort)*.**

5 **Select the phrase *Door Prize: 25 Shares of Microsoft Stock* and press Ctrl+C.**

You copied the phrase you want to translate.

6 Select the phrase *Dell computers* in the *Search for* box within the Research task pane; then press Ctrl+V, the key combination for pasting.
You replaced the previous search condition with the phrase you want to translate.

7 Click the green *Start searching* button.
The translation displays (see Figure 5.9). You can copy and paste a translation to a cell in a worksheet.

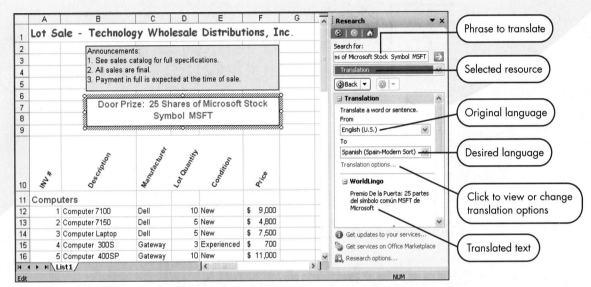

FIGURE 5.9

8 Close the Research task pane and close the *LotSize* workbook.
Continue with the next lesson, or exit Excel.

TO EXTEND YOUR KNOWLEDGE . . .

ACCESSING A THESAURUS
Figure 5.10 illustrates how to find alternative words for the entry in the current cell and insert one of the results. You can also copy an alternative word or look up words related to an alternative word.

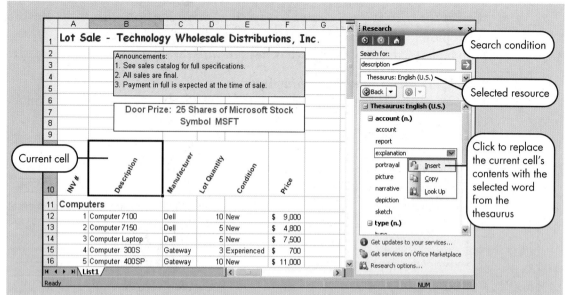

FIGURE 5.10

RESEARCHING PREMIUM CONTENT

There is no charge for much of the information that you can access using the Research task pane. Some third-party services do charge a fee to display information or to purchase books or other products. The premium content icon indicates fee-based content (see Figure 5.11).

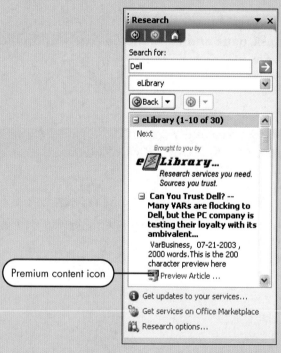

FIGURE 5.11

Generally you are not charged just for clicking a premium content icon. For example, clicking the premium content icon shown in Figure 5.11 would display a 200-character preview of a 2,000-word article. You could then subscribe to the service for a fee if you wanted to view the entire article.

LESSON 2: Linking Excel Data to a Word Document

Object Linking and Embedding (OLE) is a method of sharing data that is supported by many different programs, including all Office 2003 applications. An *object* in this context has properties, and can be referenced and used by another program. In Excel, an object can be as large as an entire workbook, or as small as a worksheet cell. Charts, clip art, and WordArt in an Excel worksheet are also examples of objects.

You can link or embed an object from a source file to a destination file. The file that contains linked or embedded data is called the *destination file.* The file providing the data to link or embed is the *source file.* For example, if you copy a section of an Excel worksheet to a Word document, the source file is the Excel workbook and the destination file is the Word document.

A *linked object* is an object in a destination file that updates whenever the data in the source file change. If files are linked, changes in the source file result in the same changes in the destination file.

An *embedded object* is an object in a destination file that does not update when the data in the source file change. Changing the data in the source file does not change the same data in the destination file.

In this lesson, you link a range of cells containing annual sales data to a sales report in Word. After creating the link you test it by changing data in the worksheet.

To Link Excel Data to a Word Document

1 **Open the Excel workbook *EE2_0502,* and save it as `SalesData01`.**
The file contains worksheet data and a chart. Now copy a range of data to a Word document.

2 **Select cells A3:E6 and then choose <u>E</u>dit, <u>C</u>opy or click the Copy button.**

3 **Start Microsoft Word, open the Word document *EE2_0503,* and save it as `SalesReport01`.**
The document consists of a title and the opening sentence in a sales report.

4 **Place the insertion point below the single sentence in the document, and choose <u>E</u>dit, Paste <u>S</u>pecial.**
The Paste Special dialog box opens.

5 **Click the *Paste <u>l</u>ink* option and then click *Microsoft Office Excel Worksheet Object* in the <u>A</u>s list box (see Figure 5.12).**

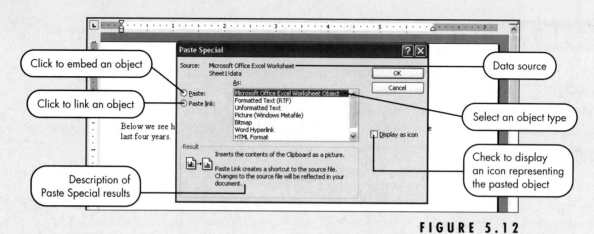

FIGURE 5.12

6 Leave the *Display as icon* option unchecked, and click OK.
The results of the Paste Special operation display in the sales report (see Figure 5.13).
Now center the object.

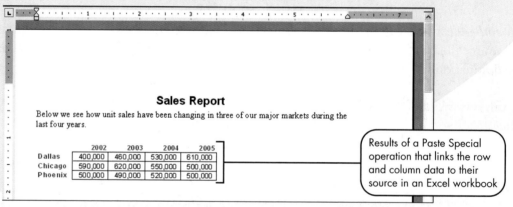

FIGURE 5.13

7 Right-click within the worksheet data and then select *Format Object* from the shortcut menu.
The Format Object dialog box opens.

8 Select the Layout tab and then select *Square* as the Wrapping style.

9 Click the *Center* option in the Horizontal alignment area, and click OK.
The inserted cells are centered horizontally. Now, test the link by changing data in the original worksheet.

10 Right-click within the worksheet object, point to *Linked Worksheet Object* on the shortcut menu, and click *Edit Link*.
If the object is not already selected, you can double-click it to produce the same results. The original source file *SalesData01* displays in Excel.

11 Press Esc to clear the marquee (the moving border) from the previous copy operation and then change the contents of cell B4 to `600,000` instead of *400,000.*

12 Display the Word document *SalesReport01* and deselect the worksheet data.
The change to 600,000 is reflected in the Word document (see Figure 5.14).

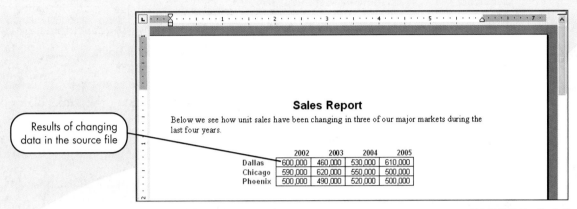

Results of changing data in the source file

Sales Report

Below we see how unit sales have been changing in three of our major markets during the last four years.

	2002	2003	2004	2005
Dallas	600,000	460,000	530,000	610,000
Chicago	590,000	620,000	550,000	500,000
Phoenix	500,000	490,000	520,000	500,000

FIGURE 5.14

If you have problems . . .

If you see 400,000 instead of 600,000, right-click within the worksheet object and choose *Update Link* on the shortcut menu.

13 Close both the Word document and the Excel workbook, saving your changes.
Continue with the next lesson, or exit Excel.

TO EXTEND YOUR KNOWLEDGE . . .

COMPARING FILE SIZE: EMBEDDED AND LINKED OBJECTS
A destination file containing an embedded object is much larger than a destination file in which the same object is linked to its source. Embedding inserts a copy of the object. Think of linking as inserting a picture of the object with a shortcut (that is, link) between the destination file and the source of the data. There are size-of-file benefits to this approach. The destination file is only a few bytes larger than it would have been without the link to data in another application. The primary disadvantage of this approach is that the link is broken if the destination file is not stored in the same location as the source file.

UPDATING LINKS

When opening a document containing links you are given the choice to update all links. The dialog box shown in Figure 5.15 presents a Yes or No option.

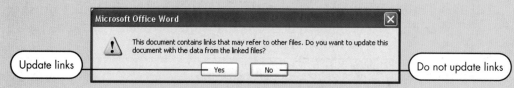

FIGURE 5.15

You can initiate a manual update of the links in your document by using Edit, Links to open the Links dialog box shown in Figure 5.16. Using the Links dialog box you can update a link manually. Use this approach if you have automatic updates turned off, or if you just want to make sure a link is updated before printing or publishing a linked document.

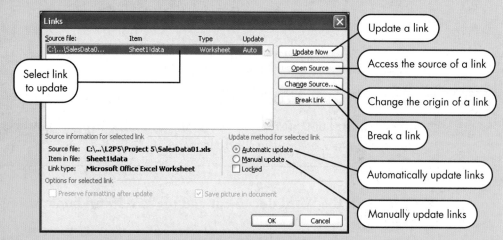

FIGURE 5.16

DISPLAYING AN OBJECT AS AN ICON

In this lesson you learned that you could link an object and display it as its source image or as an icon. The advantage of an icon is that it takes up less space and precludes its content from being printed. If the object is already inserted in its source image it can be converted to an icon. From within Word, PowerPoint, or Excel, simply choose Edit, Linked Worksheet Object, Convert. From the Convert dialog box select *Display as icon,* and click OK.

LESSON 3: Embedding Excel Data in a Word Document

Embedded data actually become a part of the destination file. Initially the results of an embed operation appear to be the same as if a link operation was executed. One major difference, however, is that if the source data in the worksheet change, the change is not reflected in the destination file. Because embedded data do not have links, you do not have to be concerned about breaking links if a source file gets moved or renamed. This is especially important if you send the file(s) to someone else.

In this lesson, you execute the same copy operation as you did in Lesson 2, except that you embed—rather than link—the annual sales data from a worksheet into the sales report. You then access Excel features from within Word, change a value, and verify that the change is not reflected in the linked worksheet.

To Embed Excel Data in a Word Document

1 Open the Excel workbook named *EE2_0502* and save it as `SalesData02`.

2 Select cells A3:E6 and then choose Edit, Copy.

3 Launch Microsoft Word, open the *EE2_0503* document, and save it as `SalesReport02`.

4 Place the insertion point below the single sentence, and choose Edit, Paste Special.
The Paste Special dialog box opens.

5 Make sure that the *Paste* option is selected (not the *Paste link* option).

6 Click Microsoft Office Excel Worksheet Object in the As list.

7 Leave the *Display as icon* option unchecked, and click OK.
The results look the same as those achieved by linking, rather than embedding (refer to Figure 5.13 in Lesson 2). Now center the embedded object.

8 Right-click within the worksheet data, select *Format Object* from the shortcut menu, select the Layout tab in the Format Object dialog box, and select *Square* as the Wrapping style.

9 Click the *Center* option in the Horizontal alignment area and then click OK.
The inserted cells are centered horizontally. Now make sure that links do not exist between the source file and the destination file. Start by accessing Excel features from within the Word document.

10 Right-click within the embedded worksheet in the *SalesReport02* document, select *Worksheet Object* from the shortcut menu, and select *Edit*.
A miniature Excel worksheet displays, and Word's menu bar and toolbars are temporarily replaced with Excel's menu bar and toolbars (see Figure 5.17).

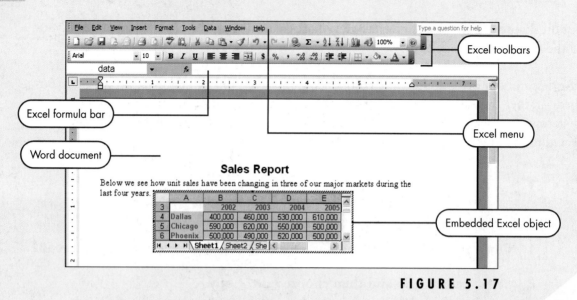

FIGURE 5.17

11 In the Excel window within Word, change the contents of cell B4 to **500,000** instead of *400,000*.

12 Click an area in the Word document that is outside the Excel window.
The object is deselected, and Word's menu and toolbars reappear.

13 Save your changes to *SalesReport02* Word document and then switch to the *SalesData02* workbook.
Making a change to an embedded worksheet in a Word document does not change the corresponding data in the Excel source file. The original value of *400,000* still displays in cell B4 of the *SalesData02* workbook. Now make a change in the source file.

14 Change the contents of cell B4 in *SalesData02* to **600,000** instead of *400,000,* and check the associated cell in the Word document.
The edited value of *500,000* in *SalesReport02* does not change. The two files are not linked in either direction.

15 Right-click the Excel object in Word.
The *Update Link* option is not available on the shortcut menu.

16 Click outside the shortcut menu to deselect it; then save and close both the Word document *SalesReport02* and the Excel workbook *SalesData02,* and exit Word.
Continue with the next lesson, or exit Excel.

LESSON 4:   Linking Excel Data to a PowerPoint Slide

When creating a PowerPoint presentation, you may want to include row and column data or a chart that already exists in an Excel worksheet. The two options you worked with in previous lessons—linking in Lesson 2, and embedding in Lesson 3—are available when integrating between Excel and any Microsoft Office application. The procedures are quite similar.

In this lesson you copy a section of an Excel worksheet to the first of two slides in a PowerPoint presentation. You paste the copied data as a link.

To Link Excel Data to a PowerPoint Slide

1 **Launch Excel if necessary, open the Excel workbook *EE2_0502*, and save it as `SalesData03`.**

2 **Select cells A3:E6 and then choose Edit, Copy.**

3 **Launch Microsoft PowerPoint, open the PowerPoint presentation named *EE2_0504*, and save it as `SalesReport03`.**
This file contains two slides that are the start of a sales report presentation.

4 **Select the first slide and then choose Edit, Paste Special.**

5 **Click *Paste link*, choose *Microsoft Office Excel Worksheet Object* in the _As_ list box, and click OK.**
The copied cells display on slide 1, but the cells are too small to read easily. Now enlarge the worksheet display.

6 **Resize and move the object similar to the size and position shown in Figure 5.18.**

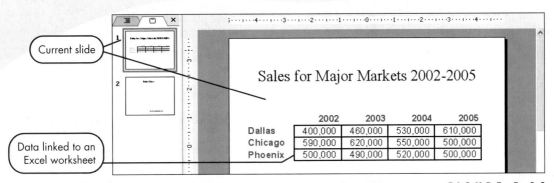

Current slide

Data linked to an Excel worksheet

Sales for Major Markets 2002-2005

	2002	2003	2004	2005
Dallas	400,000	460,000	530,000	610,000
Chicago	590,000	620,000	550,000	500,000
Phoenix	500,000	490,000	520,000	500,000

FIGURE 5.18

7 **Save your changes to the *SalesReport03* PowerPoint presentation.**
Keep both the PowerPoint file *SalesReport03* and the Excel workbook *SalesData03* open for the next lesson, in which you link an Excel chart to the second slide.

LESSON 5: Linking an Excel Chart to a PowerPoint Slide

Charts and graphics can greatly enhance a presentation. Although you can create charts within PowerPoint, its charting capability is not nearly as powerful as that found in Excel. Also, you may already have a chart within an existing Excel workbook. If you link an Excel chart to a PowerPoint slide, the chart on the slide can be updated for any changes in the Excel source file containing the chart.

In this lesson, you link an Excel chart of annual sales to the second slide in a PowerPoint presentation. You also test the links by varying the data in the Excel source file.

To Link an Excel Chart to a PowerPoint Slide

1 | **Display the Excel workbook named *SalesData03*.**

2 | **Click within a blank area of the chart to select it, and choose <u>E</u>dit, <u>C</u>opy.**
The marquee (moving border) around the chart indicates the chart has been copied to the Clipboard.

3 | **Display the PowerPoint file named *SalesReport03*.**
This file contains the two slides that are the start of a Sales Report presentation. Slide 1 already contains data linked to an Excel worksheet.

4 | **Press (PgDn) to display slide 2 and then choose <u>E</u>dit, Paste <u>S</u>pecial.**

5 | **Click *Paste <u>l</u>ink*, select *Microsoft Office Excel Chart Object* in the <u>A</u>s list box, and click OK.**
The copied chart displays on slide 2. Now enlarge the chart.

6 | **Resize and move the chart similar to the size and position shown in Figure 5.19.**

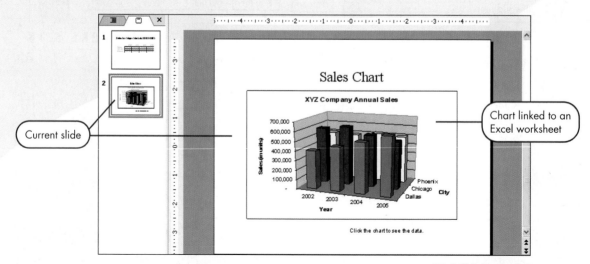

FIGURE 5.19

7 Save your changes to PowerPoint file *SalesReport03,* and close the file.

8 Test the links, as desired, by changing one or more values within the range of charted data in the Excel file *SalesData03.*

9 Open the PowerPoint file *SalesReport03* to verify that changes in the Excel source file are reflected on both slides 1 and 2. (Click *Update Links* when you see a prompt asking if you want to update the links.)

10 Close the PowerPoint file *SalesReport03* and the Excel workbook *SalesData03* without saving changes made to verify the links. Exit PowerPoint.
This concludes Lesson 5. Continue with the next lesson, or exit Excel.

LESSON 6: Importing Data from a Text File

When two applications cannot exchange data directly, you may need to save the data in a text file. Data in text form appear as a string of characters. Spaces or commas separate (delimit) fields, although other characters are sometimes used to delimit fields in a string. Excel's Text Import Wizard is available to guide you through the process of importing text data into the columns and rows of a worksheet.

In this lesson, you use the Text Import Wizard to import data from a file saved as a text file. You also proofread and edit the results. The data concern donations to the Save the Manatee fund.

To Import Data from a Text File

1 Choose File, Open.

2 Select *Text Files* in the *Files of type* drop-down list and then open the text file named *EE2_0505.*
The Text Import Wizard – Step 1 of 3 dialog box opens (see Figure 5.20). Records display in the Preview area across the bottom of the dialog box. Data fields in each record are separated by commas (name, address, city, and so on).

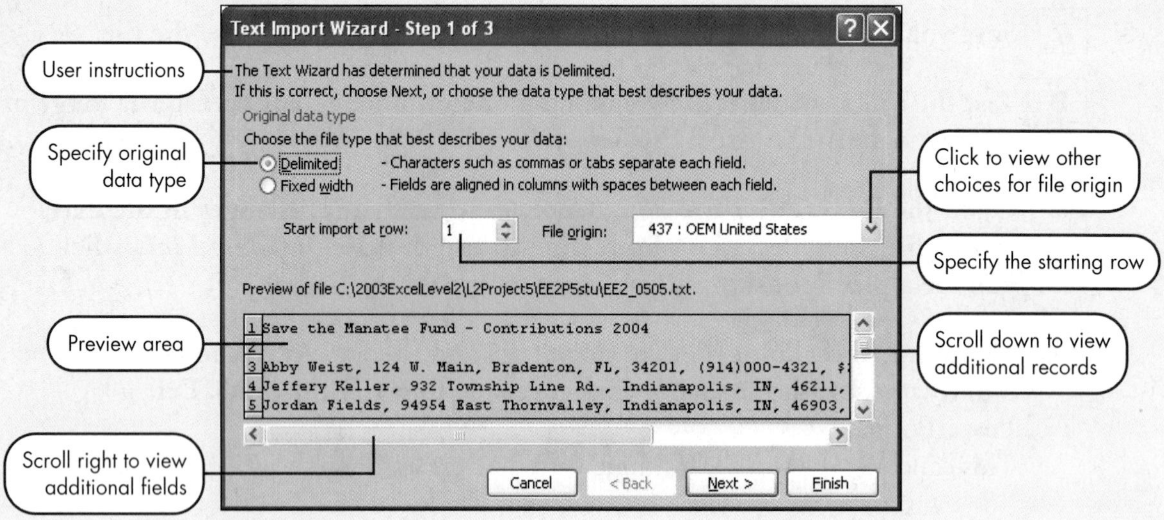

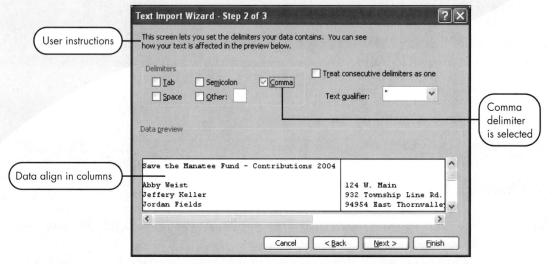

FIGURE 5.20

3 Select *Delimited* as the original data type and then click **Next**.

The Text Import Wizard – Step 2 of 3 dialog box opens. An explanation of the screen is provided at the top of the dialog box.

4 In the Delimiters area, uncheck *Tab* and then check *Comma* (see Figure 5.21).

FIGURE 5.21

5 Click **Next**.

The Text Import Wizard – Step 3 of 3 dialog box opens (see Figure 5.22).

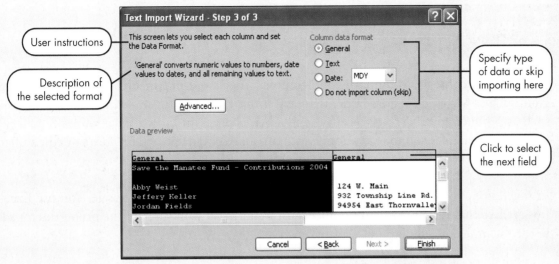

User instructions

Description of
the selected format

Specify type
of data or skip
importing here

Click to select
the next field

FIGURE 5.22

6 **Click Finish to accept the current settings.**

Excel imports the data and arranges the entries in rows (records) and columns (fields)
as shown in Figure 5.23. When you import a text file, you may need to adjust column
widths. You should also proofread the results and edit as necessary for any data errors
that might have been in the original text file.

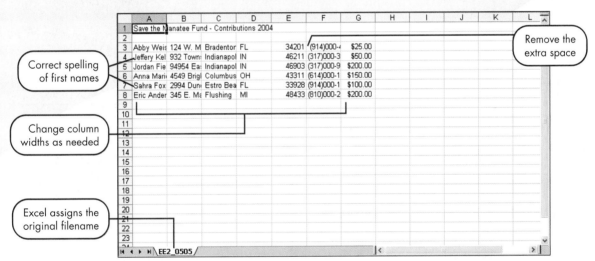

Correct spelling
of first names

Change column
widths as needed

Excel assigns the
original filename

Remove the
extra space

FIGURE 5.23

7 **Widen or narrow columns as needed.**

In addition to adjusting column widths, you should always check imported data for
errors and edit as necessary.

8 **Change *Jeffery* to Jeffrey in cell A4; then change *Sahra* to Sarah in cell A7,
and remove the extra space at the beginning of the phone number in cell F3.**

9 **Choose File, Save As, and select *Microsoft Office Excel Workbook* from the
Save as type drop-down list.**

10 **Change the filename to Manatee_Fund; then click Save, and close the workbook.**

Continue with the next lesson, or exit Excel.

LESSON 7: Importing Data from an Access Database

When data become too voluminous and complex, they are stored in a relational database program such as Microsoft Access rather than as a list in Excel. Yet for some information needs—such as producing a chart—Excel may be the better program to use. Excel's Import External Data feature enables you to reach from Excel into an Access database and create or edit a query using data in the Access database.

In this lesson, you work with an Access database that lists properties for sale. You use Excel's Import External Data feature to produce a list in an Excel worksheet of the properties for sale in the Glenn Lakes subdivision.

The lesson is intended to focus only on the mechanics of getting data from an Access database into an Excel worksheet, and does not include using the results. The sample Access database has only one table—most databases have multiple tables—which is sufficient to illustrate the process of creating a query prior to extracting data to an Excel worksheet.

To Import External Data from Access

1 Open the Excel workbook named *EE2_0506,* and save it as `Clients`.

2 Choose **D**ata, Import External **D**ata, and select *New Database Query.*

If you have problems . . .

If a message displays that Microsoft Query is not installed, click **Y**es and proceed with the installation.

The Choose Data Source dialog box opens (see Figure 5.24). If a message displays that asks whether you want help, click *No, don't provide help now.*

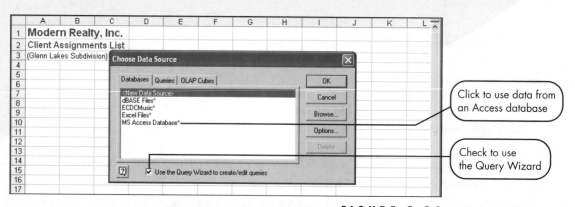

FIGURE 5.24

3 On the Databases tab, select *MS Access Database*, make sure a check mark displays in the *Use the Query Wizard to create/edit queries* check box, and click OK.

The Select Database dialog box opens. Use this dialog box to select the Access file that contains the data you want to import into Excel.

4 Select the folder containing the student data files; then select the Access database named *EE2_0507* (see Figure 5.25).

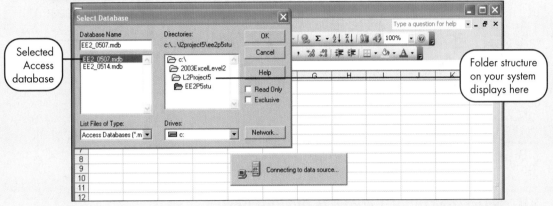

FIGURE 5.25

5 Click OK.

The Query Wizard – Choose Columns dialog box opens (see Figure 5.26). A single table named *Client Assignments* appears in the *Available tables and columns* list.

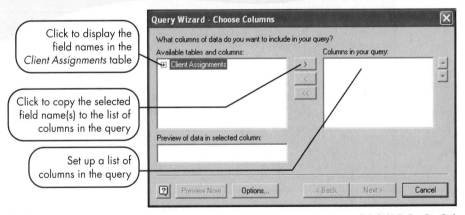

FIGURE 5.26

6 Click the + indicator next to the *Client Assignments* table name in the *Available tables and columns* list box.

7 Select the *Client Assignments* table name and then click the > button.

When you highlight a table name and click the > button, all fields in the table are transferred to the *Columns in your query* list box (see Figure 5.27). To specify fewer fields, select individual field names instead of selecting the table name. The order in which the fields are selected is the order in which they will appear in your worksheet.

As fields are selected, they are removed from the list of available fields and cannot be added to the query twice.

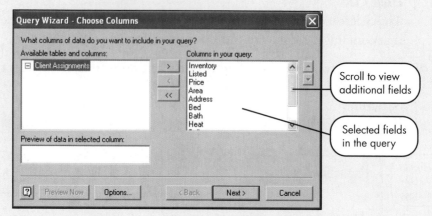

FIGURE 5.27

8 | **Click Next.**
The Query Wizard – Filter Data dialog box opens.

9 | **Select *Area* in the _Column to filter_ list box.**

10 | **In the *Only include rows where* section of the dialog box, select *equals* from the drop-down list in the first of two active text boxes under *Area* (see Figure 5.28).**

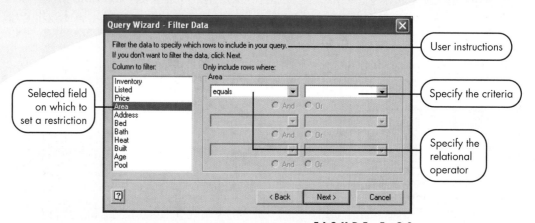

FIGURE 5.28

11 | **Click the drop-down list in the blank text box to the right of the one in which you specified the relational operator *equals,* and select *Glenn Lakes.***
You have set a filter to select only those records from the Access database in which the entry in the Area field equals *Glenn Lakes.*

12 | **Click Next.**
The Query Wizard – Sort Order dialog box opens.

13 Click the *Sort by* drop-down list; then select *Inventory,* and make sure that *Ascending* is selected.

Check that your settings match those shown in Figure 5.29.

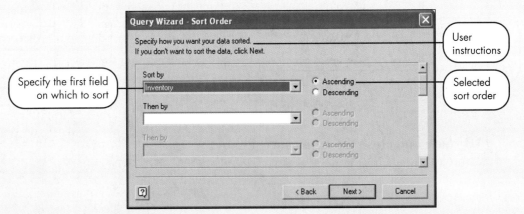

FIGURE 5.29

14 Click Next.

The Query Wizard – Finish dialog box opens.

15 Make sure that *Return Data to Microsoft Office Excel* is selected, and click Finish.

The Import Data dialog box opens, asking where you want to put the data.

16 Specify *Existing worksheet* and then click cell A5 in the worksheet.

The settings in your Import Data dialog box should match those shown in Figure 5.30.

FIGURE 5.30

17 Click OK.

The records shown in Figure 5.31 are copied from the Access database and placed in Excel's list format beginning in cell A5.

	A	B	C	D	E	F	G	H	I	J	K	L	M
1	Modern Realty, Inc.												
2	Client Assignments List												
3	(Glenn Lakes Subdivision)												
4													
5	Inventory	Listed	Price	Area	Address	Bed	Bath	Heat	Built	Age	Pool		
6	LC004	1/23/2004 0:00	172300	Glenn Lakes	3452 Cortez Street	3	2	Elec	1996	4	Y		
7	LC009	1/5/2004 0:00	170000	Glenn Lakes	1025 Wellington Circle	3	2	Elec	1998	2	Y		
8	LF005	1/15/2004 0:00	121500	Glenn Lakes	5562 Kensington Drive	4	2.5	Elec	1998	2	N		
9	LF006	2/5/2004 0:00	174600	Glenn Lakes	4874 Manatee Avenue	3	2	Elec	1995	5	Y		
10	MF003	3/6/2004 0:00	123800	Glenn Lakes	3492 54th Avenue W.	2	2	Elec	1996	4	Y		
11	MF008	3/3/2004 0:00	167200	Glenn Lakes	5778 Wellington Drive	3	2	Elec	1997	3	Y		
12	MF009	1/3/2004 0:00	180500	Glenn Lakes	6873 Wellington Drive	4	2	Elec	1997	3	Y		
13	MF014	3/3/2004 0:00	169700	Glenn Lakes	2984 44th Street West	3	2	Elec	1997	3	Y		
14													
15													

Query limited record selection to listings in the Glenn Lakes area

Field names and eight records from an Access database

FIGURE 5.31

18 **Save and close the *Clients* workbook.**
Continue with the next lesson, or exit Excel.

TO EXTEND YOUR KNOWLEDGE . . .

GETTING DATA FROM EXCEL INTO ACCESS

Excel's list capability enables you to perform sorts and filters based on data in a single worksheet that is the equivalent of one table in an Access database. By using Access, however, you can create many related tables within a database, perform queries based on multiple tables, and generate complex reports. This is necessary to avoid redundant data that occur in single data tables such as those created in Excel. Importing and exporting data between Excel and Access gives you the efficiency of both applications.

To export Excel data to an Access database, first make sure that the Excel data are in a list format—each column has a label in the first row and holds similar data, each row contains related data items, and there are no blank rows or columns within the list. Also make sure that the Excel workbook is closed. To create a new Access database, simply open the Excel workbook in Access, and follow the directions in the Link Spreadsheet Wizard. To add Excel data to an existing Access database, open the Access database where you want to copy the Excel data; on the Access File menu, select Get External Data and click Import; locate and select the workbook you want to import, click Import, and follow directions in the Import Spreadsheet Wizard. Refer to onscreen Help in Access for more information.

LESSON 8: Getting Data from the Web

You can create Web queries that enable you to retrieve tables of data or entire Web pages into Excel for analysis. A **Web query** retrieves data stored on the Internet or on your company's intranet or extranet. Keep in mind that it is your responsibility to comply with any conditions for the use of the data as determined by the creator of the site from which you retrieve data.

In the following steps, you focus on getting external data from the Web. You use a predefined query to import MSN MoneyCentral Investors data on world currency rates into an Excel worksheet. You also create a new Web query that accesses the Microsoft Corporation Web site and imports data from an annual report to stockholders.

The data can be refreshed on demand or at predetermined intervals. When you refresh the data, all of the calculations using those data are updated.

You must have an Internet connection to perform the steps in this lesson. If you are in an academic or business environment, or have a cable or DSL connection, you may already be connected. Figures reflect using Internet Explorer browser software.

To Create Web Queries

1 Connect to the Internet; then open a new workbook, and make sure that *Sheet1* is the active worksheet.

2 Choose **D**ata, Import External **D**ata, Import **D**ata.
The Select Data Source dialog box opens (see Figure 5.32). The listings in your My Data Sources subfolder might vary from those shown in the figure.

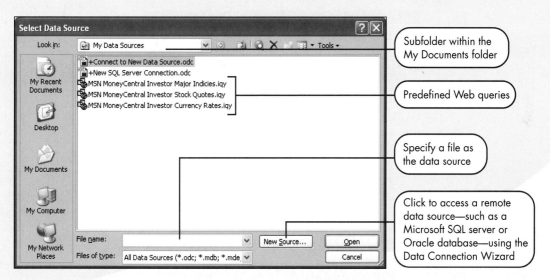

FIGURE 5.32

3 Select **MSN MoneyCentral Investor Currency Rates**, and click **O**pen.
The Import Data dialog box opens (see Figure 5.33).

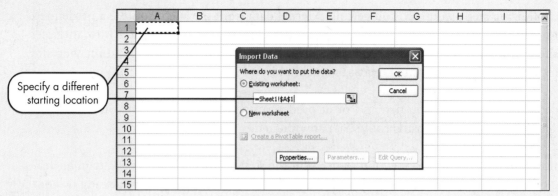

FIGURE 5.33

4 | **Make sure that *Existing worksheet* is selected; then specify cell A4 as the location, and click OK.**

After a brief delay, Excel imports the most recent data on world currency rates in a layout similar to that shown in Figure 5.34. These rates change frequently, and the values in your worksheet are likely to vary from those in the sample figure.

Link to the provider's site

	A	B	C	D	E
1					
2					
3					
4	**Currency Rates Provided by MSN MoneyCentral Investor**				
5	Click here to visit MSN MoneyCentral Investor				
6					
7	**Name**	**In US$**	**Per US$**		
8	Argentine Peso	0.34483	2.9		
9	Australian Dollar	0.6528	1.532		
10	Austrian Schilling	0.08274	12.086		
11	Bahraini Dinar	2.6526	0.377		
12	Bolivian Boliviano	0.13006	7.689		
13	Brazilian Real	0.33727	2.965		
14	British Pound	1.6164	0.619		
15	Canadian Dollar	0.71393	1.401		
16	Chilean Peso	0.00141	707		
17	Chinese Yuan	0.12081	8.277		
18	Colombian Peso	0.00035	2861		
19	Cyprus Pound	1.9417	0.515		
20	Czech Koruna	0.03545	28.207		

Sheet1 / Sheet2 / Sheet3 /

FIGURE 5.34

5 | **Enter your name in cell A1, and today's date in cell A2.**

6 | **Rename the worksheet `World Rates`, and save the workbook as `WebQueries`.**

Now use a command sequence that enables you to specify the Web site of your choice.

7 | **Display the second worksheet in the *WebQueries* workbook, and rename it `MS Data`.**

8 | **Choose Data, Import External Data, New Web Query.**

The New Web Query dialog box opens.

9 Enter `http://www.microsoft.com` in the *A_ddress* text box, and click **G_o**.
The homepage for Microsoft Corporation displays (see Figure 5.35). The current look and content is likely to vary from that shown in the figure as Microsoft updates its Web site. On a Web site, each yellow square containing a right arrow indicates a data table that you can select. If the yellow squares do not display, click Show Icons at the top of the dialog box.

FIGURE 5.35

10 Enter `annual report` in the *Search Microsoft.com for* text box, and click the Go button at the right end of the box.

11 Scroll down and browse through search results until you find a link to annual reports or other earnings data; then follow links as necessary to find a yellow square next to income-related data, and click the yellow square.
The yellow square containing an arrow switches to a green square containing a check-mark, which indicates that the associated data are selected (see the sample in Figure 5.36).

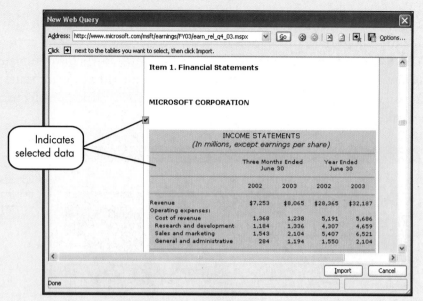

FIGURE 5.36

If you have problems . . .

Contents of Web pages change frequently. If you are not able to select a yellow square pointing to an Income Statement or other earnings-related data, select another yellow square.

12 **Click the Import button near the lower-right corner of the New Web Query dialog box.**
The Import Data dialog box opens.

13 **Click *Existing worksheet,* specify cell A4 as the location, and click OK.**
After a brief delay, Excel imports the data you selected from the Microsoft Web site (see the sample data in Figure 5.37).

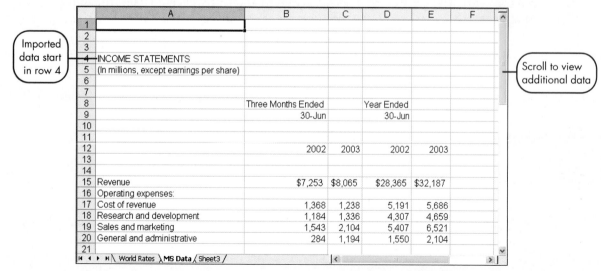

FIGURE 5.37

14 Enter your name in cell A1 and enter the current date in cell A2.

15 Save your changes to the *WebQueries* workbook and close the workbook. Continue with the end-of-project activities, or exit Excel.

TO EXTEND YOUR KNOWLEDGE . . .

SAVING A WEB QUERY
When you import data using a Web query, Excel automatically saves the Web query with your workbook. If you want to save the query so you can run it with other workbooks, click the Save Query icon in the New Web Query dialog box. The query is saved in a text file with an .iqy extension. To run a saved query, choose Data, Import External Data, Import Data, and locate the folder where the query file is stored. Select the Web query you want to run, click Open, select *Existing worksheet* or *New worksheet,* and click OK.

OTHER WAYS TO GET DATA FROM A WEB PAGE
You can use Copy and Paste commands to bring selected data from a Web page into an Excel worksheet. Select the Web page content, execute your browser's copy process, switch to the desired location in the worksheet, and click Excel's Paste button.

SUMMARY

In the initial lesson you glimpsed the power of the Research tool in Excel. You used it to look up terms in an encyclopedia and dictionary, request a stock quote, look for articles from a news service, and translate a worksheet phrase into Spanish.

The next four lessons focused on linking or embedding data from Excel to a Word document and a PowerPoint slide. In Lessons 6 and 7, you imported data from two sources—the entire contents of a text file, and selected records from an Access database. Your activities ended with several ways to get data from the Web.

You can extend your learning by reviewing concepts and terms, and by practicing variations of skills presented in the lessons. Use the following table as a guide to the numbered questions and exercises in the end-of-project learning opportunities.

LESSON	MULTIPLE CHOICE	DISCUSSION	SKILL DRILL	CHALLENGE	DISCOVERY ZONE
Using the Research Task Pane	2, 9	1, 3	1		1
Linking Excel Data to a Word Document	1, 3, 4	2	2		2
Embedding Excel Data in a Word Document	4	2		1	
Linking Excel Data to a PowerPoint Slide	5		4		2
Linking an Excel Chart to a PowerPoint Slide	5		4		2
Importing Data from a Text File	6		3		
Importing Data from an Access Database	7			2	
Getting Data from the Web	8, 10	3	5	3, 4	1

KEY TERMS

destination file	Object Linking and Embedding (OLE)	thesaurus
embedded object		third-party service
linked object	Research task pane	translate
object	source file	Web query

CHECKING CONCEPTS AND TERMS

MULTIPLE CHOICE

Circle the letter of the correct answer for each of the following.

1. What is the term that describes sharing data among Microsoft Office applications? [L2]

   a. Object Linking and Embedding (OLE)

   b. Object Sharing and Round-Tripping (OSR)

   c. Object Data Sharing (ODS)

   d. None of the above

2. When using the Research task pane, which resource provides the equivalent of the specified word or phrase in another language? [L1]

   a. Transpose

   b. Transcript

   c. Translate

   d. Transpond

3. What is the term for a file that contains a link or embedded data? [L2]

   a. Source file

   b. Destination file

   c. Application file

   d. Object file

4. Which of the following is a true statement about a file containing an embedded object? [L2, L3]

   a. The file is only a few bytes larger than it would have been without the data from another application.

   b. There is no connection between the file containing the embedded object and its source file.

   c. You can edit the connection between the file containing the embedded object and the source file.

   d. Both a and b

5. Which of the following describes a step in the process to link an Excel chart or cell range to a PowerPoint slide? [L4, L5]

   a. In Excel, select the chart and copy it.

   b. In PowerPoint, select the target slide and click the Paste button.

   c. In PowerPoint, select the target slide; then select Edit, Paste Special and click the Paste button.

   d. Both a and c

6. Which of the following is a correct statement about importing text files? [L6]

   a. When two applications cannot exchange data directly, you may need to save the data in a text file.

   b. Data in text form appear as a string of characters.

   c. Spaces or commas separate (delimit) fields.

   d. All of the above are correct.

7. Which of the following is not an accurate statement about exporting Excel data to an Access database? [L7]

   a. The Excel data must be organized in a list format.

   b. Columns must have a label in the first row and hold similar data.

   c. Each row must contain related data items.

   d. There can be one or more blank rows within the list; Access ignores the blank rows.

8. Which is not a correct statement regarding Web queries? [L8]

   a. A Web query retrieves data stored on an intranet or extranet.

   b. Because the Internet is a public resource, there are no restrictions or conditions on the use of its data.

   c. The Excel program includes several predefined Web queries.

   d. When you refresh data, all calculations using those data are updated.

9. Which task pane provides access to a thesaurus? [L1]

   a. Explore

   b. Find

   c. Research

   d. Getting Started

10. Which of the following is an accurate statement about downloading data from the Web to an Excel worksheet? [L8]

   a. Downloadable data are identified by a green square with a checkmark inside.

   b. Clicking Import downloads all selected data to a position that begins with the active cell.

   c. Both a and b

   d. Neither a nor b

DISCUSSION

1. Figure 5.38 illustrates research results. Comment on actions that you might take to generate a more manageable set of results. [L1]

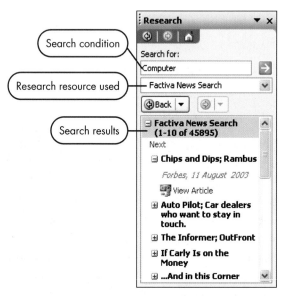

FIGURE 5.38

2. You completed an Excel worksheet that summarizes the results of last week's swim meet. Now you are about to copy the data to a report you are preparing in Word. Should you embed or link the swim meet data? Why? [L2, L3]

3. You are developing the Personal Investment worksheet shown in Figure 5.39. Currently it lists the name and ticker symbol of each stock in addition to the number of shares you own. Explain how you can use the features described in this project to help you finish the worksheet. Also explain any changes that you could or should make to improve the usefulness of the worksheet. [L1, L8]

	A	B	C	D	E	F	G	H
1	Personal Stock Portfolio							
2								
3			Cells in green can be updated					
4	Stock	Symbol	Exchange	# of Shares	Share Value	Total Value		
5	Bank of America	BAC	NYSE	100		$ -		
6	Dell Computer	Dell	NASDAQ	250		$ -		
7	Exxon Mobile	XOM	NYSE	50		$ -		
8	Barnes and Noble	BKS	NYSE	400		$ -		
9	IBM	IBM	NYSE	25		$ -		
10	ChevronTexaco	CVX	NYSE	45		$ -		
11	Ford Motor Company	F	NYSE	90		$ -		
12	Sonic Automotive	SAH	NYSE	30		$ -		
13	Total Stock Value					$ -		
14								

FIGURE 5.39

SKILL DRILL

Skill Drill exercises reinforce project skills. Each skill that is reinforced is the same, or nearly the same, as a skill presented in the project. Detailed instructions are provided in a step-by-step format.

Before beginning your first Project 5 Skill Drill exercise, complete the following steps:

1. Open the Excel file named *EE2_0508* and immediately save it as **EE2_P5drill**.

   The workbook contains an Overview sheet and five exercise sheets labeled #1-Thesaurus, #2-LinkView, #3-ImportTXT, #4-LinkBoth, and #5-GetIndices.

2. Click the Overview sheet to view the organization and content of the Project 5 Skill Drill Exercises workbook.

There are five Project 5 Skill Drill exercises. Each exercise is independent of the others, so you may complete them in any order.

Be sure to save the workbook after completing each exercise. If you need a paper copy of the completed exercise, enter your name centered in a header before printing. Other print options have already been set to print compressed to one page and to display the filename, sheet name, and current date in a footer.

Be sure to save your changes and then close the workbook if you need more than one work session to complete the desired exercises. Continue working on *EE2_P5drill* instead of starting over on the original *EE2_0508* file.

1. Looking Up a Word in a Thesaurus

You are putting the finishing touches on a worksheet that lists computers for sale. You want to replace one of the column headings with a similar word. To find a similar word using a thesaurus, follow these steps:

1. Open the *EE2_P5drill* workbook, if necessary; then select the #1-Thesaurus sheet.

2. Hold down (Alt) and click cell C12.

   Excel opens the Research task pane and copies the contents of cell C12—*Maker*—to the *Search for* box in the task pane.

3. In the box below the *Search for* box, display the resource drop-down list; then select *Thesaurus: English (U.S.)*.

4. Position the pointer on *producer* in the results area; then click the down arrow to the right, and click Insert.

   The word *Producer* replaces *Maker* in cell C12.

5. Close the Research task pane, and save your changes to the *EE2_P5drill* workbook.

2. Creating a Link and Viewing Information About Links

You maintain data in an Excel worksheet on homes available for sale. You created a memo in Word to convey information about properties available in the Glenn Lakes subdivision. Now you want to link the data in the worksheet to the Word memo so that each time the Word document is opened, the linked data can be updated. You also want to view information about links in the memo.

To create a link, and view information about links, follow these steps:

1. Open the *EE2_P5drill* workbook, if necessary; then select the #2-LinkView sheet.

2. Click cell B9, and click the Sort Descending button on the Standard toolbar.

3. Select the list range A8:I16, and click the Copy button.

4. Open the Word document *EE2_0509* and save it as **GLmemo**; then position the insertion point below the last sentence.

5. Choose Edit, Paste Special.

6. Select *Paste link,* specify pasting as a Microsoft Office Excel Worksheet Object, and click OK.

   The range of data from an Excel worksheet is linked within the Word document. Now view information about the links in the document.

7. Choose Edit, Links.

   The Links dialog box opens and lists one link. The description near the bottom of the dialog box indicates that the link is a Microsoft Office Excel Worksheet containing data from an Access query.

8. Click OK to close the dialog box.

9. Save your changes to the *GLmemo* document, and exit Word.

10. Deselect the list range in the #2-LinkView worksheet, and press (Esc) to remove the moving border from the copied range.

3. Importing Data from a Text File

You are keeping a record of the business miles you drive using Notepad, which creates a text file. Now you want to import that text file into Excel as the starting point for a worksheet that computes business expenses.

To import data to an existing worksheet from a text file, follow these steps:

1. Open the *EE2_P5drill* workbook, if necessary; then select the #3-ImportTXT sheet.

2. Click cell A4.

3. Choose Data, Import External Data, and select *Import Data.*

   The Select Data Source dialog box opens.

4. Display the *Look in* drop-down list, and select the folder containing the student data files.

5. Select the *EE2_0510* text file and then click Open.

6. Check that Delimited is selected in the Text Import Wizard – Step 1 of 3 dialog box, and click Next.

7. Make sure that a check mark displays in the *Tab* check box in the Text Import Wizard – Step 2 of 3 dialog box, and click Finish.

8. Make sure that *Existing worksheet* and *=$A$4* are the settings for the location of imported data, and click OK.

   Excel imports the text data, starting in cell A4.

9. Save your changes to the *EE2_P5drill* workbook.

4. Linking Excel Data and Chart to a PowerPoint Slide

A vital part of a PowerPoint presentation is the capability to display current data and charts. Often this information is maintained in Excel and linked to a slide presentation. In this exercise, you link an Excel pivot table and associated chart to a PowerPoint slide. A pivot table summarizes data, as explained in Project 7, "Creating PivotTable and PivotChart Reports."

To create the links, follow these steps:

1. Open the *EE2_P5drill* workbook, if necessary; then select the #4-LinkBoth sheet.

2. Open the *EE2_0511* PowerPoint file, and save it as **Mileage**.

3. Page down to display slide 2.

4. Switch to the #4-LinkBoth worksheet and then copy the range E8:F13.

5. Switch to slide 2 in the PowerPoint file *Mileage* and then click the text box on the left.

6. Choose Edit, Paste Special; then click *Paste link,* specify pasting as a Microsoft Office Excel Worksheet Object, and click OK.

   The copied data display in a small worksheet; sizing handles indicate the object is selected. For now, do not change the size or location of the copied pivot table data.

7. Switch to the #4-LinkBoth worksheet; then click within a blank area of the pie chart to select it, and click the Copy button.

8. Switch to PowerPoint; then click the graphics placeholder on the right side of slide 2 and choose Edit, Paste Special. Click *Paste link,* specify pasting as a Microsoft Office Excel Chart Object, and click OK.

9. Rearrange and resize the three objects (the title is an object) as desired to improve display. For example, you can resize the title text box and position it top-left on the slide, resize the pivot table data and position it to the right of the slide title, and enlarge the chart and center it below both of the other objects.

10. Save your changes to the *Mileage* presentation, and exit PowerPoint.

11. Deselect the pie chart in the #4-LinkBoth worksheet.

5. Getting Data from the Web on Major Investor Indices

In this project you downloaded currency rate data using the predefined Web query MS MoneyCentral Investor Currency Rates. Now you want to view information about investor indices using another predefined Web query. Follow these steps:

1. Connect to the Internet, if necessary.

2. Open the *EE2_P5drill* workbook, if necessary; then select the #5-GetIndices sheet.

3. Open the Select Data Source dialog box by choosing Data, Import External Data, Import Data.

4. Select *MSN MoneyCentral Investor Major Indices,* and click Open.

   The Import Data dialog box opens.

5. Make sure that *Existing worksheet* is selected; then specify cell A4 as the location, and click OK.

   After a brief delay, Excel imports the most recent index data.

6. Enter your name in cell A2, and today's date in cell D2.

7. Save your changes to the *EE2_P5drill* workbook.

CHALLENGE

Challenge exercises expand on or are somewhat related to skills that are presented in the lessons. Each exercise provides a brief narrative introduction, followed by instructions in a numbered-step format that are not as detailed as those in the Skill Drill section.

Before beginning your first Project 5 Challenge exercise, complete the following steps:

1. Open the *EE2_0512* workbook and save it as **EE2_P5challenge.**

   The *EE2_P5challenge* workbook contains five sheets: an Overview, and four exercise sheets named #1-Embed, #2-FromAccess, #3-WebChoice, and #4-CopyPaste.

2. Click the Overview sheet to view the organization of the Project 5 Challenge Exercises workbook.

Each exercise is independent of the others, so you may complete them in any order. Be sure to save the workbook after completing each exercise. If you need a paper copy of the completed exercise, enter your name centered in a header before printing. Other print options have already been set to print compressed to one page and to display the filename, sheet name, and current date in a footer.

If you need more than one work session to complete the desired exercises, continue working on *EE2_P5challenge* instead of starting over on the original *EE2_0512* file.

1. Embedding Excel Data in a Word Document

You prepared a memo to the Accounting department, asking for a review of your monthly expenses. Now you want to embed in the memo a copy of those expenses, which are available in an Excel worksheet.

To embed Excel data in a Word document, follow these steps:

1. Open the Word document *EE2_0513* and save it as a document named **ReviewExp**.

2. Open the *EE2_P5challenge* workbook, if necessary; then select the #1-Embed sheet.

3. Copy the range A8:E22 and then switch to the *ReviewExp* document.

4. Paste the copied Excel data after the last sentence, making sure that you embed (not link) the data as a Microsoft Office Excel Worksheet Object.

5. Access the Edit menu to verify that there is no link to the #1-Embed worksheet in the document.

6. Save your changes to the *ReviewExp* document; then close the document and exit Word.

7. Press Esc to clear the moving border, and deselect ranges as necessary in the #1-Embed worksheet.

2. Importing Access Data into an Excel Worksheet

Expense data are currently stored in an Access database, and you want to import selected data into an Excel worksheet. If you wanted to import all records with fields in the same order as they are stored in the Access database, you would choose Data, Import External Data, and select Import Data. Instead, however, you want to filter the data by the Category column so that only category 1 (Office) or category 4 (Other) records are imported. You also want the columns in a slightly different order. You can use Excel's Import External Data feature, and select *New Database Query* instead of *Import Data,* to produce the desired result.

To import Access data into an Excel worksheet, follow these steps:

1. Open the *EE2_P5challenge* workbook, if necessary; then select the #2-FromAccess worksheet and click cell A9.

2. Choose Data, Import External Data, and select *New Database Query.*

3. Choose *MS Access Database* as the data source, and specify that you want to use the Query Wizard.

4. In the Select Database dialog box, find and open the *EE2_0514* Access database.

5. Click the + sign to display fields (columns) in the Expense List table; then choose the following columns in this order: ID, Category, Expense, Date, Amount, and Client.

6. Filter the data by the Category column so that only category 1 or category 4 records are imported.

   To do this, you must use two filter lines and specify the Or button between the two specifications.

7. Sort the data by the Expense field in Ascending order.

8. Select *Return Data to Microsoft Office Excel* and then click Finish. Make sure that cell A9 in the existing worksheet is the location for imported data, and click OK.

   Imported data display starting in cell A9 of the #2-FromAccess worksheet. The Client column is blank because category 1 and 4 expenses do not have clients.

9. Reformat as needed, including changes in column widths and formatting entries in the Date column to show the date only; then save your changes to the *EE2_P5challenge* workbook.

3. Creating a Web Query

You want to import data from a site of your choice, such as one maintained by your school, a volunteer organization, or a sports organization. To import data into an Excel worksheet by creating a Web query of your choice, follow these steps:

1. Connect to the Internet, if necessary.

2. Open the *EE2_P5challenge* workbook, if necessary; then select the #3-WebChoice sheet.

3. Choose <u>D</u>ata, Import External <u>D</u>ata, New <u>W</u>eb Query.

4. Enter the URL of your choice in the *A<u>d</u>dress* text box, and click <u>G</u>o.

5. Click one or more of the yellow squares with arrows that indicate data you can select; then click the <u>I</u>mport button. Try to include numeric data in your selection(s).

6. Specify that you want to import the selected data starting in cell A4 of the existing worksheet, and complete the process to import.

7. Adjust column widths and apply formatting as desired.

8. Add documentation to the worksheet that includes your name, the date you obtained the data, and the URL for your data source.

9. Save your changes to the *EE2_P5challenge* workbook.

4. Using Copy and Paste to Get Data from the Web

You want to continue exploring methods for getting data from the Web. To use onscreen Help to learn about copying data, and apply what you learned, follow these steps:

1. Connect to the Internet, if necessary.

2. Open the *EE2_P5challenge* workbook, if necessary; then select the #4-CopyPaste sheet.

3. Display the Excel Help task pane and open the Table of Contents.

4. Browse the category *Excel and the Web* and its subtopics; then read a subtopic on copying data from a Web page.

5. Search a travel support site—such as www.Expedia.com, www.Travelocity.com, or www.VacationsToGo.com—and copy data and related images of your choice to the #4-CopyPaste sheet in the *EE2_P5challenge* workbook.

6. Reposition and resize any copied objects as desired.

7. Adjust column widths and apply formatting as desired.

8. Add documentation to the worksheet that includes your name, the date you obtained the data, and the URL for your data source.

9. Save your changes to the *EE2_P5challenge* workbook.

DISCOVERY ZONE

Discovery Zone exercises require advanced knowledge of topics presented in *Essentials* lessons, application of skills from multiple lessons, or self-directed learning of new skills.

Before beginning your first Project 5 Discovery Zone exercise, complete the following steps:

1. Open the Excel workbook named *EE2_0515* and save it as **EE2_P5discovery**.

   The *EE2_P5discovery* workbook contains three sheets: an Overview, and two exercise sheets named #1-Stock and #2-LinkHelp.

2. Select the Overview worksheet to view the organization of the Project 5 Discovery Zone Exercises workbook.

The exercises are independent of each other, so you may complete them in any order. Be sure to save the workbook after completing each exercise. If you need a paper copy of the completed exercise, enter your name centered in a header before printing. Other print options have already been set to print compressed to one page and to display the filename, sheet name, and current date in a footer.

Be sure to save your changes and close the workbook if you need more than one work session to complete the desired exercises. Then, continue working on *EE2_P5discovery* instead of starting over on the original *EE2_0515* file.

1. Getting Stock Data on the Web

You are in the process of completing a worksheet that calculates the total market value of shares held at a specific date. The worksheet—#1-Stock in the *EE2_P5discovery* workbook—includes company name, ticker symbol, stock exchange, and number of shares held for three stocks. Add stocks for four companies of your choice; then use the Research task pane as necessary to find the ticker symbol, the exchange, and the current market value per share for each stock. Enter assumed numbers for shares held. Add sufficient documentation to the worksheet—your name, date of the market values, Web sources, and so forth.

2. Getting Help on Linking

You want to learn more about topics related to linking files. Use onscreen Help to find out how to break a link and how to display a linked object as an icon. Apply text wrapping to cells A4 and A7 in the #2-LinkHelp sheet within the *EE2_P5discovery* workbook; then copy or enter text to explain how to break a link (cell A4) and how to display a linked object as an icon (cell A7).

PROJECT **6** LEVEL **2**

USING FUNCTIONS TO CREATE AND ANALYZE DATA

OBJECTIVES

IN THIS PROJECT, YOU LEARN HOW TO

- **Create data using the VLOOKUP function**
- **Create data using the HLOOKUP function**
- **Summarize data with FREQUENCY**

- **Chart the results of a frequency distribution**
- **Analyze data with COUNTIF**
- **Analyze data with SUMIF**

WHY WOULD I DO THIS?

Excel provides a variety of *functions* (predefined formulas) to help you with tasks. For instance, imagine that you are creating an Excel worksheet to track donations to a zoological society. In addition to listing each donor and the amount contributed, the society wants you to enter the associated level of giving—Stewards' Circle for $25,000 or more; Conservationists' Circle for $10,000–$24,999; and other designations for lesser amounts. There are hundreds of donors, and you hope to avoid typing the level of giving for each donor. Fortunately, Excel includes a function that can look up the donor level associated with a specific amount, and enter that level automatically.

Imagine also that you are responsible for analyzing the results of a survey conducted by a vehicle rental firm. You've entered each individual's responses in a separate row in an Excel worksheet. Now you want to generate various counts and totals automatically, instead of manually doing your analysis. Selected functions provide the tools you need.

 VISUAL SUMMARY

Excel provides hundreds of functions that are organized in categories. Some of the commonly used categories available in the Insert Function dialog box include Financial, Date & Time, Math & Trig, Statistical, Lookup & Reference, Database, and Logical. In this project, you work with five functions from three categories. This experience enables you to gain confidence in using some relatively complex functions to create and analyze data.

In Lessons 1 and 2, you work with two similar functions from the Lookup & Reference category—VLOOKUP and HLOOKUP. Figure 6.1 illustrates one of the VLOOKUP applications.

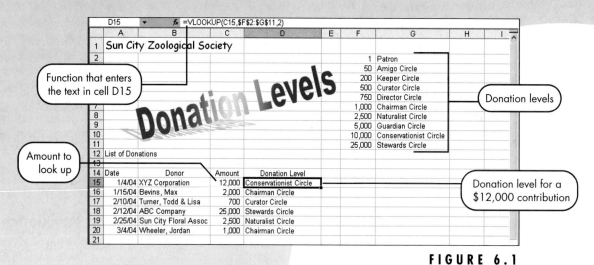

FIGURE 6.1

In Lesson 3 you use a FREQUENCY function to calculate how many times values occur within a range. You create summary data about the favorite magazine of survey respondents (see Figure 6.2) so that you can place advertising in the most popular magazines. In Lesson 4, you chart the frequency distribution results.

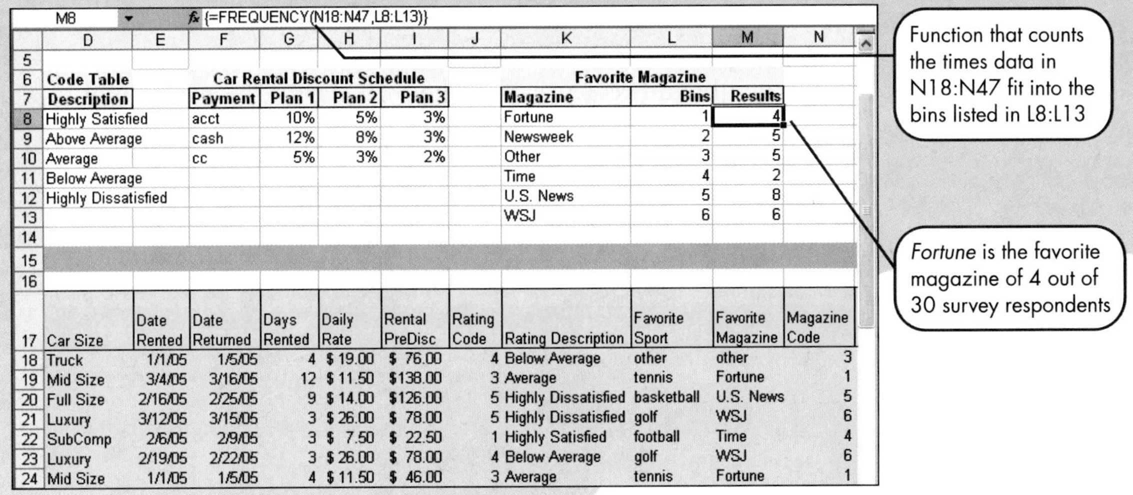

M8 ▾ fx {=FREQUENCY(N18:N47,L8:L13)}

	D	E	F	G	H	I	J	K	L	M	N
5											
6	Code Table		Car Rental Discount Schedule					Favorite Magazine			
7	Description		Payment	Plan 1	Plan 2	Plan 3		Magazine	Bins	Results	
8	Highly Satisfied		acct	10%	5%	3%		Fortune	1	4	
9	Above Average		cash	12%	8%	3%		Newsweek	2	5	
10	Average		cc	5%	3%	2%		Other	3	5	
11	Below Average							Time	4	2	
12	Highly Dissatisfied							U.S. News	5	8	
13								WSJ	6	6	
14											
15											
16											
17	Car Size		Date Rented	Date Returned	Days Rented	Daily Rate	Rental PreDisc	Rating Code	Rating Description	Favorite Sport	Favorite Magazine	Magazine Code
18	Truck	1/1/05	1/5/05	4	$ 19.00	$ 76.00	4	Below Average	other	other	3
19	Mid Size	3/4/05	3/16/05	12	$ 11.50	$138.00	3	Average	tennis	Fortune	1
20	Full Size	2/16/05	2/25/05	9	$ 14.00	$126.00	5	Highly Dissatisfied	basketball	U.S. News	5
21	Luxury	3/12/05	3/15/05	3	$ 26.00	$ 78.00	5	Highly Dissatisfied	golf	WSJ	6
22	SubComp	2/6/05	2/9/05	3	$ 7.50	$ 22.50	1	Highly Satisfied	football	Time	4
23	Luxury	2/19/05	2/22/05	3	$ 26.00	$ 78.00	4	Below Average	golf	WSJ	6
24	Mid Size	1/1/05	1/5/05	4	$ 11.50	$ 46.00	3	Average	tennis	Fortune	1

Callouts:
- Function that counts the times data in N18:N47 fit into the bins listed in L8:L13
- *Fortune* is the favorite magazine of 4 out of 30 survey respondents

FIGURE 6.2

Lessons 5 and 6 focus on using functions to count or sum the number of cells within a range that meet your specified criteria. Figure 6.3 illustrates using the COUNTIF function. You also work with the SUMIF function.

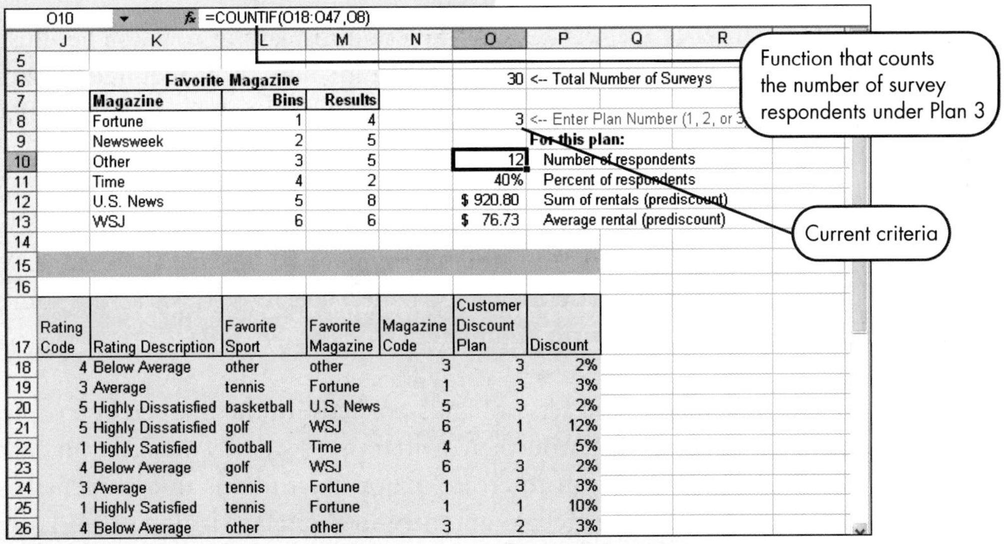

O10 ▾ fx =COUNTIF(O18:O47,O8)

	J	K	L	M	N	O	P	Q	R
5									
6		Favorite Magazine				30	<-- Total Number of Surveys		
7		Magazine	Bins	Results					
8		Fortune	1	4		3	<-- Enter Plan Number (1, 2, or 3)		
9		Newsweek	2	5			For this plan:		
10		Other	3	5		12	Number of respondents		
11		Time	4	2		40%	Percent of respondents		
12		U.S. News	5	8		$ 920.80	Sum of rentals (prediscount)		
13		WSJ	6	6		$ 76.73	Average rental (prediscount)		
14									
15									
16									
17	Rating Code	Rating Description	Favorite Sport	Favorite Magazine	Magazine Code	Customer Discount Plan	Discount		
18	4	Below Average	other	other	3	3	2%		
19	3	Average	tennis	Fortune	1	3	3%		
20	5	Highly Dissatisfied	basketball	U.S. News	5	3	2%		
21	5	Highly Dissatisfied	golf	WSJ	6	1	12%		
22	1	Highly Satisfied	football	Time	4	1	5%		
23	4	Below Average	golf	WSJ	6	3	2%		
24	3	Average	tennis	Fortune	1	3	3%		
25	1	Highly Satisfied	tennis	Fortune	1	1	10%		
26	4	Below Average	other	other	3	2	3%		

Callouts:
- Function that counts the number of survey respondents under Plan 3
- Current criteria

FIGURE 6.3

LESSON 1:   Creating Data Using the VLOOKUP Function

Excel provides several functions that you can use to look up values in a table. You can use these tools to automate data entry. For example, if you create a table with two-character major codes in one column and the associated full names of the majors in the next column—such as *FN* for Finance and *MK* for Marketing—you never have to type the full name of a major again.

If the data you want to look up are stored vertically in a table—that is, in columns—then use the VLOOKUP function. The **VLOOKUP function** looks for a specified value in the leftmost column of a table. When that value is found in a cell within the table, the function displays the contents of another cell in that same row based on the column you specify.

Does the explanation of the VLOOKUP function seem confusing? Looking at an example of the function structure and results should help to clarify the purpose of this function (see Figure 6.4).

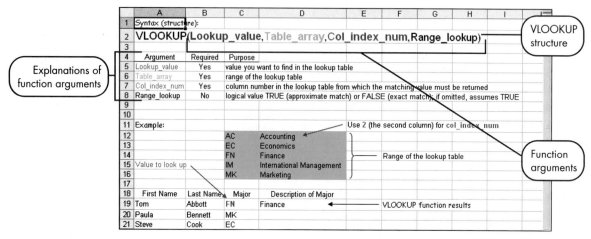

FIGURE 6.4

The syntax (structure) of the VLOOKUP function displays in row 2. The illustration shows each argument in a different color. This function includes three required arguments and one optional argument, and commas separate the arguments. Look in the range C5:C8 for explanations of the arguments.

You can specify exact or approximate matches when using the VLOOKUP function. Approximate matches enable you to work with values within a specified range. If you want to find exact matches, as is the case for major codes, specify FALSE as the fourth argument. Otherwise you can omit the fourth argument.

In this lesson, you complete two sets of hands-on steps. In the first set, you explore the syntax worksheet shown in Figure 6.4. You then switch to a second worksheet, in which you enter and copy a VLOOKUP function to create major descriptions in a student list. Each value looked up must be an exact match to an entry in the table. In the second set, you use the VLOOKUP function to create descriptions of donor level based on approximate matches. For example, VLOOKUP finds the donor level *Chairman Circle* for any donation between $1,000 and $2,499.

To Create Data Using the VLOOKUP Function (Exact Match)

1 Open the *EE2_0601* workbook, and save it as **VLOOKUP**.

2 Select the VLOOKUP syntax worksheet; then study the function syntax and explanations in rows 2–8 (refer to Figure 6.4).

3 Click cell D19; then study the example in rows 11–19 (see Figure 6.5).

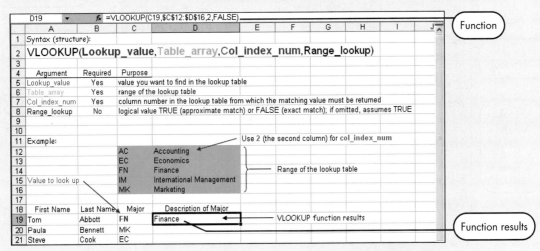

FIGURE 6.5

A blue arrow indicates the value to look up, green fill indicates the range of the lookup table, and a red arrow indicates how to specify the column from which to select the matching value.

4 Select the VLOOKUP (exact) worksheet.
The lookup table containing major codes and descriptions displays in the range C4:D8. You plan to enter a VLOOKUP function in cell D13 and copy it to the range D14:D20.

5 Select cell D13; then click the Insert Function button at the left end of the formula bar.

6 Select the *Lookup & Reference* category in the Insert Function dialog box; then select VLOOKUP as the function name, and click OK.
The Function Arguments dialog box for the VLOOKUP function displays.

7 Enter **C13** in the *Lookup_value* text box.

8 Enter **$C$4:$D$8** in the *Table_array* text box.
In this case, the range C4:D8 is an *array,* which in computing terms means an arrangement of data in a tabular form. Specifying dollar signs makes the reference to the table absolute. Doing so enables you to copy the VLOOKUP function.

9 Enter **2** in the *Col_index_num* text box.

10 Enter **FALSE** in the *Range_lookup* text box.

You entered four arguments for this VLOOKUP function (see Figure 6.6). You can enter **FALSE**, **False**, or **false** in the *Range_lookup* text box. Excel converts any lowercase letters to uppercase.

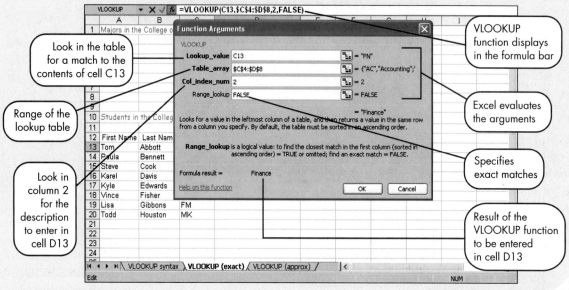

FIGURE 6.6

11 Make sure that your settings match those shown in Figure 6.6, and click OK to close the dialog box.

Finance displays in cell D13 as the description for major code *FN*.

If you have problems . . .

When cell D13 is selected, *=VLOOKUP(C13,$C$4:$D$8,2,FALSE)* should display in the formula bar. Edit the formula as needed. Be sure to include the dollar signs that make the reference to the range C4:D8 absolute before you copy the function in the next step.

---

12 Copy the function in cell D13 to the range D14:D20, and deselect the range.

The correct major descriptions display in column D except for cell D19, which holds the error value *#N/A* (see Figure 6.7). The lookup table does not contain an exact match for major code *FM* in cell C19.

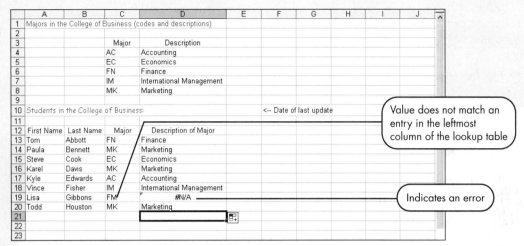

FIGURE 6.7

13 **Change the entry in cell C19 to FN instead of *FM*.**
The description *Finance* displays in cell D19.

14 **Save your changes to the *VLOOKUP* workbook.**
Keep the *VLOOKUP* workbook open for the next set of hands-on steps, or close the workbook and exit Excel.

In the previous hands-on steps, you specified FALSE as the optional *Range_lookup* argument in the VLOOKUP function. When you specify FALSE as the *Range_lookup* setting, only exact matches satisfy the lookup. If the *Range_lookup* is FALSE, you do not have to organize the values in ascending order in the first column of the lookup table.

Specify the logical value TRUE for the *Range_lookup* argument, or omit it, if the data to look up is not an exact match to an entry in the lookup table. The function finds the next largest value in the lookup table that is less than the lookup value. If the *Range_lookup* setting is TRUE or omitted, the values in the first column of the lookup table must be in ascending order to ensure correct results.

In the following hands-on steps, you use the VLOOKUP function to create descriptions of donor levels that depend on the amount donated. Omitting the *Range_lookup* argument enables the function to assign the donor level description based on a range of values.

To Create Data Using the VLOOKUP Function (Approximate Match)

1 **Open the *VLOOKUP* workbook, if necessary; then select the VLOOKUP (approx) worksheet.**
The worksheet tracks donations to the Sun City Zoological Society. The contributions needed to achieve a variety of donation levels form the lookup table in the range F2:G11 (see Figure 6.8).

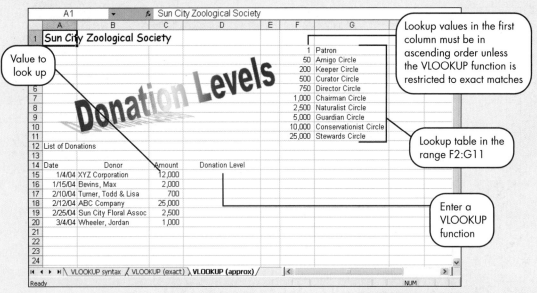

FIGURE 6.8

2 Select cell D15; then click the Insert Function button in the formula bar.

3 Select the Lookup & Reference category in the Insert Function dialog box; then select VLOOKUP as the function name, and click OK.

The Function Arguments dialog box for the VLOOKUP function displays.

4 Enter C15 in the *Lookup_value* text box.

5 Enter $F$2:$G$11 in the *Table_array* text box.

Make sure that you enter the dollar signs that make the reference to the table absolute. This is necessary because you are going to copy the VLOOKUP function.

6 Enter 2 in the *Col_index_num* text box (see Figure 6.9).

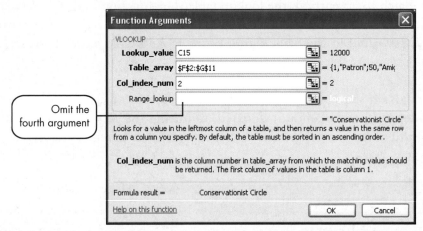

FIGURE 6.9

7 Make sure that your settings match those shown in Figure 6.9, and click OK to close the dialog box.

Conservationist Circle displays in cell D15 as the description for the donation level associated with contributing $12,000.

If you have problems . . .

When cell D15 is selected, =*VLOOKUP(C15,$F$2:$G$11,2)* should display in the formula bar. Edit the formula as needed. Be sure to include the dollar signs that make the reference to the range F2:G22 absolute before you copy the function in the next step.

---

8 **Copy the function in cell D15 to the range D16:D20, and deselect the range.**
Donation levels associated with the values in C16:C20 display in the range D16:D20 (see Figure 6.10).

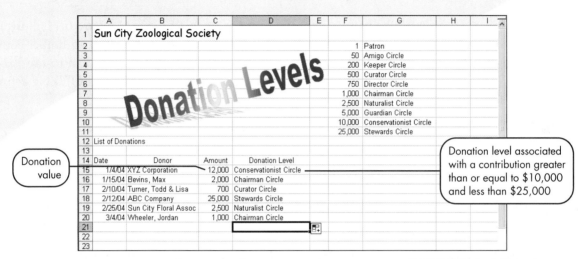

FIGURE 6.10

9 **Save your changes to the *VLOOKUP* workbook and close the workbook.**
Continue with the next lesson, or exit Excel.

TO EXTEND YOUR KNOWLEDGE . . .

USING HELP TO LEARN ABOUT LOOKUP FUNCTIONS
The link *Help on this function* appears on the Insert Function dialog box. By clicking this link, you can quickly access help about the selected function.

The Table of Contents in the Excel Help task pane provides quick access to information about all functions, including a variety of functions in the Lookup & Reference category. For example, you might want to use the MATCH function when you need to look up the position of an item in a range instead of the item itself. From the Table of Contents, select the following options in sequence: Working with Data, Function Reference, and Lookup Functions. You can then view examples and read information about the specific function(s) of your choice.

LESSON 2: Creating Data Using the HLOOKUP Function

Recall that the VLOOKUP function looks for a specified value in the leftmost column of a table array. When that value is found in a cell within the table, the function displays the contents of another cell in that same row from the column you specify.

Another function serves a similar purpose. The *HLOOKUP function* looks for a specified value in the topmost row of a table array. When that value is found in a cell within the table, the function displays the contents of another cell in that same column from the row you specify.

Looking at an example helps to clarify the purpose of this function. Figure 6.11 illustrates using the HLOOKUP function to convert the name of an organization to a number code 1 through 7. You might make a text-to-number conversion like this if you plan to use Excel's FREQUENCY function to summarize occurrences. You work with the FREQUENCY function in the next lesson.

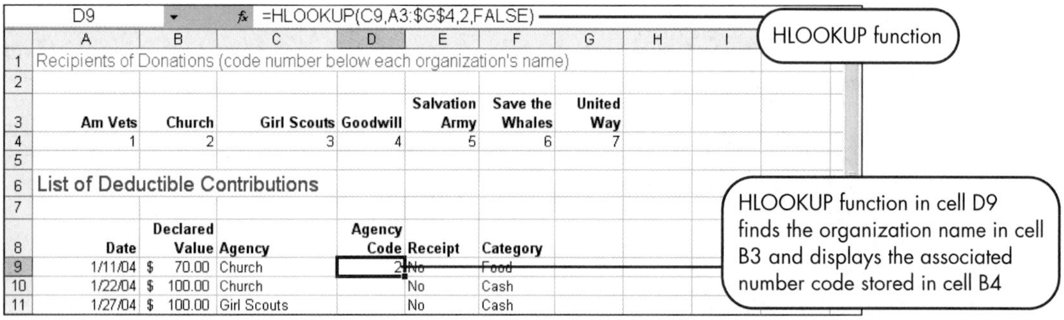

	D9		▼	*fx*	=HLOOKUP(C9,A3:$G$4,2,FALSE)					HLOOKUP function
	A	B	C	D	E	F	G	H	I	
1	Recipients of Donations (code number below each organization's name)									
2										
3	Am Vets	Church	Girl Scouts	Goodwill	Salvation Army	Save the Whales	United Way			
4	1	2	3	4	5	6	7			
5										
6	List of Deductible Contributions									
7										
8	Date	Declared Value	Agency	Agency Code	Receipt	Category				
9	1/11/04	$ 70.00	Church	2	No	Food				
10	1/22/04	$ 100.00	Church		No	Cash				
11	1/27/04	$ 100.00	Girl Scouts		No	Cash				

HLOOKUP function in cell D9 finds the organization name in cell B3 and displays the associated number code stored in cell B4

FIGURE 6.11

If the data you want to look up are stored vertically in a table—that is, in columns—use the VLOOKUP function. The "V" stands for *vertical*. If the data you want to look up are stored horizontally in a table—that is, in rows—then use the HLOOKUP function. The "H" stands for *horizontal*.

You can specify exact or approximate matches when using the VLOOKUP or HLOOKUP functions. Approximate matches enable you to work with values within a specified range.

In the following steps, you view the syntax (structure) of the HLOOKUP function, and then use it to create number codes for organization names based on exact matches to entries in the lookup table.

To Create Data Using the HLOOKUP Function (Exact Match)

1 Open the *EE2_0602* workbook, and save it as **HLOOKUP**.

2 Select the HLOOKUP syntax worksheet; then study the function syntax and explanations in rows 2–8 (see Figure 6.12).

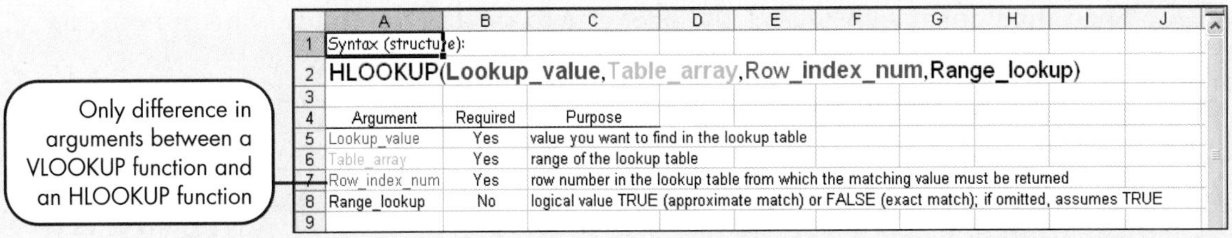

Only difference in arguments between a VLOOKUP function and an HLOOKUP function

	A	B	C	D	E	F	G	H	I	J
1	Syntax (structure):									
2	HLOOKUP(Lookup_value,Table_array,Row_index_num,Range_lookup)									
3										
4	Argument	Required	Purpose							
5	Lookup_value	Yes	value you want to find in the lookup table							
6	Table_array	Yes	range of the lookup table							
7	Row_index_num	Yes	row number in the lookup table from which the matching value must be returned							
8	Range_lookup	No	logical value TRUE (approximate match) or FALSE (exact match); if omitted, assumes TRUE							
9										

FIGURE 6.12

The syntax of the HLOOKUP function displays in row 2. The illustration shows each argument in a different color. The function includes three required arguments and one optional argument. If you want to find exact matches, specify FALSE as the fourth argument. Otherwise, you can omit the fourth argument.

3 Click cell D18; then study the example starting with row 11 (see Figure 6.13).

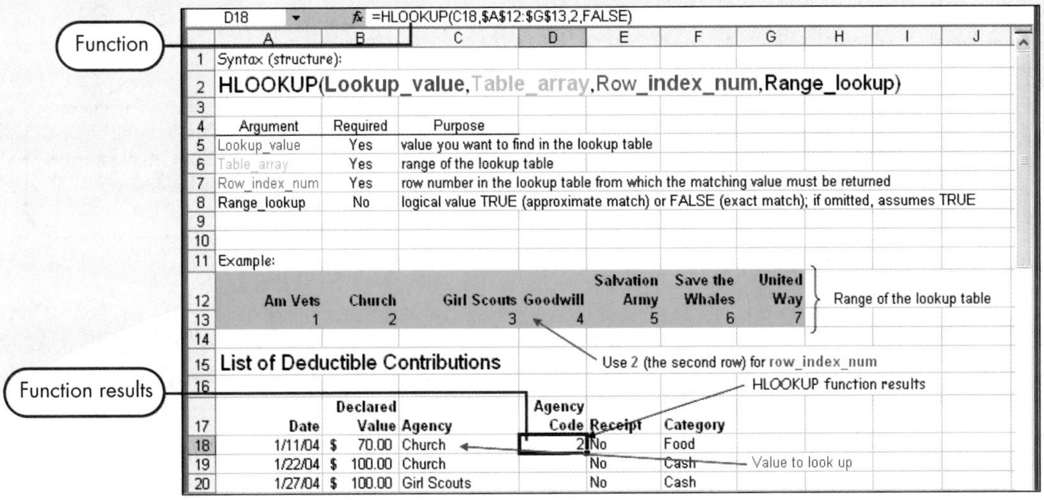

Function

D18   =HLOOKUP(C18,$A$12:$G$13,2,FALSE)

	A	B	C	D	E	F	G	H	I	J
1	Syntax (structure):									
2	HLOOKUP(Lookup_value,Table_array,Row_index_num,Range_lookup)									
3										
4	Argument	Required	Purpose							
5	Lookup_value	Yes	value you want to find in the lookup table							
6	Table_array	Yes	range of the lookup table							
7	Row_index_num	Yes	row number in the lookup table from which the matching value must be returned							
8	Range_lookup	No	logical value TRUE (approximate match) or FALSE (exact match); if omitted, assumes TRUE							
9										
10										
11	Example:									
12	Am Vets	Church	Girl Scouts	Goodwill	Salvation Army	Save the Whales	United Way			
13	1	2	3	4	5	6	7			
14										
15	List of Deductible Contributions				Use 2 (the second row) for row_index_num					
16						HLOOKUP function results				
17	Date	Declared Value	Agency	Agency Code	Receipt	Category				
18	1/11/04	$ 70.00	Church	2	No	Food				
19	1/22/04	$ 100.00	Church		No	Cash	Value to look up			
20	1/27/04	$ 100.00	Girl Scouts		No	Cash				

Function results

Range of the lookup table

FIGURE 6.13

A blue arrow indicates the value to look up, green fill indicates the range of the lookup table, and a red arrow indicates how to specify the row from which to select the matching value.

4 Select the HLOOKUP (exact) worksheet.
The lookup table containing organization names and associated code numbers displays in the range A3:G4. You plan to enter an HLOOKUP function in cell D9 and copy it to the range D10:D40.

5 Select cell D9; then click the Insert Function button in the formula bar.

6 Select the **Lookup & Reference** category in the **Insert Function** dialog box; then select **HLOOKUP** as the function name, and click **OK**.
The Function Arguments dialog box for the HLOOKUP function displays.

7 Enter **C9** in the *Lookup_value* text box.

8 Enter **$A$3:$G$4** in the *Table_array* text box.
Specifying dollar signs makes the reference to the table absolute. This is necessary because you are going to copy the HLOOKUP function.

9 Enter **2** in the *Row_index_num* text box.

10 Enter **FALSE** in the *Range_lookup* text box (see Figure 6.14).

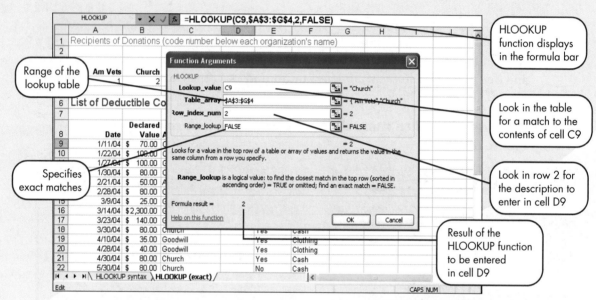

FIGURE 6.14

11 Make sure that your settings match those shown in Figure 6.14, and click **OK** to close the dialog box.
The number *2* displays in cell D9 as the number code for *Church*.

If you have problems . . .

When cell D9 is selected, *=HLOOKUP(C9,$A$3:$G$4,2,FALSE)* should display in the formula bar. Edit the formula as needed. Be sure to include the dollar signs that make the reference to the range A3:G4 absolute before you copy the function in the next step.

12 Copy the function in cell D9 to the range **D10:D40**, and deselect the range.
The correct number codes display in column D (see Figure 6.15).

	A	B	C	D	E	F	G	H	I	J
1	Recipients of Donations (code number below each organization's name)									
2										
3	Am Vets	Church	Girl Scouts	Goodwill	Salvation Army	Save the Whales	United Way			
4	1	2	3	4	5	6	7			
5										
6	List of Deductible Contributions									
7										
8	Date	Declared Value	Agency	Agency Code	Receipt	Category				
9	1/11/04	$ 70.00	Church	2	No	Food				
10	1/22/04	$ 100.00	Church	2	No	Cash				
11	1/27/04	$ 100.00	Girl Scouts	3	No	Cash				
12	1/30/04	$ 80.00	Church	2	Yes	Cash				
13	2/21/04	$ 50.00	Am Vets	1	No	Furniture				
14	2/28/04	$ 80.00	Church	2	Yes	Cash				
15	3/9/04	$ 25.00	Goodwill	4	Yes	Television				
16	3/14/04	$2,300.00	Goodwill	4	Yes	Car				
17	3/23/04	$ 140.00	Goodwill	4	No	Appliances				
18	3/30/04	$ 80.00	Church	2	Yes	Cash				
19	4/10/04	$ 35.00	Goodwill	4	Yes	Clothing				
20	4/28/04	$ 40.00	Goodwill	4	Yes	Clothing				
21	4/30/04	$ 80.00	Church	2	Yes	Cash				
22	5/30/04	$ 80.00	Church	2	No	Cash				

Data created using the HLOOKUP function

FIGURE 6.15

13 Save your changes to the *HLOOKUP* workbook, and close the workbook. Continue with the next lesson, or exit Excel.

TO EXTEND YOUR KNOWLEDGE . . .

FINDING AN APPROXIMATE MATCH WITH THE HLOOKUP FUNCTION

The *Range_lookup* argument is optional. However, if you specify FALSE as the *Range_lookup*, as you did in this lesson, only exact matches satisfy the lookup. If you specify the logical value TRUE for this component, or omit an entry for *Range_lookup*, the function uses the largest value that is less than or equal to the *Lookup_value*.

LESSON 3: Summarizing Data with FREQUENCY

You have likely seen surveys or other forms that request information on age, gender, highest year of formal education completed, annual or hourly income, and so forth. Those who analyze such data are generally interested in counting occurrences in selected categories, such as the number of respondents in each predetermined age range (20–29, 30–39, and so forth). A category is sometimes referred to as a *bin.* The counts for how often specific values occur within a set of values comprise a *frequency distribution.*

You can use Excel's *FREQUENCY function* to calculate how many times values occur within a range. The FREQUENCY function counts the occurrences of values in a range of cells and creates an array range to display results. An **array range** is a rectangular area of cells that share a common formula. Figure 6.16 illustrates how the FREQUENCY function works.

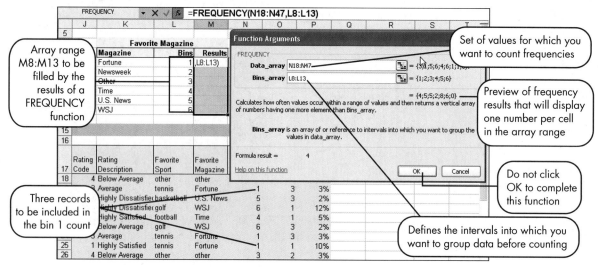

FIGURE 6.16

The FREQUENCY function generates an array. Therefore, you must enter it as an **array formula,** which means you must press the three-key combination Ctrl + ⬆Shift + ↵Enter instead of clicking OK in the Insert Function dialog box or pressing ↵Enter. You cannot edit or delete the contents of individual cells in an array. To remove the array, you select all cells in the array and press Del.

In this lesson you use the FREQUENCY function to tally the number of survey respondents who indicated a favorite magazine. You intend to place ads in the magazines mentioned most frequently. The bins are already set up as the magazine codes, arranged in ascending numeric order (see the range L8:L13 in Figure 6.16). The magazine names in the range K8:K13 are used for documentation of the bins and are not required for the function to work. However, the magazine titles make it easier to understand the frequency distribution, and they can be used as labels if you want to chart the results.

To Summarize Data with the FREQUENCY Function

1 Open the *EE2_0603* workbook and save it as `Indy500functions`.

2 Select (highlight) the range M8:M13.
You must select the entire output range for the frequency distribution before you start entering the FREQUENCY function.

3 Click the Insert Function button on the formula bar, and select *Statistical* as the function category.

4 Select FREQUENCY as the function name, and click OK.
The Function Arguments dialog box for the FREQUENCY function displays.

5 Enter `N18:N47` in the *Data_array* text box.

6 | Enter **L8:L13** in the *Bins_array* text box, but *do not* click OK or press
⏎Enter .

7 | **Check that your specifications match those shown in Figure 6.16; then press
the three-key combination Ctrl + ⬆Shift + ⏎Enter , and click any cell within
M8:M13 to deselect the range.**

Excel creates the frequency distribution in the range M8:M13 (see Figure 6.17). If
the FREQUENCY function operates as intended, the numbers *4* (Fortune), *5*
(Newsweek), *5* (Other), *2* (Time), *8* (U.S. News), and *6* (WSJ) display in the range
M8:M13.

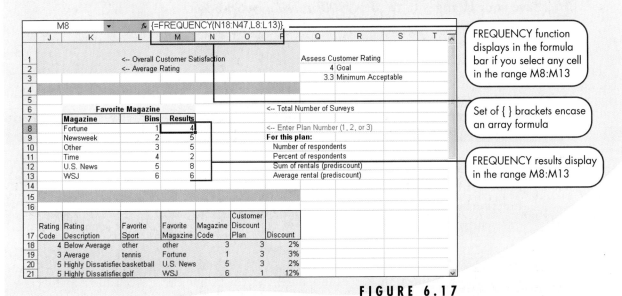

FIGURE 6.17

If you have problems . . .

If you have results only in the first cell of the range—the number 4 in cell M8—one of
two actions is the most likely reason for the problem. You may have selected only the
first cell of the result range (M8) instead of selecting M8:M13 in step 2. You may have
completed the FREQUENCY function by pressing ⏎Enter instead of pressing
Ctrl + ⬆Shift + ⏎Enter in step 7. To correct the problem, delete the contents of cells
M8:M13 and repeat steps 2–7.

If you continue to have problems, abandon the use of the Insert Function feature.
Delete the contents of cells M8:M13, select the range M8:M13, type **=FREQUENCY
(N18:N47,L8:L13)**, and press the three-key combination Ctrl + ⬆Shift + ⏎Enter .

8 | Enter **=COUNT(N18:N47)** in cell O6.
There are 30 records in the list.

9 | Enter **=SUM(M8:M13)** in cell M14.
The counts in the frequency distribution should also sum to 30.

If you have problems . . .

The results of the COUNT and SUM functions should be the same. If either result is not 30, check that you used the appropriate ranges in your calculations.

10 **Delete the contents of cell M14.**

After you check the frequency counts against the total records in the list, you no longer need the value in cell M14.

11 **Save your changes to the *Indy500functions* workbook.**

You can close the *Indy500functions* workbook now, or leave it open and continue to the next lesson.

TO EXTEND YOUR KNOWLEDGE . . .

ENTERING THE FREQUENCY FUNCTION

FREQUENCY is an array function because it returns an array of results. Array functions work differently from other functions and are entered on the worksheet differently.

Be sure you select the entire output range before attempting to enter the FREQUENCY function. You cannot enter the function in the first cell and copy the results to other cells as you do regular functions. The output range does not have to be adjacent to the bins, but it is easier to understand the results if they are adjacent.

The FREQUENCY function ignores blank cells and text entries in the *Data_array* range. If all the occurrences of numeric data to be counted exactly match bin specifications—for example, one code number representing each magazine—the bin range and output range are the same size. However, if bins represent ranges of data and not exact matches, you should include one more cell for frequency results than there are bins. The extra cell displays the count for any data items that are greater than the highest interval value stated. For example, if you want to do a frequency distribution on age, you might set bin values of 19, 34, 49 and 64. You should then specify five cells, not four, in the range for frequency results. The five cells in the output range would display counts for five age groups: 19 and under, 20 to 34, 35 to 49, 50 to 64, and 65 or older.

LESSON 4: # Charting the Results of a Frequency Distribution

When analyzing data using Excel, visualizing the data is critical to understanding what information the data convey. You may find it hard to make comparisons or draw conclusions just looking at numbers. Generally, a chart can help you to analyze or interpret the data.

In this lesson, you chart the results of a frequency distribution. On a separate sheet, you create a pie chart that converts number data to percentages. Each pie slice represents a favorite publication, such as the Wall Street Journal (WSJ) or Newsweek.

To Chart the Results of a Frequency Distribution

1 If necessary, open the *Indy500functions* workbook.

2 Select the range K8:K13 in the Sheet1 worksheet.

3 Press and hold down Ctrl, select the range M8:M13, and release Ctrl.

4 Click the Chart Wizard button on the Standard toolbar and select the default Pie chart.

5 Advance to Step 3 of 4–Chart Options, select the Titles tab, and enter `Favorite Magazine (Sample Size 30)` as the chart title.

6 Select the Data Labels tab; click *Category name* and also click *Percentage*.

7 Select the Legend tab and uncheck *Show legend*.

8 Advance to Step 4 of 4 – Chart Location; then select *As new sheet,* and click **Finish**.
Excel creates the specified chart on a sheet named Chart1 (see Figure 6.18). Each pie slice represents the contents of one cell in the frequency distribution in relation to the sum of all cell contents in the frequency distribution.

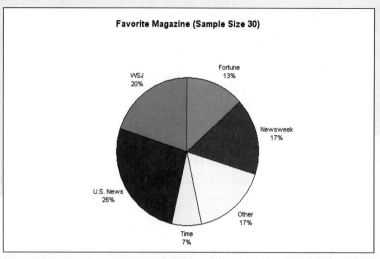

Favorite Magazine (Sample Size 30)

WSJ 20%

Fortune 13%

Newsweek 17%

U.S. News 26%

Other 17%

Time 7%

FIGURE 6.18

9 **Save your changes to the *Indy500functions* workbook.**
You can close the *Indy500functions* workbook now, or leave it open and continue to the next lesson.

LESSON 5:   Analyzing Data with COUNTIF

Excel provides a ***COUNTIF function*** that you can use to count the number of cells within a range that meet your specified criteria. The function requires two arguments—the range of cells from which the counts will be tallied, and the criteria that limit which cells in that range are counted.

To work with this function, assume that you want to analyze vehicle rental records by type of discount plan—Plan 1, Plan 2, or Plan 3. You can use this tool now to limit analysis to one plan at a time, starting with Plan 1.

To Analyze Data with COUNTIF

1 **If necessary, open the *Indy500functions* workbook.**

2 **Select cell O8 in Sheet1, and enter 1 as the plan number.**

3 **Select cell O10, click the Insert Function button on the formula bar, and select *Statistical* as the function category.**

4 **Select COUNTIF as the function name, and click OK.**
The Function Arguments dialog box for the COUNTIF function opens.

5 **Enter O18:O47 in the *Range* text box.**

6 **Enter O8 in the *Criteria* text box.**

7 Check that your specifications match those shown in Figure 6.19, and make corrections as necessary.

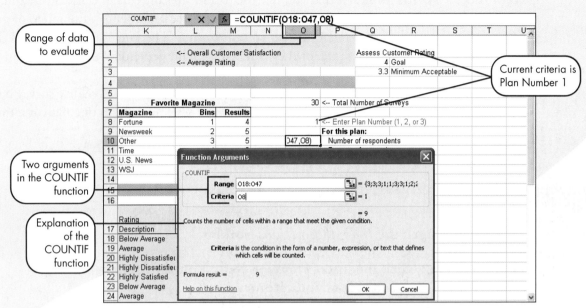

FIGURE 6.19

8 Click OK.
The number *9* displays in cell O10 as the count for Plan 1.

9 Select cell O11 and enter =O10/O6.

10 Apply a Percent, zero decimal places format to cell O11.
Plan 1 applies to 30% of survey respondents.

11 Save your changes to the *Indy500functions* workbook.
You can close the *Indy500functions* workbook now, or leave it open and continue to the last lesson.

TO EXTEND YOUR KNOWLEDGE . . .

USING COUNTIF WITH COMPARISON OPERATORS
COUNTIF criteria do not have to be exact matches. You can use COUNTIF to count values in a range that are greater than or less than a specified value. Enter the comparison number preceded by <, <=, =, >, or >= to indicate less than, less than or equal to, equal to, greater than, and greater than or equal to, respectively.

For example, assume that age data are entered in the range B10:B90 within an Excel list. Further assume that labels indicate COUNTIF criteria should be entered in cell B2 and a COUNTIF function should be entered in cell B3. To view the number of ages less than 21, enter **<21** in cell B2 and enter **=COUNTIF(B10:B90,B2)** in cell B3. To view the number of ages greater than or equal to 65, you need only change the criteria in cell B2 to **>=65**.

LESSON 6: Analyzing Data with SUMIF

Excel provides a **SUMIF function** that you can use to add the contents of cells within a range that meet your specified criteria. The function requires three arguments—the range of cells you want to evaluate, the criteria, and the actual cells to sum. The ranges entered for the first and third arguments can be the same, or they can be different, depending on the situation.

To illustrate this function, assume that you are continuing your analysis of vehicle survey data. Now, you want to sum the pre-discount rental charges by plan, limited to one plan at a time. You can use the SUMIF function to produce the desired results.

To Analyze Data with SUMIF

1 If necessary, open the *Indy500functions* workbook.

2 Select cell O12, click the Insert Function button on the formula bar, and select *Math & Trig* as the function category.

3 Select SUMIF as the function name, and click OK.
The Functions Arguments dialog box for the SUMIF function displays.

4 Enter **O18:O47** in the *Range* text box.

5 Enter **O8** in the *Criteria* text box.

6 Enter **I18:I47** in the *Sum_range* text box.

7 Check that your specifications match those shown in Figure 6.20, and make corrections as necessary.

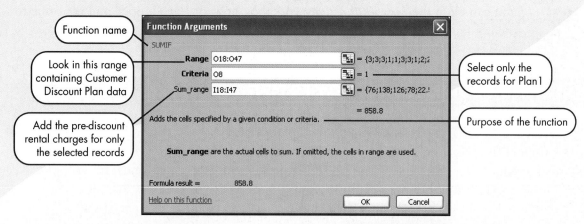

FIGURE 6.20

8 **Click OK.**

The value *858.8* displays in cell O12 as the sum for Plan 1 (see Figure 6.21).

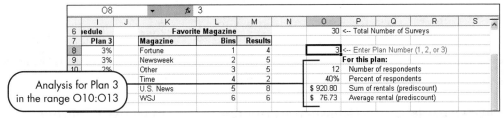

	I	J	K	L	M	N	O	P	Q	R	S
O12			fx	=SUMIF(O18:O47,O8,I18:I47)							
8	3%		Fortune	1	4		1	<-- Enter Plan Number (1, 2, or 3)			
9	3%		Newsweek	2	5			For this plan:			
10	2%		Other	3	5		9	Number of respondents			
11			Time	4	2		30%	Percent of respondents			
12			U.S. News	5	8		858.8	Sum of rentals (prediscount)			
13			WSJ	6	6			Average rental (prediscount)			
14											

SUMIF function

Sum of rentals for customers under Plan 1

FIGURE 6.21

If you have problems . . .

If your result is different from *858.8,* check that the ranges used in your function are correct, and that you entered the number 1 for the criteria in cell O8.

---

9 **Select cell O13 and enter =O12/O10.**

10 **Apply a Currency, two decimal places format to cells O12 and O13.**

The sum of the rentals under Plan 1 is $858.80 and the average rental is $95.42.

11 **Enter 3 in cell O8.**

Excel recalculates the values in the range O10:O13 to reflect Plan 3 instead of Plan 1 (see Figure 6.22). You can perform analysis on Plan 1, 2, or 3 by changing the number in cell O8.

	I	J	K	L	M	N	O	P	Q	R	S
O8			fx	3							
6	iedule		**Favorite Magazine**				30	<-- Total Number of Surveys			
7	**Plan 3**		**Magazine**	**Bins**	**Results**						
8	3%		Fortune	1	4		3	<-- Enter Plan Number (1, 2, or 3)			
9	3%		Newsweek	2	5			For this plan:			
10	2%		Other	3	5		12	Number of respondents			
			Time	4	2		40%	Percent of respondents			
			U.S. News	5	8		$ 920.80	Sum of rentals (prediscount)			
			WSJ	6	6		$ 76.73	Average rental (prediscount)			

Analysis for Plan 3 in the range O10:O13

FIGURE 6.22

12 **Save your changes to the *Indy500functions* workbook and close the workbook.**

Continue with the end-of-project activities, or exit Excel.

SUMMARY

In this project, you used functions to create and analyze data. You began by using the VLOOKUP and HLOOKUP functions to enter text based on exact and approximate matches to existing data. You used the FREQUENCY function to count how often specified data occurred within a range, and you charted the frequency distribution results. SUMIF and COUNTIF functions provided the tools to restrict analysis to data meeting specified conditions.

You can extend your learning by reviewing concepts and terms, and by practicing variations of skills presented in the lessons. Use the following table as a guide to the numbered questions and exercises in the end-of-project learning opportunities.

LESSON	MULTIPLE CHOICE	DISCUSSION	SKILL DRILL	CHALLENGE	DISCOVERY ZONE
Creating Data Using the VLOOKUP Function	3, 9	2	1, 3	3, 4	1, 2
Creating Data Using the HLOOKUP Function	4, 9	2	2		1
Summarizing Data with FREQUENCY	1, 2, 3, 5, 8, 10	1, 2	3	1	
Charting the Results of a Frequency Distribution	7		4		
Analyzing Data with COUNTIF	6	3	5	2	
Analyzing Data with SUMIF		3	6	2	

KEY TERMS

array	COUNTIF function	SUMIF function
array formula	frequency distribution	VLOOKUP function
array range	FREQUENCY function	
bin	HLOOKUP function	

CHECKING CONCEPTS AND TERMS

MULTIPLE CHOICE

Circle the letter of the correct answer for each of the following.

1. Which of the following is the key combination used to generate a frequency distribution? [L3]

   a. Ctrl + Alt + Del

   b. Ctrl + ⬆Shift + ⏎Enter

   c. Ctrl + ⏎Enter

   d. ⬆Shift + Alt + ⏎Enter

2. Which function would you use to calculate the occurrences of values in a range of cells and return a vertical array of cells containing the distribution of these occurrences? [L3]

   a. VLOOKUP

   b. HLOOKUP

   c. FREQUENCY

   d. SUMIF

3. Which of the following is true? [L1, L3]

   a. When using the VLOOKUP function, the search values in column 1 of the *Table_array* must always be in ascending order.

   b. You can use the FREQUENCY function to convert text data to numbers so the data can be summarized.

   c. Both a and b

   d. Neither a or b

4. Which of the following is a true statement about HLOOKUP? [L2]

   a. The "H" in HLOOKUP stands for *holographic*.

   b. Data to be looked up are stored in columns.

   c. You can specify exact or approximate matches.

   d. None of the above

5. Assume you are setting up bins for use in creating a frequency distribution. The first value in the bin range is $1,000, the second value in the bin range is $2,000, and the third value in the bin range is $3,000. Which of the following is a true statement? [L3]

   a. Any occurrence of $1,000 is counted in the first bin.

   b. Any occurrence of a number greater than $2,000 is counted in the second bin.

   c. Both a and b

   d. Neither a nor b

6. The COUNTIF function is capable of which of the following? [L5]

   a. Counting numbers that are greater than, less than, or equal to a specified value

   b. Counting dates that match a specified date

   c. Both a and b

   d. Neither a nor b

7. Which function produces results that you can chart? [L4]

   a. VLOOKUP

   b. HLOOKUP

   c. FREQUENCY

   d. SUMIF

8. Which of the following is true when using the FREQUENCY function? [L3]

a. You can enter the function in the first cell of the output range and copy it to the other cells in that range.

b. The output range must be adjacent to the bin range.

c. The bin range and the output range must always be the same size.

d. Blank cells in the *Data_array* range are ignored.

9. When using VLOOKUP or HLOOKUP, which of the following *Range_lookup* values will result in a search for exact values? [L1, L2]

a. TRUE

b. FALSE

c. EXACT

d. EQUAL

10. Which of the following is a rectangular area of cells that share a common formula? [L3]

a. Bin

b. Array range

c. Lookup table

d. None of the above

DISCUSSION

Use the following figure to answer the discussion questions.

	A	B	C	D	E	F	G	H	I	J
1	Residential Real Estate Listings: Glenn Lakes Realty									
2	Current Listings									
3										
4	Listed	Price	Area	Lot #	BRs	Baths	Heat	Built	Financing	
5	May-04	$ 235,000	5	329	3	2.0	Heat Pump	1999	FHA	
6	Aug-04	$ 146,500	2	20	3	3.0	Gas	1995	VA	
7	Mar-04	$ 325,000	4	453	2	2.0	Gas	1995	FHA	
8	Jul-04	$ 191,000	2	191	2	2.5	Elec	2000	OTHER	
9	Mar-04	$ 159,000	3	313	3	3.0	Elec	1997	VA	
10	Apr-04	$ 249,000	5	93	4	3.0	Gas	1995	FHA	
11	Mar-04	$ 187,500	3	40	3	2.0	Gas	1997	FHA	
12	Jul-04	$ 172,000	3	112	4	2.0	Heat Pump	2002	VA	
13	Dec-04	$ 225,000	2	113	3	3.0	Heat Pump	2001	OTHER	
14	May-04	$ 210,000	1	230	3	2.5	Heat Pump	2000	ALL	
15	Jul-04	$ 291,000	3	141	2	2.5	Heat Pump	2001	ALL	
16	Mar-04	$ 195,000	3	175	2	3.0	Gas	2002	FHA	
17	Nov-04	$ 254,000	2	178	3	2.0	Gas	2000	VA	
18	May-04	$ 230,000	5	192	4	2.0	Elec	1995	FHA	
19	Jun-04	$ 205,500	2	309	3	2.0	Heat Pump	1997	OTHER	
20	Sep-04	$ 235,000	3	333	4	2.0	Heat Pump	2002	VA	
21	Jan-04	$ 146,500	3	306	3	2.0	Heat Pump	2001	FHA	
22	Jan-04	$ 325,000	1	285	3	2.0	Gas	2001	FHA	
23	Nov-04	$ 191,000	5	54	2	3.0	Gas	1999	VA	

FIGURE 6.23

1. Refer to Figure 6.23. Describe two ways that you can use the FREQUENCY function to analyze the real estate listings data. Discuss why you cannot use FREQUENCY to analyze Heat type and Financing in the current data format in the real estate database. What would you have to do to analyze those data using FREQUENCY? [L3]

2. Refer to Figure 6.23. Assume that each entry in the Area column indicates one of five construction areas. Describe two ways that you can use the VLOOKUP (or HLOOKUP) function to analyze the real estate listings data. Think about how you can use the data as input to the FREQUENCY function to perform further analysis. [L1–L3]

3. Refer to Figure 6.23. Describe one way that you can use the SUMIF function to analyze the real estate listings data, and one way that you can use the COUNTIF function to analyze the real estate listings data. Discuss how you can combine the results from these two functions to perform additional analysis. [L5, L6]

SKILL DRILL

Skill Drill exercises reinforce project skills. Each skill that is reinforced is the same, or nearly the same, as a skill presented in the project. Detailed instructions are provided in a step-by-step format.

You use the same worksheet for all of the Project 6 Skill Drill exercises. Work through these exercises in the order presented. Be sure to save your changes and close the workbook if you need more than one work session to complete the desired exercises. Then, continue working on *EE2_P6drill* instead of starting over on the original *EE2_0604* file.

1. Using the VLOOKUP Function

Your current Residential Real Estate Listing of the Glenn Lakes subdivision lists the location of homes by construction area numbers 1 through 5. These areas now have legal names to designate each community. You want to convert the area numbers to their legal names without having to type each one individually. You can do this by using the VLOOKUP function. To use a VLOOKUP function to create data, complete the following steps:

1. Open the *EE2_0604* workbook and save it as **EE2_P6drill**.

   The VLOOKUP table has already been created in the range A8:B12. The range D20:D56 is set up to receive the names of the community areas as they are converted from area numbers in the adjacent cells C20:C56.

2. Click cell D20 in the RealEstateAnalysis worksheet; then click the Insert Function button at the left end of the formula bar.

3. Select VLOOKUP from the Lookup & Reference category and click OK.

4. Enter **C20** in the *Lookup_value* text box.

5. Enter **$A$8:$B$12** in the *Table_array* text box.

6. Enter **2** in the *Col_index_num* field and enter **FALSE** in the *Range_lookup* text box.

7. Verify that *Jacaranda* appears next to *Formula result* = in the Function Arguments dialog box.

8. Click OK.

   Jacaranda displays in cell D20 as the assigned name for area 5.

9. Copy the function in cell D20 to the range D21:D56.

10. Verify that the correct area names appear in cells D21:D56.

11. Save your changes to the *EE2_P6drill* workbook.

2. Using the HLOOKUP Function

Your residential real estate list includes fields for Heat Code and Heat Type. The Heat Type column is blank, but now that you have finished a survey of the homes in your inventory you want to display the type of heat as one of the data items. The code for type of heat has been entered in H20:H56 and a blank space has been provided for the interpretation of that code in cells I20:I56. A table has been set up in cells B15:E16 which you can use to convert the heat codes to their literal names. To use HLOOKUP to convert these codes, complete the following steps:

1. Open the *EE2_P6drill* workbook, if necessary.

2. Click cell I20, and then click the Insert Function button on the formula bar.

3. Select HLOOKUP in the Lookup & Reference category, and click OK.

4. Enter **H20** in the *Lookup_value* text box in the Function Arguments dialog box.

5. Enter **$B$15:$E$16** in the *Table_array* text box.

6. Enter **2** in the *Row_index_num* field and enter **FALSE** in the *Range_lookup* text box.

7. Verify that *Heat Pump* appears next to *Formula result* = in the Function Arguments dialog box.

8. Click OK.

9. Copy the function in cell I20 to the range I21:I56.

10. Verify that the correct type of heat appears in cells I21:I56.

11. Save your changes to the *EE2_P6drill* workbook.

3. Using VLOOKUP and Creating a Frequency Distribution

Your residential real estate list includes a field named Financing Type. You can use the FREQUENCY function to summarize the number of homes in the list based on the type of financing if you first assign a numeric equivalent to each financing type. (Recall that the FREQUENCY function can only be applied to numbers.)

You have already done some of the preliminary work. The lookup table already exists in the range D8:E12; it shows the number assigned to each financing category. The range J20:J56 consists of blank cells that will hold the financing codes. To use VLOOKUP to enter the numeric equivalents and then create a frequency distribution, complete the following steps:

1. Open the *EE2_P6drill* workbook, if necessary.

2. Click cell J20, and then click the Insert Function button on the formula bar.

3. Select VLOOKUP from the Lookup & Reference category, and click OK.

4. Enter **K20** in the *Lookup_value* text box.

5. Enter **$D$8:$E$12** in the *Table_array* text box.

6. Enter **2** in the *Col_index_num* field.

7. Enter **FALSE** in the *Range_lookup* text box, and click OK.

The financing code *3* displays in cell J20.

8. Copy the function in cell J20 to the range J21:J56.

9. Verify that the correct number codes appear in cells J21:J56.

Now that you have converted the financing type labels to numeric codes, you are ready to perform a frequency distribution to analyze the number of homes according to the financing alternatives. In the remaining steps, you type the function instead of using the Function Arguments dialog box.

10. Select cells I8:I12.

11. Enter **=FREQUENCY(J20:J56,H8:H12)**.

12. Press Ctrl+⇧Shift+↵Enter.

Excel creates the frequency distribution. The counts 6, 2, 12, 6, and 11 display in cells I8 through I12, respectively.

13. Click cell I13; then click AutoSum on the Standard toolbar and press ↵Enter.

The sum of your results should equal 37.

14. Delete the SUM function in cell I13, and save your changes to the *EE2_P6drill* workbook.

4. Charting the Results of a FREQUENCY Distribution

You are confident reading and understanding frequency results. However, you feel that other users of the data will have a better understanding of the types of financing available if they can see the frequency distribution results in the form of a pie chart. To chart the results of a frequency distribution, complete the following steps:

1. Open the *EE2_P6drill* workbook, if necessary.

2. Select the ranges G8:G12, hold down Ctrl, select cells I8:I12, and release Ctrl.

3. Select Chart Wizard from the Standard toolbar, select the default Pie chart, and then click Next to advance to Step 3 of 4.

4. Enter **Analysis of Financing Methods** in the *Chart title* text box on the Titles tab.

5. Select the Legend tab and uncheck *Show legend.*

6. Select the Data Labels tab and check the *Category name* and *Value* check boxes; then click Next.

7. Select *As new sheet* for the location of the pie chart, and then click Finish.

8. Save your changes to the *EE2_P6drill* workbook.

5. Using COUNTIF to Analyze Data

As you continue to analyze the Glenn Lakes residential listings, you want to analyze data by area, one area at a time. To begin your analysis using COUNTIF, complete the following steps:

1. Open the *EE2_P6drill* workbook, if necessary.

2. Enter **Palms** in cell J14 of the RealEstateAnalysis worksheet.

3. Select cell J16, and click the Insert Function button on the formula bar.

4. Select the *Statistical* category, select the COUNTIF function, and click OK.

5. Enter **D20:D56** in the Range text box.

6. Enter **J14** in the *Criteria* text box, and click OK; then apply a Comma, zero decimal places format to cell J16.

Excel counts the occurrences of homes in the Palms area that are listed in column D and displays the number *6* in cell J16. You can count the number of homes in a different area simply by typing the name of the new area in cell J14. When you use a separate cell for your criteria, you can easily change the criteria without editing the function itself.

7. Save your changes to the *EE2_P6drill* workbook.

6. Using SUMIF to Analyze Data

As you continue your analysis of Glenn Lakes residential listings by area, you want to know the average selling price of all homes listed in an area. You can use the results of COUNTIF and SUMIF functions to generate the desired information. Complete the following steps:

1. Open the *EE2_P6drill* workbook, if necessary.

2. Make sure that *Palms* is entered in cell J14.

3. Select cell J15, and click the Insert Function button at the left end of the formula bar.

4. Select the *Math & Trig* category, select the SUMIF function, and click OK.

5. Enter **D20:D56** in the *Range* text box.

6. Enter **J14** in the *Criteria* text box, and enter B20:B56 in the *Sum_range* text box.

7. Click OK, and apply a Currency, zero decimal places format to cell J15. Also widen column J if necessary.

Excel sums the price of homes in the Palms area; *$1,467,000* displays in cell J15.

8. Enter the formula **=J15/J16** in cell J17; then apply a Currency, zero decimal places format to cell J17.

Dividing the total price for homes in the specified area (cell J15) by the count of homes in the specified area (cell J16) calculates the average price for homes in the specified area; *$244,500* displays in cell J17 as the average price for homes in the Palms area.

9. Change the area to **Jacaranda** in cell J14.

The total price for the eight homes listed in the Jacaranda area is $1,743,000. The average price for a listed home in that area is $217,875.

10. Save your changes to the *EE2_P6drill* workbook and close the workbook.

CHALLENGE

Challenge exercises expand on or are somewhat related to skills that are presented in the lessons. Each exercise provides a brief narrative introduction, followed by instructions in a numbered-step format that are not as detailed as those in the Skill Drill section.

Before beginning your first Project 6 Challenge exercise, complete the following steps:

1. Open the file named *EE2_0605* and immediately save it as **EE2_P6challenge**.

   The *EE2_P6challenge* workbook contains four sheets: an overview, and three exercise sheets named #1-Distribution, #2-CountSum, and #3#4-VLOOKUP.

2. Click the Overview sheet to view the organization of the Project 6 Challenge Exercises workbook.

The exercises are independent of each other, so you may complete them in any order. Be sure to save the workbook after completing each exercise. If you need a paper copy of the completed exercise, enter your name centered in a header before printing. Other print options have already been set to print compressed to one page and to display the filename, sheet name, and current date in a footer. If you need more than one work session to complete the desired exercises, continue working on *EE2_P6challenge* instead of starting over on the original *EE2_0605* file.

1. Creating a Frequency Distribution Based on Ranges of Values

You want to count the number of times you made contributions within several ranges of declared values. To summarize your contributions using the FREQUENCY function, follow these steps:

1. Open the *EE2_P6challenge* workbook, if necessary; then select the #1-Distribution sheet.

2. In an area above the list of contributions, set up your choice of bins—at least three, but no more than seven. To the left of those bins, enter labels describing the bins.

3. Select the output range for the distribution.

   Because you are working with data that seldom match bin specifications, remember to include one more cell in the distribution range than you defined in the bin range.

4. Enter the FREQUENCY function to count occurrences of declared values based on the bins you set up.

5. Make sure that the total number of counts in the frequency distribution matches the number of records in the contributions list.

6. Save your changes to the *EE2_P6challenge* workbook.

2. Using COUNTIF and SUMIF to Summarize Data

You decide to analyze your contribution data by generating counts and totals. To use COUNTIF and SUMIF to generate the information you want, complete the following steps:

1. Open the *EE2_P6challenge* workbook, if necessary; then select the #2-CountSum sheet.

   For the first four analyses, labels indicate that calculated results are to display in the range A3:A6, based on conditions you specify in the range G3:G6.

2. Enter data in cell G3 and a function in cell A3 so that the number of times you donated to Goodwill (*8*) displays in cell A3.

3. Enter data in cell G4 and a function in cell A4 so that the sum of cash contributions (*$2,265*) displays in cell A4.

4. Enter data in cell G5 and a function in cell A5 so that the total declared value contributed to the church (*$1,650*) displays in cell A5.

5. Enter data in cell G6 and a function in cell A6 so that the number of times a contribution exceeded $99.99 (*10*) displays in cell A6.

6. Change the data in one or more cells within the range G3:G6 to make sure that the functions produce accurate results.

7. In rows 9 and 10 enter two more COUNTIF and/or SUMIF functions to calculate information of your choice based on the contributions data. Use the organization shown in rows 3–6, including descriptive text.

8. Save your changes to the *EE2_P6challenge* workbook.

3. Using a Simple VLOOKUP Function

You are developing a worksheet of survey results that includes a Rating Code column. Entries in that column are numbers between 1 and 5. You want to use a VLOOKUP function to enter the corresponding descriptions, such as Highly Satisfied for the number 1 and Below Average for the number 4. To enter the VLOOKUP function, complete the following steps:

1. Open the *EE2_P6challenge* workbook, if necessary; then click cell K19 in the #3#4-VLOOKUP sheet.

   The worksheet includes space in column K to enter the rating descriptions.

2. Display the Function Arguments dialog box for the VLOOKUP function.

3. Make the appropriate entries in the *Lookup_value, Table_array, Col_index_num,* and *Range_lookup* text boxes; then click OK.

4. Verify that *Below Average* displays in cell K19 as the assigned description for rating code 4.

5. Copy the function in cell K19 down the column to the last entry in the list; then widen column K, if necessary.

6. Verify that the correct rating descriptions display in column K, and save your changes to the *EE2_P6challenge* workbook.

4. Using a Complex VLOOKUP Function

You are developing a worksheet of survey results that includes a Discount column. The percentage to enter in that column depends on a customer's plan (1, 2, or 3) and that customer's method of payment (account, cash, or credit card). You want to use a VLOOKUP function to enter the percentages in column P that correspond to the types of payment in column C and the customers' discount plans in column O. To enter the VLOOKUP function, complete the following steps:

1. Open the *EE2_P6challenge* workbook and select the #3#4-VLOOKUP sheet, if necessary.

   The worksheet includes a Car Rental Discount Schedule in the range F7:I11. It also includes space in column P to enter the discount percentages.

2. Scroll to display cell A5 in the upper-left corner of the worksheet window, select cell J14, and choose <u>W</u>indow, <u>F</u>reeze Panes.

   This enables you to continue displaying data in columns A–I and rows 5–13 as you scroll to view remaining columns and rows.

3. Scroll to display data in columns O and P; then click cell P19 and open the Function Arguments dialog box for the VLOOKUP function.

   You can use VLOOKUP to create data based on two conditions—in this case, looking up the discount percent for a combination of payment type and discount plan.

4. Enter **C19** in the *Lookup_value* text box and enter **$F$9:$I$11** in the *Table_array* text box.

5. Enter **O19+1** in the *Col_index_num* text box.

   Make sure you understand how this specification tells Excel which discount table column to use. For example, cell O19 indicates Plan 3; adding the number 1 to the number 3 tells Excel to look in the fourth column in the lookup table.

6. Make the appropriate entry in the *Range_lookup* text box to ensure an exact match lookup.

7. Click OK to close the dialog box and apply a Percent, zero decimal places format to cell P19.

   The value *2%* displays in cell P19. Per the table, a credit card (cc) customer under Plan 3 gets a 2% discount.

8. Copy the function in cell P19 down the column to the last entry in the list; then click cell P22.

   Per the table, a cash customer under Plan 1 gets a 12% discount.

9. Verify that the correct discount percentages display in column P; then unfreeze the panes and save your changes to the *EE2_P6challenge* workbook.

DISCOVERY ZONE

Discovery Zone exercises require advanced knowledge of topics presented in *Essentials* lessons, application of skills from multiple lessons, or self-directed learning of new skills.

Before beginning your first Project 6 Discovery Zone exercise, complete the following steps:

1. Open the file named *EE2_0606* and immediately save it as **EE2_P6discovery**.

   The *EE2_P6discovery* workbook contains three sheets: an overview, and two exercise sheets named #1-LetterGrade, and #2-FindGrade.

2. Select the Overview worksheet to view the organization of the Project 6 Discovery Zone Exercises workbook.

The exercises are independent of each other, so you may complete them in any order. Be sure to save the workbook after completing each exercise. If you need a paper copy of the completed exercise, enter your name centered in a header before printing. Other print options have already been set to print compressed to one page and to display the filename, sheet name, and current date in a footer.

Be sure to save your changes and close the workbook if you need more than one work session to complete the desired exercises. Then, continue working on *EE2_P6discovery* instead of starting over on the original *EE2_0606* file.

1. Assigning Letter Grades Using HLOOKUP or VLOOKUP

You are evaluating the scores for an exam, which are stored in column E of the #1-LetterGrade worksheet in the *EE2_P6discovery* workbook. You want to convert each score to the corresponding letter grade of A, B, C, D, or F. (You can assign plus and minus grades as well, such as A– or B+ if you prefer.) First you must decide the minimum score for each letter grade. For example, you might decide whether 94, 92, 90, or 88 is the minimum score for an A grade. Then revise the worksheet as necessary, and execute a VLOOKUP or HLOOKUP function to enter the corresponding letter grades in column F.

2. Using MATCH and INDEX to Look Up Data

You are expanding a worksheet that lists Exam 1 scores in column E of the #2-FindGrade worksheet in the *EE2_P6discovery* workbook. You think that you can use a combination of MATCH and INDEX functions to look up an Exam 1 score by entering a student's ID number. Use onscreen Help to learn about the MATCH and INDEX functions. Apply what you have learned by entering a nested function in cell I3 that looks up the Exam 1 score associated with the ID number entered in cell C3. (Hint: Use a MATCH function as the middle argument within an INDEX function). The error message *#N/A* will display in cell I3 until you enter an ID number in cell C3.

CREATING PIVOTTABLE AND PIVOTCHART REPORTS

OBJECTIVES

IN THIS PROJECT, YOU LEARN HOW TO

- Create a pivot table

- Expand a pivot table

- Remove, hide, and show data

- Refresh a pivot table

- Create a chart from pivot table data

- Apply predefined formats to a pivot table

WHY WOULD I DO THIS?

A *pivot table* is an interactive table that quickly summarizes large amounts of data from a data source such as a list or another table. As its name suggests, you can pivot (manipulate) its rows and columns to see different comparisons of the source data. You can also expand or reduce the amount of detail shown in the table, and create a chart that plots the data.

Imagine that your responsibilities include maintaining data on 111 employees and generating reports based on that data. The available data are stored in an Excel list (see Figure 7.1).

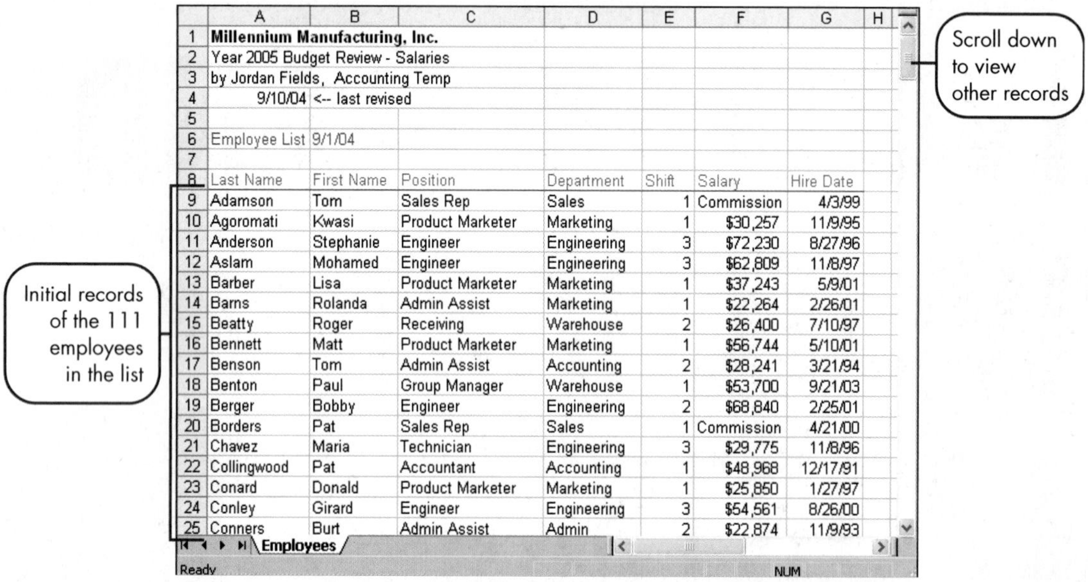

Scroll down to view other records

Initial records of the 111 employees in the list

	A	B	C	D	E	F	G	H
1	Millennium Manufacturing, Inc.							
2	Year 2005 Budget Review - Salaries							
3	by Jordan Fields, Accounting Temp							
4	9/10/04	<-- last revised						
5								
6	Employee List	9/1/04						
7								
8	Last Name	First Name	Position	Department	Shift	Salary	Hire Date	
9	Adamson	Tom	Sales Rep	Sales	1	Commission	4/3/99	
10	Agoromati	Kwasi	Product Marketer	Marketing	1	$30,257	11/9/95	
11	Anderson	Stephanie	Engineer	Engineering	3	$72,230	8/27/96	
12	Aslam	Mohamed	Engineer	Engineering	3	$62,809	11/8/97	
13	Barber	Lisa	Product Marketer	Marketing	1	$37,243	5/9/01	
14	Barns	Rolanda	Admin Assist	Marketing	1	$22,264	2/26/01	
15	Beatty	Roger	Receiving	Warehouse	2	$26,400	7/10/97	
16	Bennett	Matt	Product Marketer	Marketing	1	$56,744	5/10/01	
17	Benson	Tom	Admin Assist	Accounting	2	$28,241	3/21/94	
18	Benton	Paul	Group Manager	Warehouse	1	$53,700	9/21/03	
19	Berger	Bobby	Engineer	Engineering	2	$68,840	2/25/01	
20	Borders	Pat	Sales Rep	Sales	1	Commission	4/21/00	
21	Chavez	Maria	Technician	Engineering	3	$29,775	11/8/96	
22	Collingwood	Pat	Accountant	Accounting	1	$48,968	12/17/91	
23	Conard	Donald	Product Marketer	Marketing	1	$25,850	1/27/97	
24	Conley	Girard	Engineer	Engineering	3	$54,561	8/26/00	
25	Conners	Burt	Admin Assist	Admin	2	$22,874	11/9/93	

Employees   Ready   NUM

FIGURE 7.1

The annual budget review takes place early next month, and your supervisor has requested information based on current salary levels—total salaries for each department, average salary for each position, the number of employees on each shift by department, a chart showing total salaries for selected departments, and so forth. Using Excel's powerful PivotTable and PivotChart Wizard, you can quickly create the summary information you need.

VISUAL SUMMARY

The *PivotTable and PivotChart Wizard* guides you through the steps to summarize data in a table layout. Figure 7.2 illustrates the initial pivot table that you create in this project.

	E	F	G	H	I	J	K	L
7								
8	Shift	Salary	Hire Date			Count of Salary		
9	1	Commission	4/3/99			Department ▼	Total	
10	1	$30,257	11/9/95			Accounting	11	
11	3	$72,230	8/27/96			Admin	9	
12	3	$62,809	11/8/97			Art	5	
13	1	$37,243	5/9/01			Engineering	27	
14	1	$22,264	2/26/01			Marketing	17	
15	2	$26,400	7/10/97			R and D	9	
16	1	$56,744	5/10/01			Sales	15	
17	2	$28,241	3/21/94			Warehouse	18	
18	1	$53,700	9/21/03			Grand Total	111	
19	2	$68,840	2/25/01					

Count of employees by department

FIGURE 7.2

In subsequent lessons you explore other pivot table features. You expand a pivot table by adding row and column fields, switch from counting to summing values, set restrictions on which data display in the pivot table, and create a chart based on a pivot table. You also apply predefined formats as shown in Figure 7.3.

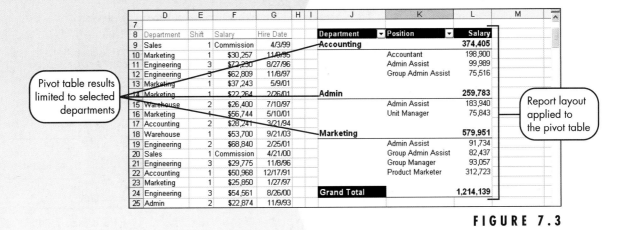

Pivot table results limited to selected departments

Report layout applied to the pivot table

FIGURE 7.3

LESSON 1:   Creating a Pivot Table

The PivotTable and PivotChart Wizard guides you through the process of creating a custom report from a list of data. The initial steps include specifying the data source, the type of report (pivot table or pivot chart), and the location of the report (a new worksheet or the existing worksheet). At that point you have two options for completing the design of the pivot table: using a Layout dialog box or making selections directly on the worksheet.

You can easily set up a pivot table directly on the worksheet by dragging the names of fields to the appropriate areas of a pivot table shell. That way you can view the data while you arrange the fields. For relatively complex pivot tables, this approach can require additional time

Project 7   Creating PivotTable and PivotChart Reports

because the data will update each time you make a change. You may prefer to design the pivot table using the Layout dialog box and then display the results when you are finished.

In this lesson you design a pivot table directly on the worksheet. You create a simple table that totals salaries by department for Millennium Manufacturing.

To Create a Pivot Table

1 **Open the *EE2_0701* workbook, and save it as `SalaryPivots`.**
The workbook is comprised of a worksheet named Employees, which contains data for 111 employees in an Excel list.

2 **Click any cell within the list range A8:G119, and choose Data, PivotTable and PivotChart Report.**
The PivotTable and PivotChart Wizard – Step 1 of 3 dialog box opens.

3 **Make sure that *Microsoft Office Excel list or database* is selected as the data source, and that *PivotTable* is selected as the report type (see Figure 7.4).**

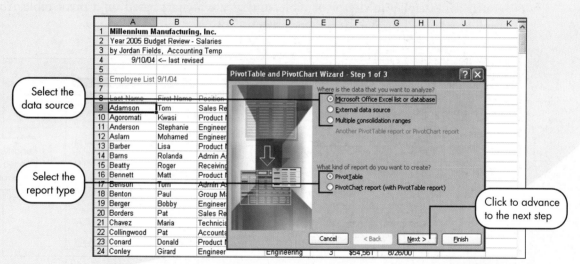

FIGURE 7.4

4 **Click Next.**
The PivotTable and PivotChart Wizard–Step 2 of 3 dialog box opens. Use this dialog box to specify the data to use for the pivot table. Because you clicked within the list before activating the Wizard, Excel automatically selects the entire list and displays *$A$8:$G$119* as the range (see Figure 7.5).

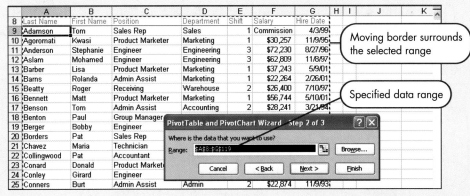

FIGURE 7.5

5 **Click Next.**
The PivotTable and PivotChart Wizard–Step 3 of 3 dialog box opens. Use this dialog box to specify creating the pivot table in a new worksheet or in the existing worksheet.

6 **Select *Existing worksheet*, and click cell J8.**
This tells Excel to position the upper-left cell of the pivot table in cell J8 in the active worksheet. *Employees!$J$8* displays in the window below the *Existing worksheet* option (see Figure 7.6).

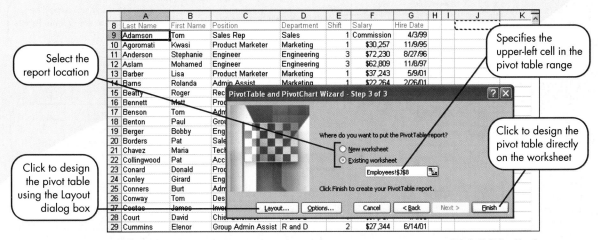

FIGURE 7.6

7 **Click Finish in the lower-right corner of the dialog box (refer to Figure 7.6).**
Excel opens the PivotTable Field List box, displays the PivotTable toolbar, and creates a shell for designing a pivot table (see Figure 7.7).

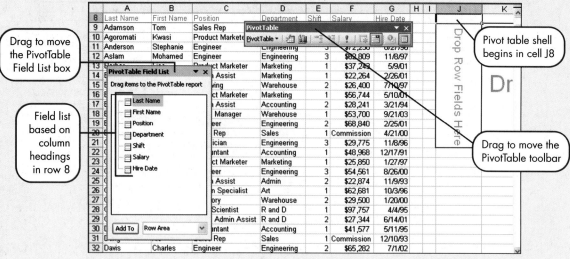

FIGURE 7.7

8 Scroll right to display the entire pivot table shell, if necessary; then click *Department* in the PivotTable Field List box (see Figure 7.8).

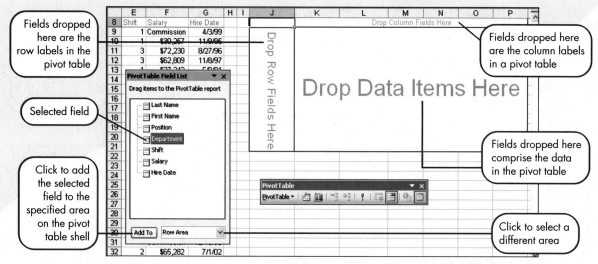

FIGURE 7.8

9 Make sure that *Row Area* is selected in the lower-right corner of the PivotTable Field List box, and click the Add To button (refer to Figure 7.8).

Excel adds the Department field as a row in the pivot table (see Figure 7.9). You can also drag the Department field to the *Drop Row Fields Here* section in the pivot table shell.

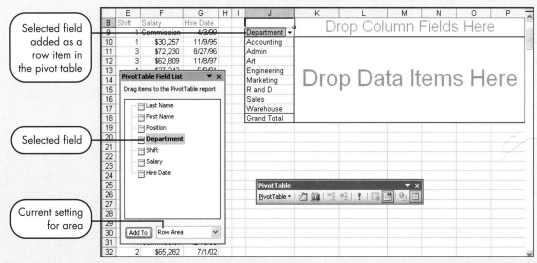

FIGURE 7.9

10 Click *Salary* in the PivotTable Field List box; then display the area drop-down list to the right of the Add To button, select *Data Area,* and click the Add To button.

Excel adds salary data to the pivot table (see Figure 7.10). You can also drag the Salary field to the *Drop Data Items Here* section in the pivot table shell. By default, the summary calculation on salary data is a count. Now change the calculation to a sum.

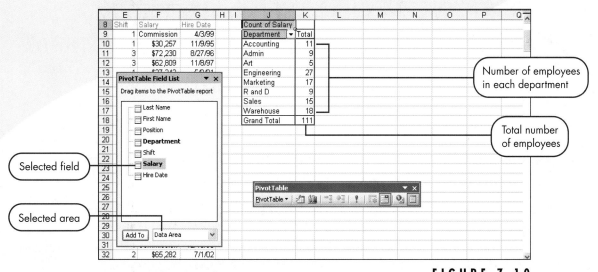

FIGURE 7.10

11 Double-click *Count of Salary* (cell J8).

The PivotTable Field dialog box opens.

12 Select *Sum* in the *Summarize by* list box (see Figure 7.11).

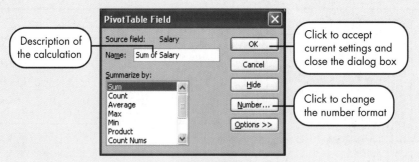

FIGURE 7.11

Sum of Salary replaces *Count of Salary* in the *Name* text box.

13 Click the **Number** button to open the Format Cells dialog box; then specify Currency format without the $ sign and with zero decimal places.

14 Click OK once to close the Format Cells dialog box; then click OK again to close the PivotTable Field dialog box.

The pivot table reflects the changes in type of summary and number formatting (see Figure 7.12).

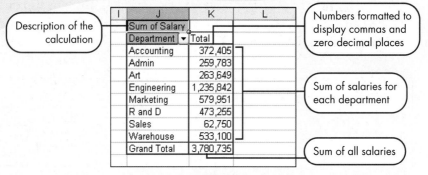

FIGURE 7.12

15 Close the PivotTable Field List box by clicking the Close button—a large X— in the upper-right corner of that box.

16 Use a similar process to close the PivotTable toolbar, and save your changes to the *SalaryPivots* workbook.

Keep the *SalaryPivots* workbook open for the next lesson, or close the workbook and exit Excel.

TO EXTEND YOUR KNOWLEDGE . . .

DELETING A PIVOT TABLE

Before you can delete a pivot table, you must select it using a three-step process. Right-click within the pivot table, choose *Select* from the shortcut menu, and click *Entire Table*. After selecting the table, choose *Edit, Clear, All*. When you delete a pivot table, the source data are not affected.

LESSON 2:   Expanding a Pivot Table

You can greatly expand a pivot table by adding more fields to it on the worksheet or to the row, column, and data areas of the Layout dialog box. For example, instead of displaying a single column with total salary for each Millennium Manufacturing department, you can add columns that provide totals for each shift within a department. You can also add rows that provide totals for each position within a department. In this lesson, you make these changes on the worksheet.

To Expand a Pivot Table

1 **Open the *SalaryPivots* workbook, if necessary.**
A pivot table showing salaries by department and in total displays in the range J8:K18.

2 **Right-click within the pivot table and select *Show Field List* from the shortcut menu.**

3 **Click *Position* in the PivotTable Field List box; then select *Row Area* and click the Add To button.**
Excel adds position data in rows to the pivot table.

4 **Click *Shift* in the PivotTable Field List box; then select *Column Area* and click the Add To button.**
Excel adds shift data in columns to the pivot table (see Figure 7.13). The summary information in the table has more than doubled as a result of adding data from two fields.

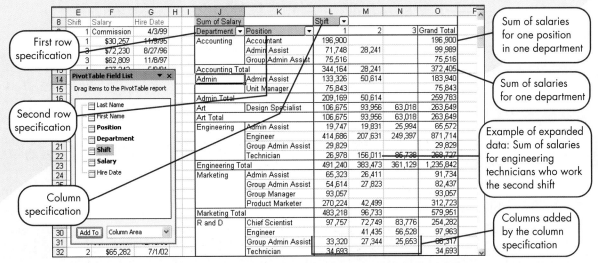

FIGURE 7.13

5 Close the PivotTable Field List box.

6 Save your changes to the *SalaryPivots* workbook.
Keep the *SalaryPivots* workbook open for the next lesson, or close the workbook and exit Excel.

TO EXTEND YOUR KNOWLEDGE . . .

CREATING A PAGE FIELD

A *page field* adds a third dimension to a pivot table report by allowing you to filter all of the data in a report by one or more fields. You can add a page field at the time you create the pivot report by selecting the field from the PivotTable Field List and adding it to the Page Area (see Figure 7.14). You can also add the page field later by modifying the design. For example, if you created a pivot table that totals salaries by department and position, you can modify it to include a page field to show data for all shifts or only the selected shift. You will use this method in Lesson 3.

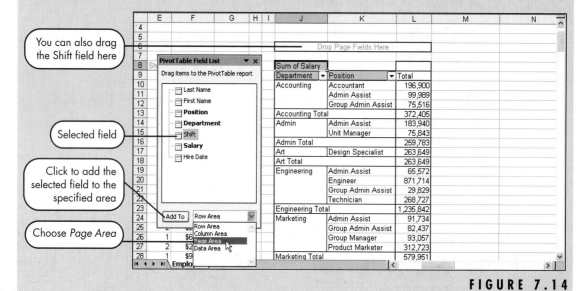

FIGURE 7.14

LESSON 3: Removing, Hiding, and Showing Data

As your information needs change, you may want to display more or less summary data in a pivot table. To quickly remove a field, drag the field button left, right, or down off the pivot table on the worksheet, or drag the field in any direction away from the PAGE, ROW, COLUMN, or DATA area in the Layout dialog box. Showing or hiding detail in a field is as easy as displaying a list of items in a field on the pivot table and checking or unchecking an item.

In this lesson, you modify the pivot table in preparation for creating a chart. You change Shift to a page field instead of a column field and hide data for the Engineering, R and D, and Warehouse departments. When you are done, only the Accounting, Administration, Art, Marketing, and Sales summary data display.

To Remove, Hide, and Show Data

1 Open the *SalaryPivots* workbook, if necessary.

2 Click the Shift button in the pivot table (cell L8), and drag it upward off the pivot table.

You removed the three columns of shift summary data from the pivot table. By dragging upward instead of to the right or left, you set up a Shift page field (see Figure 7.15).

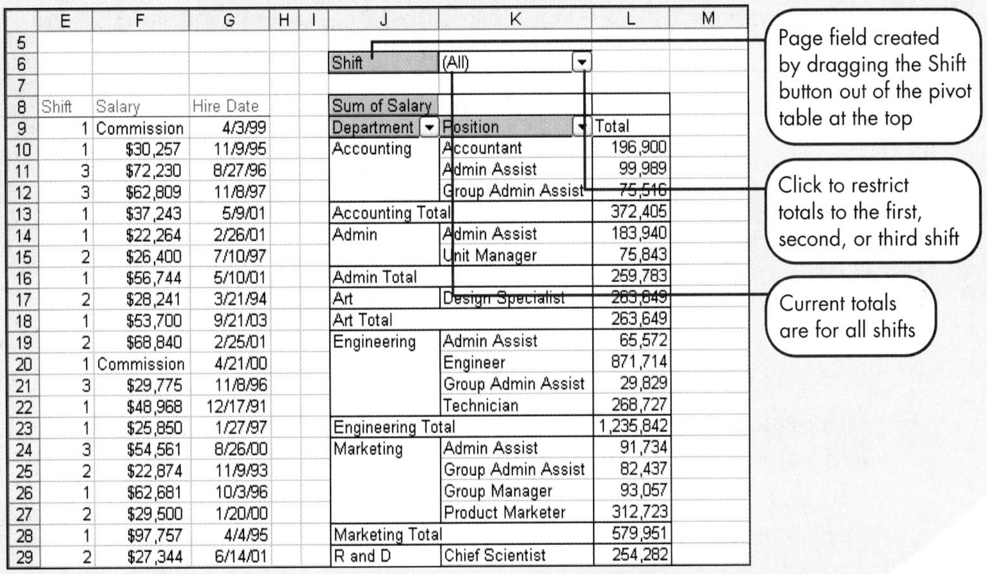

	E	F	G	H	I	J	K	L	M
5									
6						Shift	(All)	▼	
7									
8	Shift	Salary	Hire Date			Sum of Salary			
9	1	Commission	4/3/99			Department ▼	Position ▼	Total	
10	1	$30,257	11/9/95			Accounting	Accountant	196,900	
11	3	$72,230	8/27/96				Admin Assist	99,989	
12	3	$62,809	11/8/97				Group Admin Assist	75,516	
13	1	$37,243	5/9/01			Accounting Total		372,405	
14	1	$22,264	2/26/01			Admin	Admin Assist	183,940	
15	2	$26,400	7/10/97				Unit Manager	75,843	
16	1	$56,744	5/10/01			Admin Total		259,783	
17	2	$28,241	3/21/94			Art	Design Specialist	263,649	
18	1	$53,700	9/21/03			Art Total		263,649	
19	2	$68,840	2/25/01			Engineering	Admin Assist	65,572	
20	1	Commission	4/21/00				Engineer	871,714	
21	3	$29,775	11/8/96				Group Admin Assist	29,829	
22	1	$48,968	12/17/91				Technician	268,727	
23	1	$25,850	1/27/97			Engineering Total		1,235,842	
24	3	$54,561	8/26/00			Marketing	Admin Assist	91,734	
25	2	$22,874	11/9/93				Group Admin Assist	82,437	
26	1	$62,681	10/3/96				Group Manager	93,057	
27	2	$29,500	1/20/00				Product Marketer	312,723	
28	1	$97,757	4/4/95			Marketing Total		579,951	
29	2	$27,344	6/14/01			R and D	Chief Scientist	254,282	

Page field created by dragging the Shift button out of the pivot table at the top

Click to restrict totals to the first, second, or third shift

Current totals are for all shifts

FIGURE 7.15

3 Click the drop-down arrow at the right end of cell K6; then select *3* and click OK.

You used the Shift page field to display only the summary data for the third shift. The values in column L reflect totals for the third shift (see Figure 7.16).

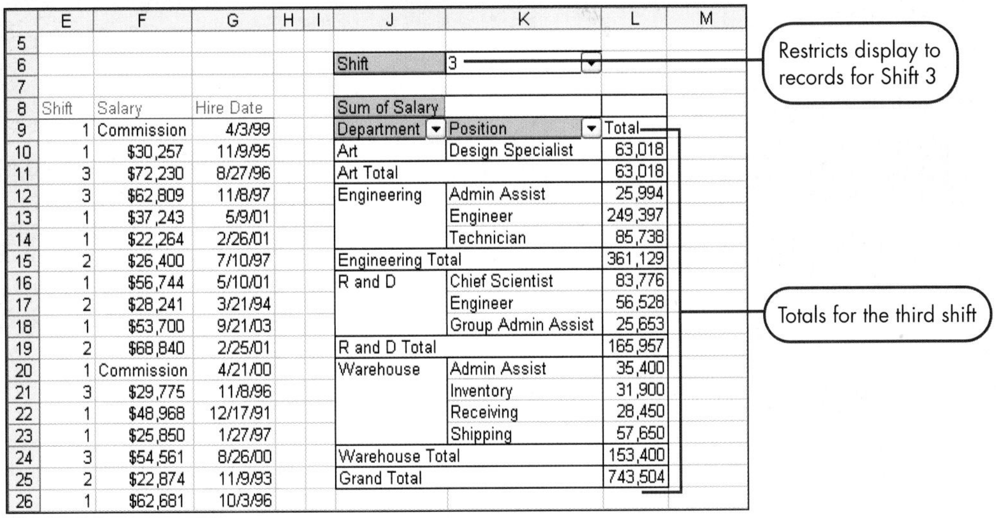

	E	F	G	H	I	J	K	L	M
5									
6						Shift	3	▼	
7									
8	Shift	Salary	Hire Date			Sum of Salary			
9	1	Commission	4/3/99			Department ▼	Position ▼	Total	
10	1	$30,257	11/9/95			Art	Design Specialist	63,018	
11	3	$72,230	8/27/96			Art Total		63,018	
12	3	$62,809	11/8/97			Engineering	Admin Assist	25,994	
13	1	$37,243	5/9/01				Engineer	249,397	
14	1	$22,264	2/26/01				Technician	85,738	
15	2	$26,400	7/10/97			Engineering Total		361,129	
16	1	$56,744	5/10/01			R and D	Chief Scientist	83,776	
17	2	$28,241	3/21/94				Engineer	56,528	
18	1	$53,700	9/21/03				Group Admin Assist	25,653	
19	2	$68,840	2/25/01			R and D Total		165,957	
20	1	Commission	4/21/00			Warehouse	Admin Assist	35,400	
21	3	$29,775	11/8/96				Inventory	31,900	
22	1	$48,968	12/17/91				Receiving	28,450	
23	1	$25,850	1/27/97				Shipping	57,650	
24	3	$54,561	8/26/00			Warehouse Total		153,400	
25	2	$22,874	11/9/93			Grand Total		743,504	
26	1	$62,681	10/3/96						

Restricts display to records for Shift 3

Totals for the third shift

FIGURE 7.16

4 Click the drop-down arrow for cell K6, select *(All)*, and click OK.

5 Display the Department drop-down list (cell J9).

Check marks in front of department names indicate the pivot table currently displays summary data for all departments (see Figure 7.17). Clicking a check mark deselects the item and temporarily hides the related data in the pivot table.

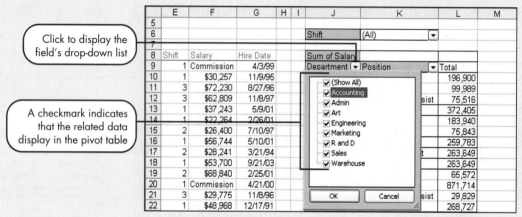

FIGURE 7.17

6 Uncheck the Engineering, R and D, and Warehouse items in the Department drop-down list; then click OK.

Summary data for the Engineering, R and D, and Warehouse departments do not display in the pivot table (see Figure 7.18).

	E	F	G	H	I	J	K	L	M
5									
6						Shift	(All)		
7									
8	Shift	Salary	Hire Date			Sum of Salary			
9	1	Commission	4/3/99			Department	Position	Total	
10	1	$30,257	11/9/95			Accounting	Accountant	196,900	
11	3	$72,230	8/27/96				Admin Assist	99,989	
12	3	$62,809	11/8/97				Group Admin Assist	75,516	
13	1	$37,243	5/9/01			Accounting Total		372,405	
14	1	$22,264	2/26/01			Admin	Admin Assist	183,940	
15	2	$26,400	7/10/97				Unit Manager	75,843	
16	1	$56,744	5/10/01			Admin Total		259,783	
17	2	$28,241	3/21/94			Art	Design Specialist	263,649	
18	1	$53,700	9/21/03			Art Total		263,649	
19	2	$68,840	2/25/01			Marketing	Admin Assist	91,734	
20	1	Commission	4/21/00				Group Admin Assist	82,437	
21	3	$29,775	11/8/96				Group Manager	93,057	
22	1	$48,968	12/17/91				Product Marketer	312,723	
23	1	$25,850	1/27/97			Marketing Total		579,951	
24	3	$54,561	8/26/00			Sales	Sales Manager	62,750	
25	2	$22,874	11/9/93				Sales Rep	0	
26	1	$62,681	10/3/96			Sales Total		62,750	
27	2	$29,500	1/20/00			Grand Total		1,538,538	
28	1	$97,757	4/4/95						

FIGURE 7.18

7 Save your changes to the *SalaryPivots* workbook.

Keep the *SalaryPivots* workbook open for the next lesson, or close the workbook and exit Excel.

TO EXTEND YOUR KNOWLEDGE . . .

USING THE PIVOTTABLE TOOLBAR

If the PivotTable toolbar is not visible, select View, Toolbars, PivotTable or right-click the pivot table and select *Show PivotTable Toolbar* to display it. The PivotTable toolbar provides buttons to execute common pivot table tasks (see Figure 7.19). For example, the last button is a toggle button. If the PivotTable Field List box is not visible, you can click the Show Field List button to display it. If the PivotTable Field List box is visible, you can click the Hide Field List button to close it. You use several buttons on the toolbar in subsequent lessons.

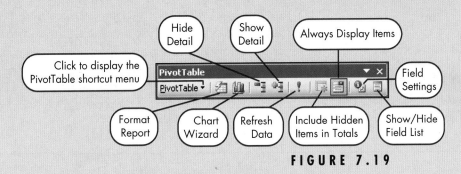

FIGURE 7.19

DISPLAYING THE TOP OR BOTTOM ITEMS IN A FIELD

You can display a user-specified number of top or bottom items in a pivot table field. Click within the pivot table, click PivotTable on the PivotTable toolbar, and select *Sort and Top 10*. In the *AutoSort options* area, select Manual, Ascending, or Descending. In the *Top 10 AutoShow* area, click On. In the *Show* box, select *Top* or *Bottom,* and in the box to the right, specify the number of items to display. In the *Using field* box, click the data field to use for calculating the top or bottom items and then click OK.

LESSON 4:   Refreshing a Pivot Table

If you change data in a worksheet and the new figures impact a summary calculation in a pivot table, Excel does not automatically update the pivot table. After making changes to the worksheet, you must *refresh* (recalculate) the pivot table.

A word of caution is in order to avoid using invalid data to make decisions. Because you are accustomed to Excel recalculating a worksheet automatically, it's easy to overlook refreshing any pivot tables that incorporate the changed data. In complex pivot tables, errors in summary amounts are difficult to detect visually; therefore, you should acquire the habit of refreshing pivot tables after any change in worksheet data.

In this lesson you change worksheet data, check for changes in pivot table amounts, refresh the pivot table, and check amounts again.

To Refresh a Pivot Table

1 Open the *SalaryPivots* workbook, if necessary, and make sure that the PivotTable Field List box does not display.

2 Scroll the worksheet to display column A, starting with row 8.
Currently the salary for accountant Pat Collingwood is $48,968 (cell F22).

3 Scroll right as needed to display the entire pivot table.
The sum of salaries for accountants is $196,900 (cell L10).

4 Change the contents of cell F22 to $50,968 instead of *$48,968*.
You changed the salary of an accountant, but the sum of salaries for accountants in the pivot table did not change ($196,900 in cell L10). Just looking at the summary data, it is not apparent that the pivot table contains an error.

5 Right-click anywhere within the pivot table, and choose *Refresh Data*.
The sum of salaries for accountants increases from $196,900 to $198,900 in cell L10 (see Figure 7.20).

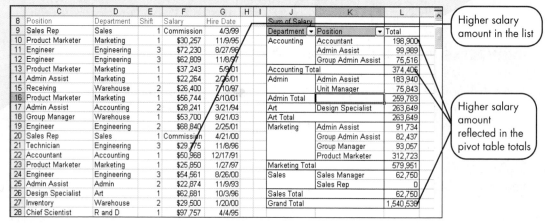

FIGURE 7.20

6 Save your changes to the *SalaryPivots* workbook.
Keep the *SalaryPivots* workbook open for the next lesson, or close the workbook and exit Excel.

TO EXTEND YOUR KNOWLEDGE . . .

OTHER WAYS TO SELECT REFRESH

Refresh Data is an option on the shortcut menu that displays when you right-click within a pivot table. You can also choose the menu sequence Data, Refresh Data or click the Refresh Data button on the PivotTable toolbar (refer to Figure 7.19).

LESSON 5:   Creating a Chart from Pivot Table Data

A pivot table displays summary data in rows and columns. Creating a chart based on pivot table data can be an effective means to interpret the data. You can create a chart quickly by right-clicking within an existing pivot table and then selecting *PivotChart* from the shortcut menu. You can also use the PivotTable and PivotChart Wizard to create both a chart and its related table at the same time.

For either method, Excel automatically creates a column chart on a separate sheet. You can then edit the *PivotChart* report just as you would any Excel chart—adding and deleting data points, changing chart type, applying number formats, and so forth. You can use any chart type except XY (scatter), bubble, and stock.

In this lesson, you create a column chart based on the pivot table in the *SalaryPivots* workbook. You then hide the Art and Sales department salary data, which limits the chart to Accounting, Admin, and Marketing salaries. You also convert the column chart to a line chart.

To Create and Modify a Chart Based on Pivot Table Data

1 **Open the *SalaryPivots* workbook, if necessary.**

2 **Right-click any cell in the pivot table (J8:L27), and select *PivotChart* on the shortcut menu.**
Excel creates a column chart on a separate sheet based on the visible data in the pivot table (see Figure 7.21). Department and Position buttons display centered below the chart, and the Shift button displays in the top-left corner.

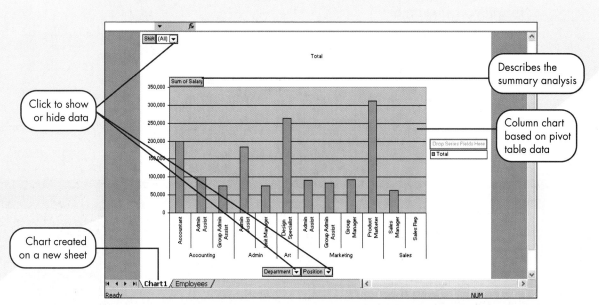

FIGURE 7.21

3 Display the Department drop-down list; then uncheck *Art* and *Sales,* and click OK.
The columns depicting Art and Sales department data disappear from the chart.

4 Right-click a blank area within the chart, and select *Chart Type* from the shortcut menu.
The Chart Type dialog box opens.

5 Select *Line* in the *Chart type* section of the dialog box, and click OK.
A line chart replaces the column chart (see Figure 7.22).

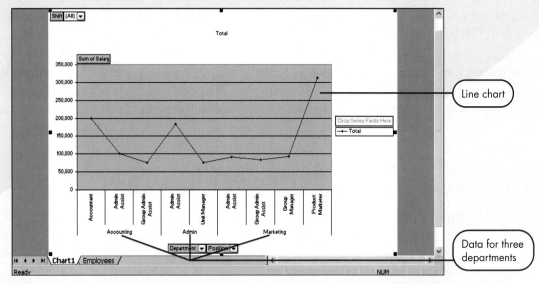

FIGURE 7.22

6 Click in the gray area outside the chart to deselect it, and click the Employees sheet tab.
The data you hid in the chart are also hidden in the pivot table results. Only the Accounting, Admin, and Marketing data display in the pivot table.

7 Save your changes to the *SalaryPivots* workbook.
Keep the *SalaryPivots* workbook open for the next lesson, or close the workbook and exit Excel.

TO EXTEND YOUR KNOWLEDGE . . .

HOW CHANGES IN PIVOT TABLE DATA AFFECT A RELATED CHART
If a chart is based on pivot table data—which in turn summarize worksheet data—you should understand the impact on the chart of a change in underlying worksheet data. Such a chart will only be updated when its associated pivot table is refreshed.

CREATING A STATIC CHART BASED ON PIVOT TABLE DATA
You can convert an existing PivotChart report to a static chart—also known as a nonpivoting chart—by deleting the associated PivotTable report. Alternatively, you can delete the worksheet containing the data used to create the chart if you no longer need the data. You cannot change the charted data in a static chart.

LESSON 6: Applying Predefined Formats to a Pivot Table

A variety of predefined formats can be applied to pivot tables. These formats not only improve the aesthetics of a table, they focus the reader's attention on different areas of the table. Some formats work better than others, depending on the layout and complexity of the pivot table. You should experiment with different types of formats to see which best presents your data.

In this lesson, you apply a table format to a pivot table, switch to a report format, change the fields in the report, and add a field to the table using the PivotTable and PivotChart Wizard Layout dialog box.

To Apply Predefined Formats to a Pivot Table

1 Open the *SalaryPivots* workbook and select the Employees worksheet, if necessary.

2 Make sure that the entire pivot table in the range J8:L22 displays; then click any cell within this range.
The pivot table displays in the PivotTable Classic format—the default format automatically assigned to new pivot tables.

 3 Click the Format Report button on the PivotTable toolbar.

 If you have problems . . .

If the PivotTable toolbar is not in view, right-click within the pivot table and then select *Show PivotTable Toolbar.*

The AutoFormat dialog box opens (see Figure 7.23). Report formats—the indented formats—display first. An **indented format** supports the presentation of pivot table data in categories and subcategories. Each subcategory is offset to the right from its main category.

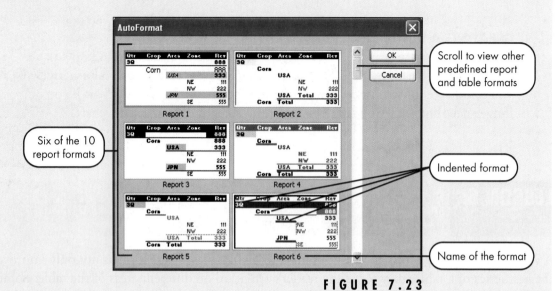

FIGURE 7.23

4 **Scroll down to view the remaining report formats and the table formats.**
Ten table formats—the nonindented formats—display after the report formats. A *nonindented format* does not offset subcategories within categories in a PivotTable report. The last two choices are *PivotTable Classic* (the default) and *None*.

5 **Double-click the Table 1 format (the description displays below the associated format), click anywhere outside the table to deselect it, and scroll to view the entire pivot table.**
The pivot table displays in the Table 1 format (see Figure 7.24).

Salary	Department			
Position	Accounting	Admin	Marketing	Grand Total
Accountant	198,900			198,900
Admin Assist	99,989	183,940	91,734	375,663
Group Admin Assist	75,516		82,437	157,953
Group Manager			93,057	93,057
Product Marketer			312,723	312,723
Unit Manager		75,843		75,843
Grand Total	374,405	259,783	579,951	1,214,139

Department is a column field

Table 1 format (one of 10 nonindented formats)

FIGURE 7.24

6 **Click a cell within the pivot table, and click the Format Report button on the PivotTable toolbar.**

7 **Double-click the Report 1 format, and click anywhere outside the table to deselect it.**
The pivot table displays in the Report 1 format (see Figure 7.25).

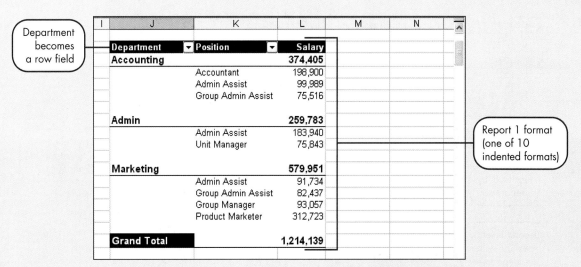

FIGURE 7.25

8   **Display the Department drop-down list (cell J8), and uncheck the three fields currently in the pivot table—Accounting, Admin, and Marketing.**

9   **Check two fields—Engineering and R and D—and click OK.**
The pivot table continues to display the Report 1 format.

10   **Click within the pivot table, display the PivotTable drop-down list in the PivotTable toolbar, and select *PivotTable Wizard.***
The PivotTable and PivotChart Wizard – Step 3 of 3 dialog box opens.

11   **Click the Layout button in the lower-left corner of the dialog box.**
Now add the Shift data as a row item in the PivotTable report.

12   **Click the Shift field button from the list of buttons on the right, and drag it to the ROW area below the Position field on the diagram.**
Three field buttons are now in the row area in the order—from top to bottom—Department, Position, and Shift (see Figure 7.26).

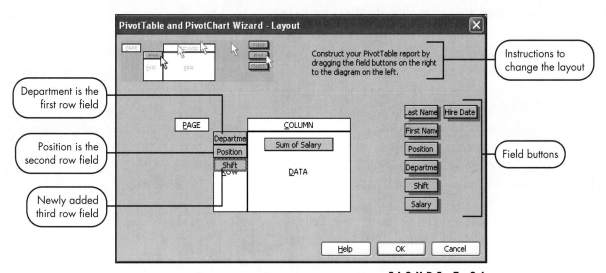

FIGURE 7.26

13 Click OK, and click Finish.

14 Close the PivotTable Field List box and the PivotTable toolbar.
The report displays the layered (indented) layout shown in Figure 7.27.

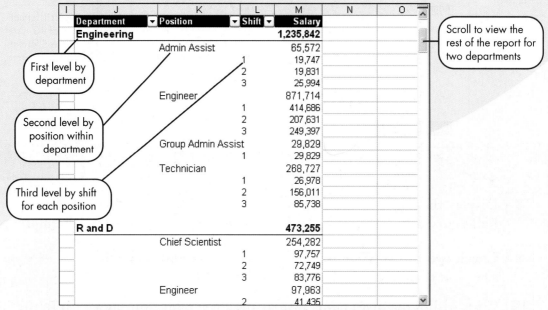

FIGURE 7.27

15 Save your changes to the *SalaryPivots* workbook and close the workbook.
Continue with end-of-project exercises or exit Excel.

TO EXTEND YOUR KNOWLEDGE . . .

REMOVING A PREDEFINED FORMAT
To immediately remove a predefined format after applying it, choose Edit, Undo AutoFormat. To remove a predefined format later, and any other character and cell formats applied manually, select the range with unwanted formatting, open the AutoFormat dialog box, and choose None. You may not get the results you want, however, because Excel simply removes effects such as borders, shading, italics, and changes in font size. Because cell contents remain in place, the action does not move any fields, change display to indented or nonindented format, or remove blank lines inserted between items in rows.

SUMMARY

You began this project by creating a simple pivot table directly on the worksheet. In subsequent lessons you learned how to add and remove fields, hide and show fields, refresh a pivot table, and create a chart from pivot table data. You completed the project by applying predefined formats. These experiences provided only a glimpse of the power of pivot tables.

You can extend your learning by reviewing concepts and terms, and by practicing variations of skills presented in the lessons. Use the following table as a guide to the numbered questions and exercises in the end-of-project learning opportunities.

LESSON	MULTIPLE CHOICE	DISCUSSION	SKILL DRILL	CHALLENGE	DISCOVERY ZONE
Creating a Pivot Table	1, 4, 7	1, 2	1, 4	1, 3	1, 2
Expanding a Pivot Table	10	3	2, 3	2, 4	
Removing, Hiding, and Showing Data	6	3	6		
Refreshing a Pivot Table	5		4		
Creating a Chart from Pivot Table Data	2, 8, 9	2	6	3	
Applying Predefined Formats to a Pivot Table	3		5	2, 4	2, 3

KEY TERMS

indented format

nonindented format

page field

pivot table

PivotTable and PivotChart Wizard

refresh

CHECKING CONCEPTS AND TERMS

MULTIPLE CHOICE

Circle the letter of the correct answer for each of the following.

1. Which of the following is a true statement? [L1]
   a. To delete a pivot table, right-click within it and then select <u>D</u>elete from the shortcut menu.
   b. To delete a pivot table, click within the pivot table to select it and then press Del.
   c. Both a and b
   d. Neither a nor b

2. Which of the following chart types cannot be used to chart pivot table data? [L5]
   a. Line
   b. XY (scatter)
   c. Column
   d. All of the above

3. If you want to apply an indented format to a pivot table, which of the following predefined formats would produce the desired result? [L6]
   a. Report 1
   b. PivotTable Classic
   c. Table 1
   d. None of the above

4. Which of the following is a summary calculation available in a pivot table? [L1]
   a. Max
   b. Average
   c. Both a and b
   d. Neither a nor b

5. Which of the following is a term associated with updating the data in a pivot table after a change in the data source for the table? [L4]
   a. Recalculate
   b. Redo
   c. Refresh
   d. None of the above

6. Which is a way to delete a field from a PivotTable report using the mouse? [L3]
   a. Drag the field to the left, off of the pivot table.
   b. Drag the field to the right, off of the pivot table.
   c. Drag the field upward, off of the pivot table.
   d. Both a and b

7. Which of the following can be specified using the PivotTable and PivotChart Wizard? [L1]
   a. Source data for the table
   b. Type of PivotTable report
   c. Location of the report
   d. All of the above

8. Which of the following is an accurate statement about charts based on a pivot table? [L5]
   a. Charts based on pivot data are limited to XY(scatter), bubble, and stock chart types.
   b. Charts based on pivot tables update automatically whenever the data change.
   c. Charts based on pivot tables update only when the pivot table is refreshed.
   d. Both a and c

9. Why can't a static chart based on pivot table data be updated? [L5]

   a. The data are based on absolute cell references.

   b. The underlying data have been deleted.

   c. The static chart is actually a JPEG graphic.

   d. None of the above

10. Which PivotTable report element enables you to filter records? [L2]

   a. Page field

   b. Row field

   c. Column field

   d. Data field

DISCUSSION

1. The Glenn Lakes Volunteers list shown in Figure 7.28 includes data about the organization's volunteers and their activities. Describe two variations of pivot tables you could create to summarize data in the list. Be specific as to the type of summary calculation, and include at least one row field and one column field in each of your examples. [L1]

	A	B	C	D	E	F	G
1	GLENN LAKES VOLUNTEERS						
2	Time and Expense Summary: 1st Quarter 2004						
3							
4	Name	Date of Service	Organization	Hours Vol	Expenses	Miles	
5	Juarez, Ernesto	2-Jan-04	Meals on Wheels	3	$ 11.00	188	
6	Anderson, Stephanie	3-Jan-04	Big Sisters	8	$ 7.00	182	
7	Keller, Jeffrey	3-Jan-04	Hospice	6	$ 25.00		
8	Enloe, Ree	4-Jan-04	Big Sisters	4	$ 6.00	71	
9	Fox, Matthew	5-Jan-04	Pet Rescue	2	$ 14.00		
10	Anderson, Stephanie	7-Jan-04	Hospice	2	$ 5.00	102	
11	Anderson, Stephanie	8-Jan-04	Pet Rescue	5	$ 25.00	160	
12	Fox, Matthew	11-Jan-04	Red Cross	6	$ 16.00		
13	Rosenfeld, Mary	11-Jan-04	Big Brothers	7	$ 10.00	136	
14	Juarez, Ernesto	13-Jan-04	Cortez Food Pantry	6	$ -	170	
15	Jones, David	16-Jan-04	Big Sisters	8	$ 24.00		
16	Rosenfeld, Mary	19-Jan-04	Meals on Wheels	6	$ 8.00	98	
17	Juarez, Ernesto	20-Jan-04	Hospice	2	$ 10.00	147	
18	Martinez, Juan	20-Jan-04	Meals on Wheels	4	$ 22.00		
19	Martinez, Juan	21-Jan-04	Big Brothers	6	$ 2.00		

Qtr 1

Ready   NUM

FIGURE 7.28

2. Refer to the Glenn Lakes Volunteers list shown in Figure 7.28, and describe a meaningful PivotChart report that you could create to interpret data in the list. Be specific as to the type of chart and the data shown along the Y-axis and X-axis. [L1, L5]

3. Refer to the Glenn Lakes Volunteers list shown in Figure 7.28, and describe how you might incorporate a Page field in a pivot table. Explain how the results would better serve your information needs than hiding or removing data. [L2, L3]

SKILL DRILL

Skill Drill exercises reinforce project skills. Each skill that is reinforced is the same, or nearly the same, as a skill presented in the project. Detailed instructions are provided in a step-by-step format.

Before beginning your first Project 7 Skill Drill exercise, complete the following steps:

1. Open the file named *EE2_0702* and immediately save it as **EE2_P7drill**.

    The workbook contains an overview sheet and six exercise sheets named #1-New Table, #2-Expand Table, #3-Add Counts, #4-Refresh, #5-AutoFormat, and #6-PivotChart.

2. Click the Overview sheet to view the organization and content of the Project 7 Skill Drill Exercises workbook.

Each exercise is independent of the others, so you may complete the exercises in any order. Be sure to save the workbook after completing each exercise. If you need a paper copy of the completed exercise, enter your name centered in a header before printing. Other print options have already been set to print compressed to one page and to display the filename, sheet name, and current date in a footer.

Be sure to save your changes and close the workbook if you need more than one work session to complete the desired exercises. Continue working on *EE2_P7drill* instead of starting over on the original *EE2_0702* file.

1. Creating a Pivot Table

You keep track of your charitable contributions in an Excel list. Now you would like to find out how much you gave to each agency during the year. To get the information you need by creating a pivot table, follow these steps:

1. Open the *EE2_P7drill* workbook, if necessary; then select the #1-New Table sheet.

2. Click any cell in the list range A13:E42.

3. Choose Data, PivotTable and PivotChart Report, and click the Next button.

    This accepts the default settings for data and type of report—a pivot table based on an Excel list.

4. Verify that the specified range is *$A$13:$E$42*, and click the Next button.

5. Click *Existing worksheet*, click G14, and click Finish.

    Excel creates a shell for a pivot table on the worksheet.

6. Click *Agency* in the PivotTable Field List box, make sure that *Row Area* is selected in the lower-right corner of the PivotTable Field List box, and click the Add To button.

    Excel adds the Agency field as a row in the pivot table.

7. Click *Declared Value* in the PivotTable Field List box. Display the area drop-down list to the right of the Add To button, select *Data Area,* and click the Add To button.

   A pivot table displaying a summary of contributions by agency displays in the range G14:H22. The Grand Total of contributions is *4685.*

8. Click outside the table to deselect it, and save your changes to the *EE2_P7drill* workbook.

2. Expanding a Pivot Table

You can expand a pivot table by adding one or more column, row, and data fields. Assume that you created a simple pivot table to sum contributions by agency. Now expand that table to show subtotals by agency based on whether or not a receipt was provided. To expand a pivot table, follow these steps:

1. Open the *EE2_P7drill* workbook, if necessary; then select the #2-Expand Table sheet.

2. Click within the pivot table.

   The PivotTable Field List box displays.

3. Click *Receipt* in the PivotTable Field List box.

4. Display the area drop-down list to the right of the Add To button in the PivotTable Field List box, select *Column Area,* and click the Add To button.

   Two new columns display between the Agency and Grand Total columns. The total of contributions for which no receipt was provided is *685.* Contributions confirmed by receipts total *4000.*

5. Save your changes to the *EE2_P7drill* workbook.

3. Displaying Counts in a Pivot Table

As you analyze your contributions during the past year, you want to know how many times you made a contribution to each agency. To display counts in a pivot table, follow these steps:

1. Open the *EE2_P7drill* workbook, if necessary; then select the #3-Add Counts sheet.

2. Right-click any cell in the pivot table, and select *PivotTable Wizard* from the shortcut menu.

3. Click the Layout button.

4. Drag the Declared Value field button onto the DATA area.

   Two *Sum of Declared Value* buttons display in the DATA area.

5. Double-click the upper of the two *Sum of Declared Value* buttons.

   The PivotTable Field dialog box opens.

6. Select *Count* in the *Summarize by* list box, and click OK.

   Count of Declared Value displays in the DATA area above *Sum of Declared Value.*

7. Click OK and then click Finish.

   The table expands to include counts of contributions. You made three contributions to the Salvation Army with a total declared value of *135.* You made seven contributions to Goodwill with a total declared value of *2660.*

8. Save your changes to the *EE2_P7drill* workbook.

4. Creating, Editing, and Refreshing a Pivot Table

After creating a pivot table, you discover an error in the amount of a contribution to the Girl Scouts. You need to edit the worksheet data and refresh the pivot table. To create a pivot table, change data, and refresh the pivot table, follow these steps:

1. Open the *EE2_P7drill* workbook, if necessary; then select the #4-Refresh sheet.

2. Click any cell in the list range A13:E42.

3. Choose Data, PivotTable and PivotChart Report, and click the Next button.

4. Verify that the specified range is *$A$13:$E$42,* and click the Next button.

5. Click *Existing worksheet,* click cell G14, and click Finish.

6. Click *Agency* in the PivotTable Field List box, make sure that *Row Area* is selected in the lower-right corner of the PivotTable Field List box, and click the Add To button.

7. Click *Declared Value* in the PivotTable Field List box. Display the area drop-down list to the right of the Add To button, select *Data Area,* and click the Add To button.

   The total for contributions to the Girl Scouts (*100*) displays in cell H18 of the pivot table.

8. Click cell B41 in the list of contributions, and change *100* to **200**.

   Note that cell H18 still displays *100* as the total for contributions to the Girl Scouts organization.

9. Right-click any cell in the pivot table, and select *Refresh Data* from the shortcut menu. Alternatively, click within the pivot table and then click the Refresh Data button on the PivotTable toolbar.

   Now cell H18 displays the correct amount—*200.*

10. Save your changes to the *EE2_P7drill* workbook.

5. Applying a Predefined Format to a Pivot Table

Your pivot table format is acceptable for your personal or interoffice use; however, to prepare your table for use with presentation graphics, you want to apply one of Excel's AutoFormats. To apply a predefined format to a pivot table, follow these steps:

1. Open the *EE2_P7drill* workbook, if necessary; then select the #5-AutoFormat sheet.

2. Set zoom level to **75%**, and scroll to view the pivot table to the right of the data.

   The pivot table is wider than it is tall, displaying agencies in columns and categories in rows. Now apply a report format to produce an indented effect that is easier to view and print.

3. Click any cell in the pivot table, and click the Format Report button on the PivotTable toolbar. If the PivotTable toolbar is not in view, right-click within the pivot table and select *Show PivotTable Toolbar.*

4. Select Report 4, click OK, and click outside the pivot table to deselect it.

   Data are now displayed in three columns, with indenting that clearly defines the levels of detail in rows.

5. Set zoom level to **100%**, and save your changes to the *EE2_P7drill* workbook.

6. Creating a Chart Based on Pivot Table Data

You think it might be easier to compare the amounts donated to various agencies if you see the data in a column chart. To create a chart based on data in a pivot table, follow these steps:

1. Open the *EE2_P7drill* workbook, if necessary; then select the #6-PivotChart sheet.

2. Right-click any cell in the pivot table.

3. Choose *PivotChart.*

   A column chart displays on a new worksheet named Chart1. Much higher amounts were contributed in total to Church and Goodwill than to the other four categories.

4. Display the field drop-down list for Agency at the bottom of the chart.

5. Uncheck the Church and Goodwill agencies, and click OK.

   Excel hides the data for the two agencies receiving the largest contributions. The Y-axis scale shifts to illustrate more clearly the differences between amounts contributed to the other four agencies.

6. Select the #6-PivotChart worksheet.

   Hiding data in a chart also hides the data in the associated pivot table.

7. Close the PivotTable Field List box and the PivotTable toolbar; then save your changes to the *EE2_P7drill* workbook.

CHALLENGE

Challenge exercises expand on or are somewhat related to skills that are presented in the lessons. Each exercise provides a brief narrative introduction, followed by instructions in a numbered-step format that are not as detailed as those in the Skill Drill section.

Before beginning your first Project 7 Challenge exercise, complete the following steps:

1. Open the file named *EE2_0703* and immediately save it as **EE2_P7challenge**.

   The *EE2_P7challenge* workbook contains five sheets: an overview, and four exercise sheets named #1-MaxMin, #2-Modify, #3-PivotChart, and #4-MultiCalc.

2. Click the Overview sheet to view the organization of the Project 7 Challenge Exercises workbook.

Each exercise is independent of the others, so you may complete them in any order. Be sure to save the workbook after completing each exercise. If you need a paper copy of the completed exercise, enter your name centered in a header before printing. Other print options have already been set to print compressed to one page and to display the filename, sheet name, and current date in a footer.

If you need more than one work session to complete the desired exercises, continue working on *EE2_P7challenge* instead of starting over on the original *EE2_0703* file.

1. Creating Summary Data Using MAX or MIN

As you analyze current residential real estate listings, you decide to display the highest selling price for a home in each area. Next you want to switch the display to the lowest price at which someone could buy into each area. To do this, you can use Max and Min summary calculations, respectively. To create summary data using Max or Min, and format the results to Currency with zero decimal places, follow these steps:

1. Open the *EE2_P7challenge* workbook, if necessary; then select the #1-MaxMin worksheet.

2. Click any cell within the database, and activate the PivotTable and PivotChart Wizard.

3. Specify that you want to create a pivot table in the current worksheet starting in cell K5.

4. Lay out the pivot table to include Area as a row field and Price as the data item.

5. Specify Max as the summary calculation on Price.

   Max of Price displays in cell K5. The second column displays the highest asking price for a home in the corresponding area. For example, the highest asking price for a home in Champions Village is *156400.*

6. Change the summary calculation from Max to Min.

   Excel replaces the prices in the second column with the lowest asking price for a home in each corresponding area. For example, the lowest asking price for a home in Champions Village is *102900.*

7. Double-click *Min of Price* in cell K5, and click the <u>N</u>umber button in the PivotTable Field dialog box.

8. Specify Currency format with $ sign and zero decimal places.

   Numbers display with the specified format. The Grand Total (in this case, the minimum of the listed values) is *$74,500.*

9. Deselect the pivot table, close the toolbar, and save your changes to the *EE2_P7challenge* workbook.

2. Changing the Number and Location of Fields in a Pivot Table

You created a pivot table that displays the counts of homes in each area—the list of areas in one column, and the counts in the adjacent column to the right. Now you want to add counts for type of heat, and number of bedrooms within each type of heat category. That way you can easily answer a question such as "How many of the three-bedroom homes in Glenn Lakes have electric heat?" To change the number and location of fields in a pivot table, follow these steps:

1. Open the *EE2_P7challenge* workbook, if necessary; then select the #2-Modify worksheet.

2. Click within the pivot table (K5:L17). Use the PivotTable Field List box to add two fields to the Row Area—first Bed; then Heat.

3. Click *Area* in the PivotTable Field List box and then add it to the Column Area.

   Adding the Area field to the Column Area removes it from the Row Area. Excel computes the requested counts in a pivot table that extends across many columns. Scroll to view counts at a detailed level. For example, there are five three-bedroom homes with electric heat in the Glenn Lakes area.

4. Apply the Report 6 AutoFormat to the pivot table.

5. Deselect the pivot table, close the toolbar, and save your changes to the *EE2_P7challenge* workbook.

3. Creating a PivotChart Report Using Its Wizard

You know how to create a chart from an existing pivot table. Now you want to create a chart and its associated pivot table at the same time. To create a PivotChart report, follow these steps:

1. Open the *EE2_P7challenge* workbook, if necessary; then select the #3-PivotChart worksheet.

2. Click any cell in the list range A5:I40, and activate the PivotTable and PivotChart Wizard.

3. Specify that you want to create a PivotChart report with the corresponding pivot table located at cell K5 of the current worksheet.

   Excel creates a blank Chart1 worksheet.

4. Use the PivotTable Field List box in the Chart1 worksheet to set up two fields: *Price* in the Data Area of the chart, and *Area* as the Category Axis.

5. Change *Sum of Price* to *Average of Price*.

6. Click the worksheet tab named #3-PivotChart.

   Excel automatically created the pivot table on which the chart is based.

7. Format the numbers in the pivot table to Currency (no dollar sign, zero decimal places), and deselect the pivot table.

8. Switch back to the Chart1 worksheet. Add titles and other documentation as appropriate, and change display of Y-axis values to include commas and dollar signs with zero decimal places.

9. Close any open box or toolbar, and save your changes to the *EE2_P7challenge* workbook.

4. Specifying More Than One Summary Calculation

For each area in the residential listings database, you want to know the number of homes available for sale and the average price. To specify more than one summary calculation, follow these steps:

1. Open the *EE2_P7challenge* workbook, if necessary; then select the #4-MultiCalc worksheet.

2. Click any cell within the database, and activate the PivotTable and PivotChart Wizard.

3. Specify that you want to create a pivot table in the current worksheet starting in cell K5, and access the PivotTable and PivotChart Wizard – Layout dialog box.

4. Lay out the pivot table to include *Area* as a <u>R</u>OW field and *Price* as a <u>D</u>ATA item two times.

5. Specify *Count* as the summary calculation on the first Price data item, and specify *Average* as the summary calculation on the second Price data item.

6. Close or exit as needed to generate the pivot table.

7. Widen column K as desired, and change the format of numbers in the pivot table to comma, zero decimal places.

   The table displays in PivotTable Classic format. Eight houses are listed for sale in Glenn Lakes, at an average price of *159,975*.

8. Apply a Table 6 predefined format.

   Notice that Excel does not retain number formatting when you apply a predefined format.

9. Change the display of numbers to Comma format, zero decimal places.

10. Deselect the pivot table, close the toolbar, and save your changes to the *EE2_P7challenge* workbook.

DISCOVERY ZONE

Discovery Zone exercises require advanced knowledge of topics presented in *Essentials* lessons, application of skills from multiple lessons, or self-directed learning of new skills.

Before beginning your first Project 7 Discovery Zone exercise, complete the following steps:

1. Open the file named *EE2_0704* and immediately save it as **EE2_P7discovery**.

   The *EE2_P7discovery* workbook contains four sheets: an overview, and three exercise sheets named #1-MultiPivot, #2-PageField, and #3-Group.

2. Select the Overview worksheet to view the organization of the Project 7 Discovery Zone Exercises workbook.

Each exercise is independent of the others, so you may complete them in any order. Be sure to save the workbook after completing each exercise. If you need a paper copy of the completed exercise, enter your name centered in a header before printing. Other print options have already been set to print compressed to one page and to display the filename, sheet name, and current date in a footer.

Be sure to save your changes, and close the workbook if you need more than one work session to complete the desired exercises. Continue working on *EE2_P7discovery* instead of starting over on the original *EE2_0704* file.

1. Analyzing Data Using Multiple Pivot Tables

Your supervisor has asked you to review the shipping data for Great Wilderness Outfitters, Inc. (GWO). This analysis already contains a great deal of information about GWO's shipping performance. The list begins in row 10 on the #1-MultiPivot sheet of the *EE2_P7discovery* workbook. It contains data on the day of the week an order was taken and which shift processed the order.

Discovery Zone   **245**   LEVEL 2

Through PivotTable and PivotChart reports you can determine in more detail the day of the week and which shift has the best or worst performance. Generate and save as many variations of pivot tables as you need to help you identify the problem areas.

2. Including a Page Field in a Pivot Table

You want to gain experience setting up page fields in a pivot table. Use onscreen Help to learn more about page fields, and then display the #2-PageField worksheet in the *EE2_P7discovery* workbook. Create a pivot table with a page field of your choice; also apply an appropriate pre-defined table or report format. Make sure you set up a page field that is useful for analyzing the charitable contributions data. After you create the pivot table, use the Page drop-down button to page through different views of your data.

3. Grouping Items in a Pivot Table

You are analyzing employee-related data on the #3-Group worksheet in the *EE2_P7discovery* workbook. Use onscreen Help to learn about grouping records. Set up a pivot table that shows the number of employees hired each year, and apply the predefined report or table format of your choice.

4. Getting Online Training on Pivot Tables

You know the basics for setting up PivotTable and PivotChart reports. Now you want to expand your knowledge. Access Microsoft's online training, and work through several levels of interactive training on pivot tables.

CREATING HYPERLINKS AND USING COLLABORATIVE TOOLS

OBJECTIVES

IN THIS PROJECT, YOU LEARN HOW TO

- Create a hyperlink between worksheets in an Excel workbook

- Create a hyperlink between a Word document and an Excel worksheet

- Create a hyperlink between a PowerPoint slide and an Excel worksheet

- Track changes in a workbook

- Accept or reject changes

- Edit a shared workbook

- Merge workbooks

- Explore digital signatures

WHY WOULD I DO THIS?

While working with multiple applications and collaborating with others on end products, you are likely to encounter a *hyperlink*—a link in a document that you can click to jump to another location, open another file, or start a process such as sending an e-mail or transferring a file. Hyperlinks in Web pages enable you to link to other locations in the current Web site and to other Web sites. You can create your own hyperlinks in Microsoft Office applications that refer to other application files, other locations within the current file, or Internet links.

Excel also provides a variety of collaborative tools. You can, for example, track the changes that you and others make to a workbook, and accept or reject each change. Individuals can also work on copies of a workbook and then merge the changes. You can even certify that a workbook you send to someone else is an unaltered version. These features support a dynamic collaborative process that promotes working smarter by sharing ideas and information.

👁 VISUAL SUMMARY

You start this project by creating and using three hyperlinks—a link to another worksheet in the current Excel workbook (see Figure 8.1), a link from a Word document to an Excel worksheet, and a link from a PowerPoint slide to an Excel worksheet.

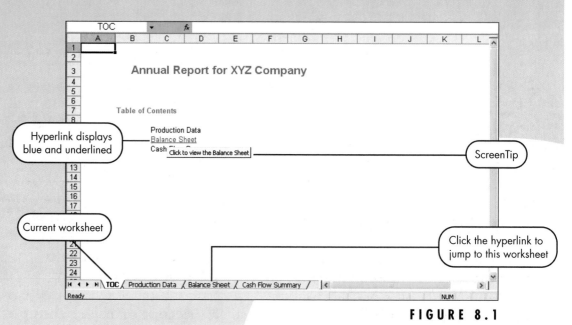

FIGURE 8.1

You also turn on and use a feature that tracks changes in a workbook. Each change can be accepted or rejected. Excel automatically attaches a note that identifies the user who made the change, specifies the date and time the change was made, and provides a description of the change (see Figure 8.2).

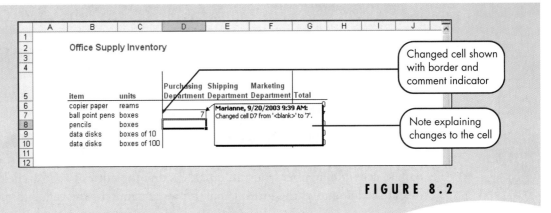

FIGURE 8.2

You also edit three shared workbooks and merge the resulting workbooks into a single workbook (see Figure 8.3). In the last lesson, you learn to digitally certify that a file has not been altered.

FIGURE 8.3

LESSON 1: Creating a Hyperlink Between Worksheets in an Excel Workbook

A hyperlink can be text—which generally displays blue and underlined—or a picture. When you position the mouse pointer on a hyperlink, the pointer changes to a hand, which indicates that the text or picture is an item you can click.

You can set up a hyperlink to provide a quick means to move from one location to another by clicking on the link. If the hyperlink is set up in an Excel worksheet, the connection can be to a position within the same worksheet, to another worksheet in the same workbook, to another workbook, to another application, or to a place within a Web site. You can attach a ScreenTip—a form of onscreen documentation—to a hyperlink. The ScreenTip displays each time that you position the mouse pointer on the hyperlink.

In this lesson, you open a workbook containing a very preliminary design for a company's annual report. You set up hyperlinks between two worksheets.

To Create a Hyperlink Between Worksheets

1 **Open the *EE2_0801* workbook, and save it as `Annual_Report`.**

The workbook contains the beginnings of a layout for an annual report. The first worksheet, named TOC, is the Table of Contents. Now create a hyperlink to jump to the start of the Balance Sheet and another link to jump back to the top of the TOC worksheet.

2 **Click cell A1 in the TOC worksheet, and name the cell `TOC`.**

Although you can jump to specific cells, it is easier and less confusing to jump to named cells. Remember, you can quickly name the current cell by clicking the *Name* box at the left end of the formula bar, typing a name for the cell, and pressing ⏎Enter.

3 **Click cell A3 in the Balance Sheet worksheet, name the cell `BalSheet`, and save the workbook.**

4 **Click cell C10 in the TOC worksheet; then click Insert Hyperlink on the Standard toolbar.**

The Insert Hyperlink dialog box opens. You can also open the dialog box by choosing Hyperlink on the Insert menu, or by right-clicking a cell and selecting *Hyperlink* from the shortcut menu.

5 **In the *Link to* area—a column along the left side of the dialog box—click *Place in This Document*.**

An outline of cell references and defined names displays in the Insert Hyperlink dialog box (see Figure 8.4)

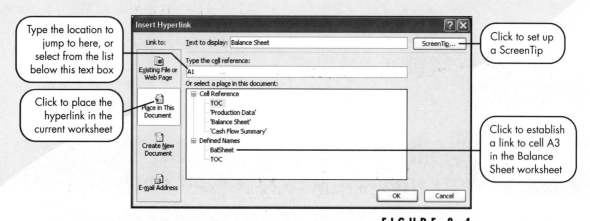

Type the location to jump to here, or select from the list below this text box

Click to place the hyperlink in the current worksheet

Click to set up a ScreenTip

Click to establish a link to cell A3 in the Balance Sheet worksheet

FIGURE 8.4

6 **Click *BalSheet,* the first name listed under Defined Names.**

If you have problems . . .

If you do not see BalSheet, you may need to expand the Defined Names outline by clicking the "+" outline symbol next to it.

7 | Click the ScreenTip button in the upper-right corner of the dialog box, and type `Click to view the Balance Sheet` in the ScreenTip text box.

You must be using Microsoft Internet Explorer version 4.0 or later to take advantage of the ScreenTip feature shown in Figure 8.5.

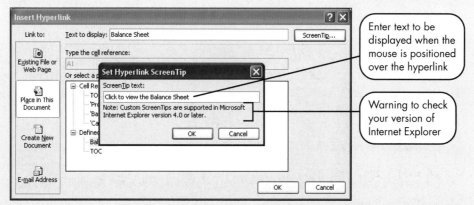

FIGURE 8.5

8 | Click OK to close the Set Hyperlink ScreenTip dialog box, and then click OK to close the Insert Hyperlink dialog box.

Balance Sheet in cell C10 displays blue and underlined, indicating it is a hyperlink (refer to Figure 8.1). Now test the link.

9 | Position the pointer on the blue underlined text in cell C10.

The pointer changes to a hand, and the ScreenTip *Click to view the Balance Sheet* displays.

10 | Click the hyperlinked text in cell C10.

Excel jumps to the destination for the hyperlink, cell A3 in the Balance Sheet worksheet. Once you have followed a hyperlink its color changes from blue to another color, indicating it has been used. The hyperlink color will change back to blue after the workbook has been closed and reopened.

11 | Click cell E1 in the Balance Sheet worksheet, enter `TOC`, and then create a hyperlink in cell E1 to the cell named *TOC* in the Table of Contents worksheet (include a ScreenTip `Click to view the Table of Contents`).

To complete this step, follow a procedure similar to steps 4–8 above.

12 | Click the new hyperlink.

If the *TOC* hyperlink is set up properly, cell A1 in the TOC worksheet becomes the active cell. Test your links several times until you are comfortable using links in a workbook.

13 | Save your changes to the *Annual_Report* workbook, and close the workbook.

Continue with the next lesson, or exit Excel.

TO EXTEND YOUR KNOWLEDGE . . .

REMOVING AND RESTORING A HYPERLINK

To remove a hyperlink and its associated text, right-click the hyperlink and select *Clear Contents*. You can also click the cell containing the hyperlink, hold down the mouse button until the pointer becomes a cross, release the mouse button, and press Del.

To remove a hyperlink without removing its associated text, right-click the hyperlink and select *Remove Hyperlink*. If you remove a hyperlink in error, use Edit, Undo to restore it.

USING THE HYPERLINK FUNCTION

Another option for creating a hyperlink is the HYPERLINK function. The format for this function is =*HYPERLINK(Link_location,Friendly_name)*. Use HYPERLINK to jump to an Internet, intranet, or extranet site or a document stored on your system. For example, the function =*HYPERLINK("http://www.microsoft.com", "Microsoft home page")* provides a link to Microsoft's Web site. To link to a document stored on your system, replace the first argument in the sample function with the full path and document name.

REDIRECTING A HYPERLINK

On occasion it may become necessary to redirect a hyperlink to a new location. Right-click the hyperlink, select *Edit Hyperlink,* and edit the destination. If the hyperlink was created using the HYPERLINK function, then you must edit the formula.

COPYING OR MOVING A HYPERLINK

When it becomes necessary to duplicate or move a hyperlink, the process is similar to copying and pasting text or other objects. Right-click the hyperlink to be moved or copied, select either *Copy* or *Cut,* position the pointer at the new location, and paste the hyperlink.

CHANGING THE APPEARANCE OF HYPERLINKS

Hyperlinks initially display blue and underlined, which tends to be the standard for links on Web sites, links within e-mail, and so forth. However, the appearance of a hyperlink that you create is entirely under your control, and you can apply any formatting you choose—font, color, size, shading, and so on. To change the formatting of a hyperlink, right-click it and choose *Format Cells* from the shortcut menu. Make your desired selections from the Format Cells dialog box, and click OK.

ASSIGNING A HYPERLINK TO A TOOLBAR BUTTON OR MENU COMMAND

If a hyperlink is used frequently from many different worksheets, you can assign a hyperlink to a toolbar button or menu command. Onscreen Help explains the process.

LESSON 2: Creating a Hyperlink Between a Word Document and an Excel Worksheet

You can easily set up hyperlinks between Microsoft Office applications. For example, you can create a hyperlink in an Excel worksheet that jumps to a specific location in a Word document. You can also create a hyperlink in a Word document that jumps to an Excel worksheet.

Assume you are writing a sales report in Microsoft Word, and you want its readers to be able to quickly see data in an Excel worksheet to support statements made in the report. If the report is a formal one, to be distributed widely throughout the organization, you would probably copy or link the worksheet data to the Word document. Then its readers could view the worksheet data as they read the report online or in hard copy format. If you want the worksheet data to be available but not included in the report itself, create a hyperlink to the worksheet data. If you choose the hyperlink approach, the workbook referenced in the hyperlink must continue to be stored in the location captured in the hyperlink.

In this lesson, you open a Word document containing the initial lines in a sales report, and create a hyperlink in that report to supporting data stored in an Excel workbook. You then test the hyperlink.

To Create a Hyperlink Between a Word Document and an Excel Worksheet

1 Launch Word; then open *EE2_0802* and save it as `WordLink.doc`.
A *Sales Report* document opens.

2 Select the phrase *(Click to view the Excel data)*; then choose Insert, Hyperlink.

3 In the *Link to* area on the left side of the dialog box, click *Existing File or Web Page*.
Filenames used in previous hyperlinks may appear in the dialog box if you have used the hyperlink feature before.

4 In the *Look in* box, select the folder in which you are storing the student files that accompany this text; then select the Excel workbook *EE2_0803*.

5 Click the ScreenTip button, type `Click to view the associated Excel file`, and click OK.

6 Click OK to close the Insert Hyperlink dialog box.
The hyperlinked text *(Click to view the Excel data)* displays blue and underlined. Now test the hyperlink.

7 **Position the pointer on the hyperlink.**

You see the ScreenTip that you defined and the message *CTRL + click to follow link* in bold (see Figure 8.6).

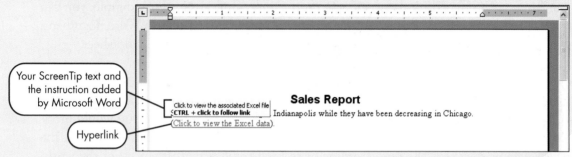

FIGURE 8.6

8 **Press and hold Ctrl and then click the hyperlink in the Word document.**

The Sales Data worksheet displays (see Figure 8.7). When Excel is accessed through a hyperlink, the Web toolbar displays automatically.

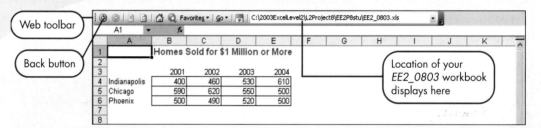

FIGURE 8.7

9 **Click the Back button on the Web toolbar.**

The word-processed report displays.

10 **Save and close the *WordLink* document, and exit Word.**

11 **Close the *EE2_0803* Excel workbook without saving it.**

Continue with the next lesson, or exit Excel.

TO EXTEND YOUR KNOWLEDGE . . .

SETTING A HYPERLINK TO EXCEL DATA

When you set a hyperlink to an Excel worksheet from another Office application, the link accesses the first worksheet of the workbook. Make sure that the Excel data you want to display are in the first worksheet, or store the data in their own workbook.

CHANGING A HYPERLINK IN WORD

Over time you may need to change an existing hyperlink. This is an easy process in Word or any other Office application. Right-click the current hyperlink, choose *Edit Hyperlink* from the shortcut menu, and edit as desired—such as revising the destination.

LESSON 3: Creating a Hyperlink Between a PowerPoint Slide and an Excel Worksheet

You can create a hyperlink in Excel that jumps to a specific slide in a PowerPoint presentation. You can also create a hyperlink in a PowerPoint presentation that jumps to a worksheet cell in an Excel workbook. The latter situation is far more common. Creating the hyperlink in PowerPoint makes it possible to reference Excel data without making the data the primary focus of the slide. The worksheet data would not be visible on the slide, but during the presentation you could activate the hyperlink and display the associated worksheet data in Excel.

In this lesson, you open a PowerPoint presentation file containing a single slide with a chart based on Excel data. The chart is not linked to the corresponding Excel file. You create a hyperlink between the chart on the PowerPoint slide and the Excel worksheet on which the chart is based, and test the link.

To Create a Hyperlink Between a PowerPoint Slide and an Excel Worksheet

1 Launch PowerPoint; then open the *EE2_0804* presentation and save it as `PPTlink`.
The PowerPoint presentation consists of a single slide—a chart based on data in the *EE2_0805* Excel workbook. There are no links between the two files.

2 Click the PowerPoint chart to select it, and choose <u>I</u>nsert, Hyper<u>l</u>ink.

3 In the *Link to* area on the left side of the dialog box, click *E<u>x</u>isting File or Web Page.*

4 Select but do not open the Excel workbook *EE2_0805* from the location in which you are storing the student files that accompany this text.
The file *EE2_0805* is highlighted.

5 Click the Scree<u>n</u>Tip button, enter `Click the chart to view the associated Excel data`, and click OK.

6 Click OK to close the Insert Hyperlink dialog box, and click outside the chart to deselect it.
You created a hyperlink to use during a PowerPoint slide show. Now verify that the hyperlink works as intended.

 7 Start the PowerPoint slide show by clicking the Slide Show button near the lower-left corner of the screen or selecting <u>V</u>iew, Slide Sho<u>w</u>.
The single slide containing a chart displays in Slide Show view.

8 Position the pointer on the chart but do not click the chart.

The ScreenTip *Click the chart to view the associated Excel data* appears (see Figure 8.8).

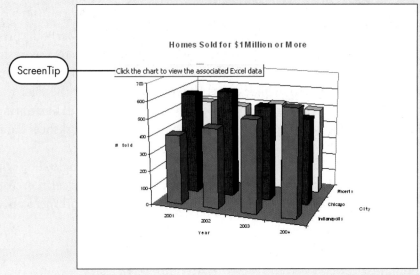

FIGURE 8.8

If you have problems . . .

The ScreenTip will disappear after a few seconds. This is normal. If you want to see the ScreenTip again move the mouse off and back on the chart and it will reappear.

9 Click within the chart on the slide.

Clicking the chart opens Excel and displays the first worksheet in the *EE2_0805* workbook (see Figure 8.9).

FIGURE 8.9

10 Click the Back button on the Web toolbar to jump back to the PowerPoint presentation.

11 Press Esc to end the slide show.

12 Save your changes to *PPTlink* presentation and exit PowerPoint.

This concludes Lesson 3, the last of three lessons on hyperlinks. Continue with the next lesson, or exit Excel.l

13 Close the Web toolbar, and close the *EE2_0805* workbook without saving it.

TO EXTEND YOUR KNOWLEDGE . . .

CHANGING A HYPERLINK IN POWERPOINT

As you modify a PowerPoint slide show, you might need to make changes to one or more hyperlinks. To change hyperlink text, select the text and type the new text. To change the destination of an existing hyperlink, select the hyperlink; choose Insert, Hyperlink; and type or select the new destination.

REMOVING A HYPERLINK FROM A CHART

To remove a hyperlink from a chart, select the chart; select Insert, Hyperlink; and click the Remove Link button.

LESSON 4:   Tracking Changes in a Workbook

Excel enables you to track the changes in a workbook, whether you make all of the changes yourself or multiple users are involved. In a work environment, it is common practice for two or more people to collaborate on developing or editing a workbook. Each user needs to know what changes the others have made.

Change tracking records row and column insertions and deletions, moves and copies, and changes to cell contents. The feature does not track formatting changes to cells or data, hiding or unhiding rows or columns, and adding or changing comments.

You can only track changes in a shared workbook. A ***shared workbook*** is a workbook that is set up to enable multiple users to make changes. When the setting to track changes is active, the word *[Shared]* displays to the right of the filename in the title bar. While in Shared mode, certain operations are not available. For example, you cannot delete a worksheet while a workbook is shared.

In this lesson, you work with an office supply inventory model. Imagine that the workbook is available to many users on a network. After opening the workbook, you save it using a different name. You then turn on the track changes feature and prepare to monitor changes made by different users.

To Track Changes in a Workbook

1 Open the *EE2_0806* workbook, and save it as `Inventory`.

2 Choose **T**ools, **T**rack Changes, **H**ighlight Changes.
The Highlight Changes dialog box opens (see Figure 8.10).

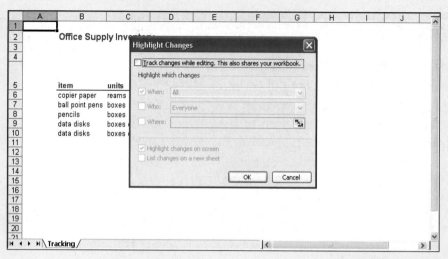

FIGURE 8.10

3 | Click the *Track changes while editing* check box at the top of the dialog box.
This setting activates Shared mode.

4 | Check the *When* check box and select *All* from the drop-down list, if necessary.
The *When* check box determines the extent of tracking changes. Selecting *All* (the default) causes all changes to be tracked. Other options include *Since I last saved, Not yet reviewed,* and *Since date.* If you select the last option, Excel provides a prompt to enter the date.

5 | Check the *Who* check box, and select *Everyone* from the drop-down list.
Options on the *Who* drop-down list include *Everyone* and *Everyone but Me.* The latter might be used if you were a supervisor or wanted to monitor only the changes that other people in your workgroup made to the workbook.

6 | Leave the *Where* check box unchecked.
If you check *Where,* you can select specific cells to be monitored.

7 | Check the *Highlight changes on screen* check box, if necessary (see Figure 8.11).
This setting creates a cell comment for every cell that is changed.

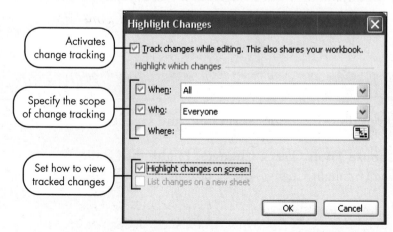

FIGURE 8.11

8 **Click OK. When a message box appears asking if you want to continue the save operation, click OK.**

The word *[Shared]* displays in the title bar. Tracking changes automatically shares the workbook even though you may be the only one making changes.

9 **Save your changes to the *Inventory* workbook.**

This concludes Lesson 4, the first of three lessons on change tracking. Continue with the next lesson, or close the workbook and exit Excel.

TO EXTEND YOUR KNOWLEDGE . . .

SETTING THE NUMBER OF DAYS TO TRACK CHANGES

When you turn on change tracking, the history is kept for 30 days. When you turn off change tracking or stop sharing the workbook, all change history is deleted.

You can increase or decrease the number of days that changes are tracked. Choose Tools, Share Workbook and then select the Advanced tab in the Share Workbook dialog box. Type the desired number of days in the *Keep change history for* spinner box, and click OK.

LESSON 5: Accepting or Rejecting Changes

Excel provides three ways to view tracked changes—onscreen highlighting, a History worksheet, and a dialog box in which you can accept or reject each change. You are using the first method when you view a shared workbook onscreen. Excel outlines changes with a different color for each user, and displays a note when you position the pointer on a changed cell. The note includes the name of the user who made the change, the date and time of the change, and a description of the change.

A *History worksheet* is a temporary worksheet that provides detailed information about changes in a list form—one change per row. To view and print the History worksheet, check *List changes on a new sheet* when turning on *Track changes while editing* in the Highlight Changes dialog box.

You can also view your changes in sequence in a dialog box that enables you to accept or reject each change. When multiple users revise a tracked document, generally one person makes the final decision on whether to keep or discard the suggested changes. It is a good idea to accept or reject changes on a regular basis, to keep the display of revisions made to other changes at a minimum.

In this lesson you use the first and third methods to view tracked changes. You make a change in the Office Supply model, and view information about the change onscreen. You then make a second change, and use the Accept or Reject Changes dialog box to accept one change and reject the other.

To Accept or Reject Changes

1 **Open the *Inventory* workbook, if necessary.**
The workbook is in Shared mode; *[Shared]* displays in the title bar.

If you have problems . . .

If the workbook is not currently shared, choose Share Workbook on the <u>T</u>ools menu, click the Editing tab, and check the *<u>A</u>llow changes by more than one user at the same time* check box.

2 **Enter the number 7 in cell D7.**
Excel automatically displays a border around the cell and inserts a comment, as evidenced by the small triangular comment indicator in the upper-left corner of the cell.

3 **Position the mouse pointer on cell D7.**
The attached comment displays. It identifies the user—by name or computer number—who made the change, specifies the date and time the change was made, and provides a description of the change (see the sample in Figure 8.12).

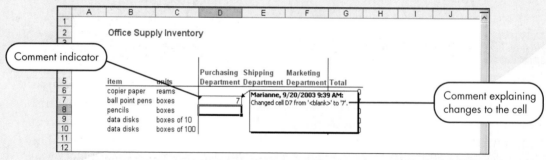

FIGURE 8.12

4 **Enter the number 5 in cell D9.**

5 **Choose <u>T</u>ools, Track Changes, <u>A</u>ccept or Reject Changes.**
A message box displays with the following text: *This action will now save the workbook. Do you want to continue?*

6 **Click OK.**
The Select Changes to Accept or Reject dialog box opens (see Figure 8.13).

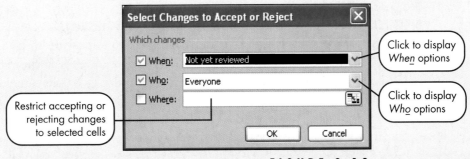

FIGURE 8.13

7   If necessary, check the *When* box, and select *Not yet reviewed* from the drop-down list.

8   If necessary, check the *Who* box, and select *Everyone* from the drop-down list.

9   Click OK.
The Accept or Reject Changes dialog box opens (see Figure 8.14).

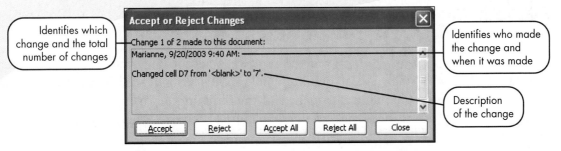

FIGURE 8.14

10   Click the **A**ccept button to accept the first change.
Information about the second change displays in the Accept or Reject Changes dialog box.

11   Click the **R**eject button to reject the second change.
Only the change made to cell D7 remains in the worksheet.

12   Save your changes to the *Inventory* workbook.
This concludes Lesson 5. Continue with the next lesson, or close the workbook and exit Excel.

TO EXTEND YOUR KNOWLEDGE . . .

REMOVING A WORKBOOK FROM SHARED USE

To remove a workbook from shared use, choose <u>T</u>ools, Share Wor<u>k</u>book, and then select the Editing tab. Make sure that you are the only person listed in the *Who has this workbook open now* section. Remove the check mark from the *<u>A</u>llow changes by more than one user at the same time* check box, and click OK.

NOTIFICATION OF CHANGES TO A FILE OR DISCUSSION
When working in a shared environment, you can subscribe to be notified by e-mail of changes to a file or discussion on your network or Web site. The network administrator must create a discussion server in order to participate. Once this is done, you subscribe to a discussion. You can specify the conditions for which you want to be notified of changes to a file or discussion, the e-mail address where notifications are to be sent, and how often you want to receive notifications.

SUMMARY OF CHANGE TRACKING
Excel can track the following changes to shared workbooks: edits of cell contents; data moved or copied; and rows, columns, and cells that are inserted or deleted. Certain changes cannot be tracked by Excel. These revisions include changes to sheet names, insertions and deletions of worksheets, cell and data formatting, hiding and unhiding rows and columns, adding and changing comments, recalculations, and unsaved changes.

LESSON 6: Editing a Shared Workbook

In the previous lesson, you learned the process to accept or reject changes by evaluating changes made by a single user in one workbook. In this lesson, you simulate changes made by two users—the Purchasing department and the Shipping department—in the same workbook. You view the changes and end the simulation of multiple users.

To Edit a Shared Workbook

1 **Open the *Inventory* workbook, if necessary.**
The workbook is in Shared mode; *[Shared]* displays in the title bar. Now create the simulation by revising the username on the General tab in the Options dialog box.

If you have problems . . .

If the workbook is not currently shared, choose *Share Workbook* on the <u>T</u>ools menu, click the Editing tab, and check the *<u>A</u>llow changes by more than one user at the same time* check box.

2 **Choose <u>T</u>ools, <u>O</u>ptions.**

3 **Click the General tab, and make note of the current entry in the *User <u>n</u>ame* text box (see the sample shown in Figure 8.15).**
Make sure that you remember the original username, so that you can restore it near the end of this lesson.

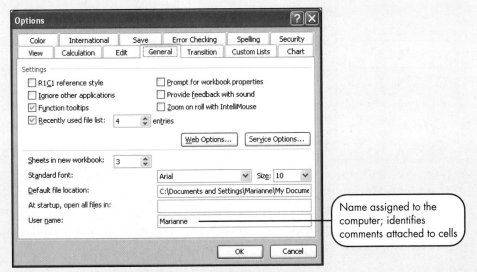

Name assigned to the computer; identifies comments attached to cells

FIGURE 8.15

4 | **Change the *User name* text box entry to Purchasing, and click OK.**
This changes the name of your computer temporarily to simulate multiple users making changes to the worksheet. At the end of the exercise you will change the username back to its original setting. In a normal situation, people on different computers with different usernames would be making these changes.

If you have problems . . .

If you are working in a computer lab or a networked environment, you may not be able to change the username on your system and complete this lesson. Instead, read the remaining steps and the To Extend Your Knowledge feature at the end of this lesson to gain an understanding of related processes.

5 | **Enter the number 50 in cell D6, save the workbook, and position the mouse pointer on cell D6.**
The comment indicates the change was made by *Purchasing*.

6 | **Choose Tools, Options; click the General tab, change the *User name* text box entry to Shipping, and click OK.**

7 | **Enter the number 10 in cell E7, save the workbook, and position the mouse pointer on cell E7.**
The comment indicates that the change was made by *Shipping*.

8 | **Choose Tools, Track Changes, Accept or Reject Changes, and then click OK.**
The Accept or Reject Changes dialog box opens (see Figure 8.16).

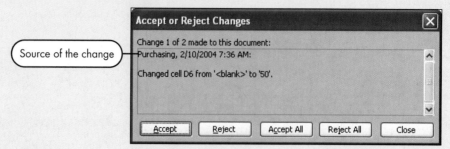

FIGURE 8.16

At this point, you could proceed to accept or reject changes made by multiple users the same way you accepted or rejected changes made by a single user in the previous lesson. Instead, you will restore the appropriate username, and save your changes to the shared workbook.

9 **Click Close.**

The Accept or Reject Changes dialog box closes without accepting or rejecting any changes. Now end the simulation of multiple users by restoring the original username, and save your changes.

10 **Choose Tools, Options, and then select the General tab.**

11 **Change the *User name* text box entry to its original specification, and click OK.**

12 **Save your changes to the *Inventory* workbook, and close the workbook.**

This concludes Lesson 6, the last of three lessons on change tracking. You can continue with the next lesson, or exit Excel.

TO EXTEND YOUR KNOWLEDGE . . .

CONFLICTING CHANGES TO A SHARED WORKBOOK

When two users try to save changes that affect the same cell, Excel displays the Resolve Conflicts dialog box for one of the users. The user can click *Accept Mine*, *Accept All Mine*, *Accept Other*, or *Accept All Others*. You can see how you and others resolved past conflicts by viewing the History worksheet.

LESSON 7:   Merging Workbooks

Often two or more people collaborate on the development of a workbook by working on different copies of the file. If you want to merge copies of a shared workbook in which users have made changes, Excel requires that each copy be set up to maintain the history of changes.

If you intend to merge workbooks, set up Shared mode in the original workbook and make copies for others to edit. All copies of the workbook must remain in the Shared mode while being modified. Collaborators can work on their copies from remote locations on a network or download them to their computers. When editing is complete, you must merge all the workbooks into one before you accept or reject changes.

In the following steps, you open a shared workbook that contains only the labels and formulas for displaying annual sales data from three stores (see Figure 8.17).

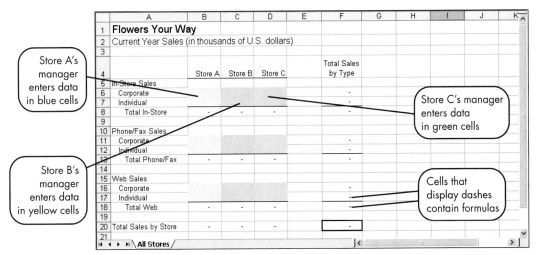

FIGURE 8.17

Assume that you previously distributed copies of this shared workbook to the managers of three stores. You requested that each manager keep the Shared mode active and fill in the appropriate data in column B (Store A), column C (Store B), or column D (Store C). Now each store manager has returned a copy with numbers added, and you want to merge those three copies into the original workbook.

In the following steps, you open the four files involved in the merge and save them under different names. Doing so enables you to work through the steps more than once. You then merge the changes in workbooks that contain store-specific data into the original workbook.

To Merge Workbooks

1 | **Open the *EE2_0807* workbook, and save it as Store_A.**
Shared mode is active. The blue cells display data entered by the manager of store A (see Figure 8.18). Notice that *[Shared]* appears next to the filename in the title bar at the top of the screen indicating that Shared mode is active.

	A	B	C	D	E	F	G	H	I	J	K
1	Flowers Your Way										
2	Current Year Sales (in thousands of U.S. dollars)										
3											
4		Store A	Store B	Store C		Total Sales by Type					
5	In-Store Sales										
6	Corporate	108				108					
7	Individual	321				321					
8	Total In-Store	429	-	-		429					
9											
10	Phone/Fax Sales										
11	Corporate	450				450					
12	Individual	225				225					
13	Total Phone/Fax	675	-	-		675					
14											
15	Web Sales										
16	Corporate	57				57					
17	Individual	11				11					
18	Total Web	68	-	-		68					
19											
20	Total Sales by Store	1,172	-	-		1,172					
21											

All Stores

FIGURE 8.18

2 Close the *Store_A* workbook.

3 Open the *EE2_0808* workbook and save it as `Store_B`.
Shared mode is active. The yellow cells display data entered by the manager of store B (see Figure 8.19).

	A	B	C	D	E	F	G	H	I	J	K
1	Flowers Your Way										
2	Current Year Sales (in thousands of U.S. dollars)										
3											
4		Store A	Store B	Store C		Total Sales by Type					
5	In-Store Sales										
6	Corporate		111			111					
7	Individual		371			371					
8	Total In-Store	-	482	-		482					
9											
10	Phone/Fax Sales										
11	Corporate		425			425					
12	Individual		229			229					
13	Total Phone/Fax	-	654	-		654					
14											
15	Web Sales										
16	Corporate		65			65					
17	Individual		14			14					
18	Total Web	-	79	-		79					
19											
20	Total Sales by Store	-	1,215	-		1,215					
21											

All Stores

FIGURE 8.19

4 Close the *Store_B* workbook.

5 Open the *EE2_0809* workbook and save it as `Store_C`.
Shared mode is active. The green cells display data entered by the manager of store C (see Figure 8.20).

	A	B	C	D	E	F	G	H	I	J	K
1	Flowers Your Way										
2	Current Year Sales (in thousands of U.S. dollars)										
3											
4		Store A	Store B	Store C		Total Sales by Type					
5	In-Store Sales										
6	Corporate			96		96					
7	Individual			305		305					
8	Total In-Store	-	-	401		401					
9											
10	Phone/Fax Sales										
11	Corporate			510		510					
12	Individual			241		241					
13	Total Phone/Fax	-	-	751		751					
14											
15	Web Sales										
16	Corporate			89		89					
17	Individual			17		17					
18	Total Web	-	-	106		106					
19											
20	Total Sales by Store	-	-	1,258		1,258					
21											

All Stores

FIGURE 8.20

6 **Close the *Store_C* workbook.**
The previous steps enabled you to create copies of original student data files and to view the data that you will merge into a fourth workbook. Next, you begin the merge process.

7 **Open the *EE2_0810* workbook and save it as `Merge_Workbooks`.**
Shared mode is active. The workbook includes one worksheet named All Stores. Labels and formulas are in place, and colors indicate cells that will hold data about each store's sales (refer to Figure 8.17).

8 **Choose Tools, Compare and Merge Workbooks.**
The Select Files to Merge Into Current Workbook dialog box opens.

9 **In the *Look in* box, display the folder containing your *Store_A, Store_B, Store_C,* and *Merge_Workbooks* files (see the sample in Figure 8.21).**

FIGURE 8.21

10 **Hold down Ctrl; then click each of the three files you want to merge (refer to Figure 8.21) and release Ctrl.**
You selected the files named *Store_A, Store_B,* and *Store_C.*

11 **Click OK.**
The dialog box closes and Excel executes the merge. Data display for each store, one column at a time, in the *Merge_Workbooks* file (see the complete results in Figure 8.22).

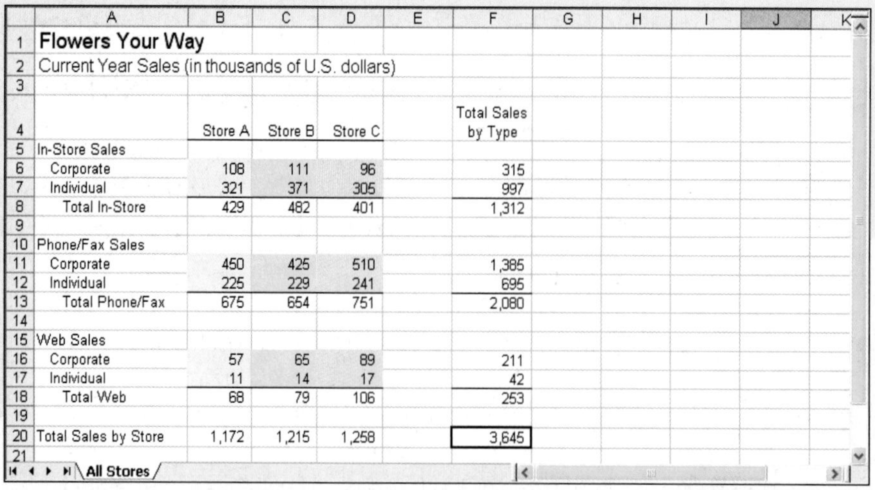

	A	B	C	D	E	F	G	H	I	J	K
1	Flowers Your Way										
2	Current Year Sales (in thousands of U.S. dollars)										
3											
4		Store A	Store B	Store C		Total Sales by Type					
5	In-Store Sales										
6	Corporate	108	111	96		315					
7	Individual	321	371	305		997					
8	Total In-Store	429	482	401		1,312					
9											
10	Phone/Fax Sales										
11	Corporate	450	425	510		1,385					
12	Individual	225	229	241		695					
13	Total Phone/Fax	675	654	751		2,080					
14											
15	Web Sales										
16	Corporate	57	65	89		211					
17	Individual	11	14	17		42					
18	Total Web	68	79	106		253					
19											
20	Total Sales by Store	1,172	1,215	1,258		3,645					
21											

All Stores

FIGURE 8.22

12 Activate Excel's change tracking feature, and accept all changes.

13 Save your changes to the *Merge_Workbooks* file, and close the workbook. Continue with the last lesson, or exit Excel.

LESSON 8:   Exploring Digital Signatures

Microsoft Office 2003 includes a feature to digitally sign a document. A *digital signature* confirms that the document has not been altered since the document was signed. You can open and view a digitally signed file, but if you edit it, the signature is removed.

You use a digital certificate to create a digital signature. A *digital certificate* confirms that the document originated from the signer. Most digital certificates are obtained from commercial sources that act as certification authorities. A system administrator in a networked environment can also issue an internal digital certificate that indicates the subject file is certified by the organization's internal security.

To create a signed file, you must have a digital certificate loaded on your computer system. Make sure that all changes to the file have been made, and the file saved, before you attach the digital signature.

In the following steps, you explore dialog boxes associated with digital signatures. After you open a self-signed Excel workbook, you access the Security tab on the Tools, Options menu and view information about the digital certificate. You also save the signed file, which removes the digital signature.

To Explore Digital Signatures

1 **Open the *EE2_0811* workbook, but do not save it at this time.**

The bracketed information *[Signed, unverified]* displays in the title bar. *Signed* indicates there is a digital certificate attached, and *unverified* indicates that the document is self-signed, as opposed to being issued by a commercial certifying organization.

2 **Click Tools, Options, and select the Security tab.**

3 **Click the Digital Signatures button.**

The Digital Signature dialog box opens (see Figure 8.23).

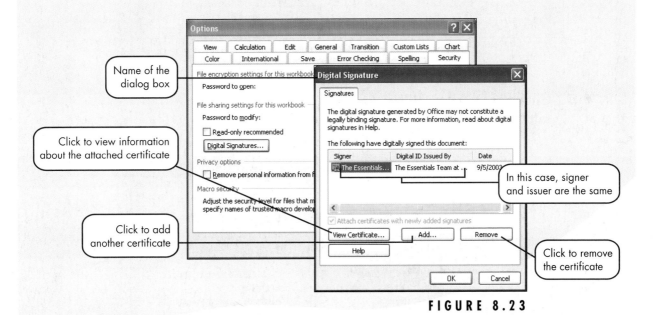

FIGURE 8.23

4 **Click the View Certificate button.**

The Certificate dialog box opens (see Figure 8.24). Your screen might display slightly different dates.

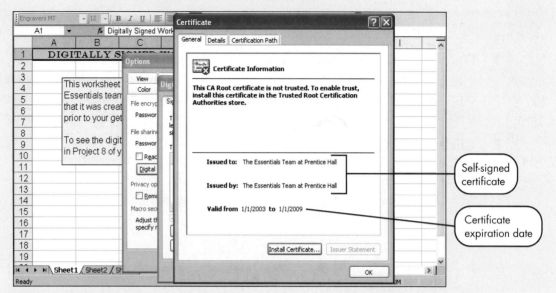

FIGURE 8.24

5 **Click the Details tab.**

Information about the certificate displays (see Figure 8.25).

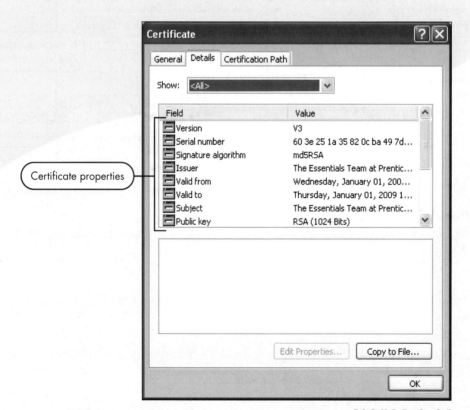

FIGURE 8.25

6 **Click OK three times to close the three open dialog boxes.**

The original worksheet in the self-signed workbook displays.

7 Click <u>F</u>ile, Save <u>A</u>s; then save the workbook as `Signature` in the folder where you are saving your solutions to this text.

The warning message shown in Figure 8.26 appears; it indicates that saving the file will remove all signatures.

Warning message

FIGURE 8.26

8 Click OK.

This saves the workbook under the new name with the digital signature removed.

9 Click <u>T</u>ools, <u>O</u>ptions.

10 Make sure that the Security tab is active, and click the <u>D</u>igital Signatures button.

There are no digital signatures listed for this workbook.

11 Close the two open dialog boxes, and close the *Signature* workbook.

Continue with the exercises at the end of the project, or exit Excel.

TO EXTEND YOUR KNOWLEDGE . . .

GETTING HELP ON DIGITAL SIGNATURES

Onscreen Help provides general information about digital signatures. Enter `digital signature` in the *Type a question for help* box, and select *About digital signatures.*

GETTING HELP ON CREATING A SELF-SIGNED DIGITAL CERTIFICATE

You can create a digital certificate yourself using the Selfcert.exe program. However, certificates that you create yourself generate a warning message if the security level is set to High or Medium.

You can use online Help to learn more about the purpose for and process of creating a self-signed digital certificate. To quickly view the related information, enter `Create your own digital certificate` in the *Type a question for help* box, and select the topic that matches your Help request.

SUMMARY

The initial three lessons, on hyperlinks, explained how to set up connections between locations within a workbook and between Excel and other Microsoft applications. Subsequent lessons described features that support the collaborative process. First you explored using features that enable more than one person to edit a workbook at the same time. Topics included designating a workbook as shared, tracking changes, accepting or rejecting tracked changes, and editing a shared workbook. You also merged workbooks being modified by three users and learned about digital signatures.

You can extend your learning by reviewing concepts and terms, and by practicing variations of skills presented in the lessons. Use the following table as a guide to the numbered questions and exercises in the end-of-project learning opportunities.

LESSON	MULTIPLE CHOICE	DISCUSSION	SKILL DRILL	CHALLENGE	DISCOVERY ZONE
Creating a Hyperlink Between Worksheets in an Excel Workbook	4, 6	3	1, 2, 3, 5, 6	1, 3, 4	3
Creating a Hyperlink Between a Word Document and an Excel Worksheet	5, 6				3
Creating a Hyperlink Between a PowerPoint Slide and an Excel Worksheet	6				3
Tracking Changes in a Workbook	1, 2, 3		4		1
Accepting or Rejecting Changes	7			2	
Editing a Shared Workbook	8	2			2
Merging Workbooks	9	1			2
Exploring Digital Signatures	10			5	

KEY TERMS

change tracking   digital signature   hyperlink

digital certificate   History worksheet   shared workbook

CHECKING CONCEPTS AND TERMS

MULTIPLE CHOICE

Circle the letter of the correct answer for each of the following.

1. Which of the following is true? [L4]

   a. Tracking automatically sets up a shared workbook.

   b. You can delete a worksheet if its workbook is currently in Shared mode.

   c. Both a and b

   d. Neither a or b

2. Which of the following is not an option when determining the extent of change tracking? [L4]

   a. All

   b. Since I last saved

   c. Not yet reviewed

   d. Between these dates

3. Which of the following is not captured by change tracking? [L4]

   a. Formatting changes

   b. Changes to cell contents

   c. Row and column insertions and deletions

   d. Moves and copies

4. A hyperlink set up in Excel can be a link to which of the following? [L1]

   a. A Web page

   b. Another worksheet in the same workbook

   c. Another application, such as Microsoft Word

   d. All of the above

5. Which is a change you can make to a hyperlink in Word? [L2]

   a. Point the hyperlink to a different workbook.

   b. Change the hyperlink text, but not the hyperlink.

   c. Convert hyperlink text to normal text.

   d. All of the above

6. Which of the following is a special effect you can associate with a hyperlink? [L1–3]

   a. Password protection

   b. Choice of format styles

   c. Both a and b

   d. Neither a or b

7. Which of the following is a means of viewing tracked changes? [L5]

   a. Onscreen highlighting

   b. A history worksheet

   c. A dialog box in which you can accept or reject each change

   d. All of the above

8. Which of the following is not a true statement about the Resolve Conflicts dialog box? [L6]

   a. The Resolve Conflicts dialog box appears when you attempt to save a worksheet twice.

   b. Options to resolve conflicting changes include Accept Mine, Accept All Mine, Accept Other, and Accept All Others.

   c. You can check the History worksheet to see how changes were dealt with in the past before making a decision.

   d. Both a and b

9. Which of the following is *not* accurate if you intend to merge changes from copies of the same workbook? [L7]

    a. You should activate Shared mode before making copies of the original workbook to distribute for editing.

    b. You should keep Shared mode active while editing a workbook to be merged.

    c. You must accept or reject pending changes in workbooks before merging the workbooks.

    d. Collaborators can work on their copies of a workbook from remote locations and a network.

10. Which of the following is a source for digital certificates? [L8]

    a. A commercial certifying organization

    b. A system administrator

    c. An individual creating a self-signed certificate

    d. All of the above

DISCUSSION

1. Describe a situation not used in your textbook that would be appropriate for merging workbooks. Describe the process for setting up shared workbooks and the process for merging those workbooks after they have been used. [L7]

2. Some changes are not tracked when Excel's change tracking is active—such as formatting changes to cells or data, hiding or unhiding rows or columns, and any changes to features unavailable in shared workbooks. Use onscreen Help to learn about the features that are not available in shared workbooks, and describe at least eight of them. Include information about alternatives, if available. [L6]

3. Describe a situation not used in your textbook that would be appropriate for using hyperlinks in the same workbook; your sample workbook should include multiple worksheets. Discuss how hyperlinks make navigating the workbook easier than the traditional navigation methods of selecting a worksheet and scrolling to the desired location. Also describe the process of creating a hyperlink. [L1]

SKILL DRILL

Skill Drill exercises reinforce project skills. Each skill that is reinforced is the same, or nearly the same, as a skill presented in the project. Detailed instructions are provided in a step-by-step format.

Before beginning your first Project 8 Skill Drill exercise, complete the following steps:

    1. Open the workbook named *EE2_0812* and immediately save it as **EE2_P8drill**.

        The workbook contains an Overview sheet and six sheets named #1-Create Link, #2-Edit Link, #3-Remove Link, #4-Track, #5-Redirect, and #6-HYPERLINK.

    2. Click the Overview sheet to view the organization and content of the Project 8 Skill Drill Exercises workbook.

Each exercise is independent of the others, so you may complete them in any order. Be sure to save the workbook after completing each exercise. If you need a paper copy of the completed exercise, enter your name centered in a header before printing. Other print options have already been set to print compressed to one page and to display the filename, sheet name, and current date in a footer.

If you need more than one work session to complete the desired exercises, continue working on *EE2_P8drill* instead of starting over on the original *EE2_0812* file.

1. Creating a Hyperlink Within a Worksheet

You work for Real Estate for Tomorrow, Inc., and you manage a list of residential real estate for sale. You want to create a hyperlink within the worksheet to the mailing address for the firm. To create the hyperlink, follow these steps:

1. Open the *EE2_P8drill* workbook, if necessary; then select the #1-Create Link sheet.
2. Enter **Mailing Address** in cell A6.
3. Click cell M3, name the cell **address**, and save the workbook.
4. Click cell A6, and select Insert, Hyperlink.
5. In the *Link to* area—a column along the left side of the dialog box—click *Place in This Document*.

    An outline of cell references and defined names displays in the Insert Hyperlink dialog box.
6. Click *address* under Defined Names.
7. Click the ScreenTip button in the upper-right corner of the dialog box, and enter **Click to view the firm's mailing address** in the ScreenTip text box.
8. Click OK to close the Set Hyperlink ScreenTip dialog box, and then click OK to close the Insert Hyperlink dialog box.

    Mailing Address in cell A6 displays blue and underlined, indicating it is a hyperlink. Now test the link.
9. Position the pointer on the blue underlined text in cell A6.

    The pointer changes to a hand, and the ScreenTip *Click to view the firm's mailing address* displays.
10. Click the hyperlinked text in cell A6.

    Excel jumps to cell M3, the destination for the hyperlink.
11. Save your changes to the *EE2_P8drill* workbook.

2. Editing a Hyperlink

You work for Real Estate for Tomorrow, Inc., and you manage a list of residential real estate for sale. You want to improve the display of data by changing the destination cell in a hyperlink. To edit the hyperlink, follow these steps:

1. Open the *EE2_P8drill* workbook, if necessary; then select the #2-Edit Link sheet.

2. Click the *Contact us!* hyperlink in cell A5.

   Excel jumps to cell M3. Depending on your display settings, you may not be able to see the complete phone and fax numbers.

3. Right-click the *Contact us!* hyperlink in cell A5, and select *Edit Hyperlink* from the shortcut menu.

4. In the *Type the cell reference* text box, change *M3* to **O3** (be sure to type the letter *O* instead of a zero).

5. Click OK, and then click the edited link in cell A5.

   Excel jumps to cell O3. You see the complete phone and fax numbers.

6. Save your changes to the *EE2_P8drill* workbook.

3. Removing a Hyperlink

You work for Real Estate for Tomorrow, Inc., and you manage a list of residential real estate for sale. You want to delete data about real estate agents from the worksheet. To remove the hyperlink to agent names and delete the associated data, follow these steps:

1. Open the *EE2_P8drill* workbook, if necessary; then select the #3-Remove Link sheet.

2. Right-click the *Agent List* hyperlink in cell A5, and select *Remove Hyperlink* from the shortcut menu.

   The hyperlink is removed. The text *Agent List* no longer displays blue and underlined.

3. Delete the contents of cell A5 and the range M3:M7.

4. Save your changes to the *EE2_P8drill* workbook.

4. Tracking Changes in a Worksheet

You work for Real Estate for Tomorrow, Inc., and you manage a list of residential real estate for sale. You want to track changes in the selling prices of several homes, so that a coworker can easily double-check your work. To turn on the change tracking feature and make a change, follow these steps:

1. Open the *EE2_P8drill* workbook, if necessary; then select the #4-Track sheet.

2. Choose <u>T</u>ools, <u>T</u>rack Changes, <u>H</u>ighlight Changes.

   The Highlight Changes dialog box opens.

3. Click the *<u>T</u>rack changes while editing* check box at the top of the dialog box.

4. Check the *Whe<u>n</u>* check box and select *All* from the drop-down list, if necessary.

5. Check the *Wh<u>o</u>* check box, and select *Everyone* from the drop-down list.

6. Leave the *Whe<u>r</u>e* check box unchecked.

7. Check the *Highlight changes on <u>s</u>creen* check box, if necessary, and click OK.

8. When a message box appears asking if you want to continue the save operation, click OK.

   Notice that *[Shared]* displays in the title bar. The change tracking feature is active.

9. Change the amount in cell B23 from *226,000* to **219,900**.

Excel automatically displays a border around the cell and inserts a comment, as evidenced by the small triangular comment indicator in the upper-left corner of the cell.

10. Position the mouse pointer on cell B23.

The attached comment displays. It identifies the user—by name or computer number—who made the change, specifies the date and time the change was made, and provides a description of the change. Now, find out what happens if you turn off change tracking.

11. Choose <u>T</u>ools, Share Wor<u>k</u>book; then uncheck the *<u>A</u>llow changes by more than one user at the same time* check box on the Editing tab, and click OK.

Excel accepts the change and the comment indicator disappears.

12. Save your changes to the *EE2_P8drill* workbook.

5. Redirecting and Removing Hyperlinks

You want to improve your ability to work with hyperlinks. Maintenance activities include removing a hyperlink, editing a hyperlink including its accompanying ScreenTip, and redirecting the destination of the hyperlink. To practice maintaining hyperlinks, follow these steps:

1. Open the *EE2_P8drill* workbook, if necessary; then select the #5-Redirect sheet.

2. Right-click cell A5 and select *<u>R</u>emove Hyperlink*.

Notice that the hyperlink has been removed but the cell content remains. Now edit a hyperlink by changing the ScreenTip.

3. Right-click cell A7 and select *Edit <u>H</u>yperlink*.

4. Select *Screen<u>T</u>ip* and replace the Screen<u>T</u>ip text with **This is a good source for custom maps**.

5. Click *OK* twice to return to the worksheet.

6. Position the mouse pointer over the hyperlink to see the new ScreenTip.

Make any corrections that are necessary. Now redirect a hyperlink from one URL to another.

7. Right-click cell A9 and select *Edit <u>H</u>yperlink*.

8. Replace the Web site URL in the *Add<u>r</u>ess* text box with **http://www.time.gov/**

9. Replace the contents of the *<u>T</u>ext to display* text box with **U.S. Time Zone Information**.

10. Click *Screen<u>T</u>ip* and replace the Screen<u>T</u>ip text with **Click to access the official U.S. time**.

11. Click OK twice, position the mouse pointer over cell A9, and then verify that the ScreenTip is correct.

12. Connect to the Internet, if necessary; then click cell A9 to make sure that the hyperlink works.

13. Close your browser, and save your changes to the *EE2_P8drill* workbook.

6. Using the HYPERLINK Function

You have been enhancing your ability to navigate within Excel workbooks and between Excel and other Office applications such as Word and PowerPoint. To do this you have been using the Insert Hyperlink option. Now you want to work with an alternative means of hyperlinking—the HYPERLINK function. To use the HYPERLINK function to access a Web site, follow these steps:

1. Open the *EE2_P8drill* workbook, if necessary; then select the #6-HYPERLINK sheet.

2. Select cell B5, and click the Insert Function button at the left side of the formula bar.

3. Select *HYPERLINK* from the Lookup & Reference category in the Insert Function dialog box, and click OK.

   The Function Arguments dialog box for the HYPERLINK function opens.

4. Type `http://www.microsoft.com/` in the *Link_location* text box.

5. Type `"Microsoft Home Page"` in the *Friendly_name* text box; then click OK.

   You created a hyperlink to the Microsoft Web site. The text you typed as the *Friendly_name* argument displays blue and underlined in cell B5.

6. Connect to the Internet, if necessary; then click the hyperlink.

   The home page for Microsoft Corporation displays.

7. Click your browser's Back button to return to the worksheet. (If the Back button is not active, click the Excel worksheet's button on the taskbar at the bottom of the screen or close the browser.)

8. Repeat steps 2 and 3 using cell B7; then type `http://www.msnbc.com` as the *Link_location.*

9. Click within the *Friendly_name* box; then click cell A7.

   Excel uses the contents of cell A7 as the *Friendly_name* argument. You see = *"MSNBC News"* at the right end of the *Friendly_name* box.

10. Click OK; then click the newly created link to the MSNBC News site.

11. Use the HYPERLINK function to create a hyperlink in cell B9; specify `http://www.usatoday.com` as the *Link_location,* and the contents of cell A9 as the *Friendly_name.*

12. After making sure that the link in cell B9 works as intended, close your browser and save your changes to the *EE2_P8drill* workbook.

CHALLENGE

Challenge exercises expand on or are somewhat related to skills that are presented in the lessons. Each exercise provides a brief narrative introduction, followed by instructions in a numbered-step format that are not as detailed as those in the Skill Drill section.

Before beginning your first Project 8 Challenge exercise, complete the following steps:

1. Open the workbook named *EE2_0813* and immediately save it as **EE2_P8challenge**.

    The *EE2_P8challenge* workbook contains five sheets: an Overview, and sheets named #1-SetLinks, #2-AcceptReject, #3-Web, and #4-Send.

2. Click the Overview sheet to view the organization of the Project 8 Challenge Exercises workbook.

Each exercise is independent of the others, so you may complete them in any order. Be sure to save the workbook after completing each exercise. If you need a paper copy of the completed exercise, enter your name centered in a header before printing. Other print options have already been set to print compressed to one page and to display the filename, sheet name, and current date in a footer.

If you need more than one work session to complete the desired exercises, continue working on *EE2_P8challenge* instead of starting over on the original *EE2_0813* file.

1. Creating Hyperlinks Within a Large Worksheet

You are managing an employee database in an Excel worksheet. You want to set up hyperlinks to various areas within the worksheet. To create and test the links, follow these steps:

1. Open the *EE2_P8challenge* workbook, if necessary; then select the #1-SetLinks sheet.

2. Use navigation keys and Print Preview to learn the organization and content of the worksheet.

3. Set up four hyperlinks in the worksheet using the following range names and cell references:

    Criteria in cell F3, jumping to cell C12

    Database in cell F4, jumping to cell C21

    DropDownLists in cell F5, jumping to cell T1

    Extract in cell F6, jumping to cell K134

4. Enter **List of hyperlinks** in cell A131, and set a hyperlink jumping to cell F3.

5. Copy the hyperlink in cell A131 to cells K136 and R1.

6. Make sure that each link in the range F3:F6 jumps to the appropriate area in the worksheet, and that each *List of hyperlinks* link jumps to cell F3.

7. Save your changes to the *EE2_P8challenge* workbook.

2. Accepting or Rejecting Tracked Changes

You are managing a Transportation Model worksheet. You want to track changes in that worksheet as you make them, followed by accepting or rejecting each change when you are done. To activate Excel's change tracking feature, make changes, and accept or reject each change, follow these steps:

1. Open the *EE2_P8challenge* workbook, if necessary; then select the #2-AcceptReject sheet.

2. Turn on tracking of all changes by everyone.

3. Change the shipping cost per unit in cell H8 to **3.40**.

4. Replace all occurrences of *Chicago* with **St. Louis**.

5. Change the capacity value in cell J17 from *20,000* to **22,000**.

6. Activate accepting and rejecting changes for changes by everyone not yet reviewed.

7. Accept the change in city and shipping cost per unit, but reject the change in capacity.

8. Disable tracking changes while editing, which removes the workbook from shared use.

9. Save your changes to the *EE2_P8challenge* workbook.

3. Creating a Hyperlink to a Web Site

You developed a worksheet to track annual revenues for three cities over a four-year period. Now you want to create a hyperlink to a Web site for the first city. To create the hyperlink to a Web site, follow these steps:

1. Open the *EE2_P8challenge* workbook, if necessary; then select the #3-Web sheet.

2. Replace *Baltimore* in cells A7 and A13 with the name of the major city that is closest to where you live.

3. Find the government-sponsored URL for the city you specified in step 2.

4. Click cell A13, and start the process to insert a hyperlink in the current document.

5. Specify that you want to create a link to a Web page.

6. Enter the URL for your selected city in the *Address* text box, and click OK.

7. Make sure that the hyperlink to your city's Web site works; then close your browser and save your changes to the *EE2_P8challenge* workbook.

4. Creating an E-mail Hyperlink

You are the Phoenix sales director, and you developed a worksheet to track annual revenues for three cities over a four-year period. Now you want to create a hyperlink to your e-mail address. To create the hyperlink, follow these steps:

1. Open the *EE2_P8challenge* workbook, if necessary; then select the #4-Send sheet.

2. Click cell A15, and start the process to insert a hyperlink in the current document.

3. Select the *E-mail Address* option in the Insert Hyperlink dialog box.

4. Enter your personal e-mail address in the *E-mail address* text box, and click OK.

5. Save your changes to the *EE2_P8challenge* workbook.

5. Getting Help Using Digital Signatures

In today's environment of increasing computer security problems, you are concerned that files and e-mail you send are causing concern to recipients. You viewed a workbook that was digitally signed and want to learn more about digital signatures. To learn more about digital signatures using onscreen Help, follow these steps (if the training session mentioned in steps 2 through 4 is not available, skip to step 5):

1. Connect to the Internet, if necessary; then display an Excel worksheet and enter **digital signature** in the *Type a question for help* text box.

2. Start the training session titled *Help protect yourself: Security in Office.*

   This 20–30 minute training session provides an overview of passwords, viruses, certificates, and other security topics.

3. Select *Trust, certificates, and security settings* from the Overview list on the left side of the screen, and click the digital signature topic.

4. Work through other topics in the training session, as desired; then restore display of the Search Results task pane.

5. Read the Help topics *About digital signatures* and *Create your own digital certificate* (substitute other topics, if necessary).

6. Switch to the Research task pane; then select *All Research Sites* and search for digital signatures.

7. Select *MSN Search* and look for topics on digital signatures. When you are finished, close your browser and any open dialog boxes or task panes.

DISCOVERY ZONE

Discovery Zone exercises require advanced knowledge of topics presented in *Essentials* lessons, application of skills from multiple lessons, or self-directed learning of new skills.

Each exercise is independent of the others, so you may complete them in any order. The second exercise on merging workbooks requires working with one other person.

1. Displaying and Printing a History Worksheet

You want to make several changes in a workbook and view the changes in a History worksheet. Open the *EE2_0814* workbook and save it as **EE2_P8discovery1**. Turn on change tracking and make the following changes: Center the column headings in row 3; change the contents of cell B4 from *145,000* to **150,000**; change the name of the worksheet from *GlennLakes GC* to **Year 2004**; and insert a row between *Golf Lessons* (row 5) and *Other Revenue* (row 6). Save your changes to the *EE2_P8discovery1* workbook. Display and print a History worksheet, and note that centering the column headings in row 3—a formatting change—is not listed. Close the workbook. (Reminder: Whether you save the file or not as you close it, Excel does not retain the History worksheet.)

2. Merging Workbooks

You (Person #1) are going to make changes to a workbook. Select someone else (Person #2) to make changes to a copy of the same workbook. After all changes are made, merge the workbooks. Follow the instructions below in three stages—prepare to edit, make changes, and merge the workbooks.

Prepare to Edit (Person #1): Open the *EE2_0815* workbook, enable change tracking, and save the workbook as **Edit1**. Make a copy of the *Edit1* workbook, change the name of the copy to **Edit2**, and distribute the copy to Person #2.

Make Changes (Person #1): Open the *Edit1* workbook, and make sure that change tracking is enabled. Change the contents of cell B4 from *145,000* to **150,000** and save your change.

Make Changes (Person #2): Open the *Edit2* workbook, and make sure that change tracking is enabled. Insert a row between *Golf Lessons* (row 5) and *Other Revenue* (row 6). Enter **Pro Shop Sales** in column A of the newly inserted row. Save your changes to the *Edit2* workbook, and return a copy of the revised workbook to Person #1.

Merge Workbooks (Person #1): Make sure that the revised workbooks *Edit1* and *Edit 2* are in the same folder, and open the *Edit1* workbook, if necessary. Select the option to merge workbooks from the <u>T</u>ools menu, and select the *Edit2* workbook to merge into the current workbook. Complete the merge; then turn off Shared mode and save the result as **EE2_P8discovery2**.

3. Creating Hyperlinks to Navigate Between Three Office Applications

In your position as treasurer for the Glenn Lakes Golf Club, you have put together an Excel workbook (*EE2_0816.xls*) and PowerPoint presentation (*EE2_0817.ppt*) for the joint Board of Directors and Members meeting next month. You want to distribute the packet in both hard copy and electronic form to each of the board members. In addition, the electronic version will be available to members on the club's Web site. Before you finalize the Word, PowerPoint, and Excel documents, you want to set up numerous hyperlinks between the applications. Open the *EE2_0816* workbook and save it as **EE2_P8discovery3**. Explore the workbook and notice its organization: a table of contents sheet; three revenue statements for 2003 through 2005; and a worksheet containing three charts, each successive chart below the previous one. Create hyperlinks to navigate between the five worksheets.

Next open the *EE2_0817* PowerPoint presentation and save it as **EE2_P8discovery4**. Explore the presentation and note that there is an initial slide including a table of contents and three additional slides—each containing a revenue chart for a year. Create hyperlinks to navigate between the worksheet in *EE2_P8discovery3* and the presentation in *EE2_P8discovery4*.

Open the *EE2_0818* document in Word, and save it as **EE2_P8discovery5**. Read the cover memo carefully; then create hyperlinks to the workbook and the PowerPoint presentation. Don't forget the e-mail address for the treasurer. Assume that you will display this memo as the first document during your computer presentation at the board meeting.

INTEGRATING PROJECTS

Essentials 2003: Microsoft Excel (Level 2)

The Integrating Projects exercises are designed to provide additional hands-on practice in working with Excel. Each exercise requires the application of skills from multiple projects; a cross-reference accompanying each exercise title tells you which projects introduced the skills applied in the exercise. The exercises are independent and can be worked in any order.

You follow a checklist as you create and enhance each complete end product. Many of the exercises include opportunities to make decisions about the best approach and features to use in a particular situation.

1 USING SORT, AUTOFILTER, AND COUNTIF TO ANALYZE CRUISE DATA

You are working with an Excel list of the Year 2005 cruises that depart from Tampa, Florida, for locations in the Caribbean, Mexico, and Central America. These cruises return to the same port. You want to correct a misspelling, add some formatting to the worksheet, and begin some preliminary analysis that includes sorting, filtering, and using the COUNTIF function.

Based on Projects 1, 2, 3, and 6

IP Exercise Checklist

❑ Open the *EE2_IP01* workbook, and save it as `Cruises_FormatCount`.

❑ Review the current content and organization of the single worksheet named *Sort*. There are data on 215 cruises in the list range A8:I223.

❑ Use the Replace All feature to change *Carribbean* to its correct spelling `Caribbean`.

❑ Below the worksheet title *Schedule of Cruises: Depart/Return TAMPA,* insert and size WordArt with the text `Year 2005`. Rotate the WordArt as desired.

❑ In the area to the right of the worksheet title and WordArt, insert and size a cruise-related clip of your choice. Change brightness and/or contrast as desired.

❑ Attach a comment to cell F8 explaining the rating system—from 1 (lowest) to 6 (highest).

❑ Sort the list so that records appear in ascending order first by area, then by number of days, then by departure date.

❑ Make two copies of the Sort worksheet, and rename the new sheets `Filter` and `COUNTIF`. (You create these copies so that you can save all of your solutions. For your own worksheets, you would keep only one set of data.)

❑ Reposition the worksheets, as necessary, so that they are in order left to right: Sort, Filter, and COUNTIF.

❑ Activate AutoFilter for the list on the Filter sheet; then set a filter to display the 10-day cruises.

❑ Redisplay all records; then set a filter to display only the 7-day Caribbean cruises rated 4 or higher.

❑ Select the COUNTIF sheet; then enter and label a COUNTIF function above the list that counts the number of cruises for a specific number of days. Set up a separate cell to hold the search condition.

❑ Below the initial COUNTIF function, set up and label two meaningful COUNTIF functions of your choice.

❑ Enter your name and the date in a location of your choice on the Sort sheet; then save your changes to the *Cruises_FormatCount* workbook, and close the workbook.

CREATIVE SOLUTION

Based on Projects
1, 4, 6, 7, and 8

2 USING FREQUENCY AND PIVOT TABLES TO ANALYZE CRUISE DATA

You are working with an Excel list of the Year 2005 cruises that depart from Tampa, Florida, for locations in the Caribbean, Mexico, and Central America. These cruises return to the same port. After you make a few formatting changes, you plan to use the FREQUENCY function and pivot tables to generate summary data.

IP Exercise Checklist

❑ Open the *EE2_IP02* workbook, and save it as **Cruises_FreqPivot**.

❑ Make sure that FREQUENCY is the current worksheet; then flip the block arrow horizontally and change its rotation and position as desired. Apply fill color of your choice.

❑ Starting in column L to the right of the Excel list, create a well-labeled frequency distribution. The distribution should count the number of cruises that have the same sailing period (4-day cruises, 5-day cruises, and so on).

❑ Create a second, well-labeled frequency distribution of your choice to the right of the first one.

❑ Create a hyperlink below the last record in the list. (Remember to maintain a blank row after the last record in the list.) Specify a link to cell A9, and include a ScreenTip that indicates a jump to the top of the list.

❑ Create a second hyperlink at the top of the worksheet that jumps to the cell below the first hyperlink. Include an appropriate ScreenTip to indicate a jump to the bottom of the list.

❑ Switch to the Pivot worksheet; then create a pivot table starting in cell K12 that counts the number of cruises that have the same sailing period (4-day cruises, 5-day cruises, and so on).

❑ Expand the pivot table to provide a page field for cruise lines and columns that show counts for Caribbean cruises and Mexico/Central America cruises.

❑ Apply an AutoFormat of your choice to the pivot table.

❑ To the right of the first pivot table, create a second pivot table that counts the cruises departing Tampa each month—in total, and for each cruise line. Apply formatting as desired. (Hint: Use onscreen Help to learn about grouping dates in a pivot table.)

❑ Create a third pivot table of your choice on a new worksheet, and apply formatting as desired. Name the new sheet **Pivot3-yourname** (substitute your last name in place of *yourname*), and position it as the last sheet in the workbook.

❑ Save your changes to the *Cruises_FreqPivot* workbook, and close the workbook.

3 FORMATTING AND PROTECTING SALES DATA

Based on Projects 2, 3, 4, and 5

You are using Excel to develop a monthly earnings report. The only change you want to make in content is to find an alternative word to replace another one. You also want to apply an AutoFormat to data about salespersons. After you complete your edits, you plan to protect the worksheet at two levels—protecting formula cells, and requiring a password to open the file.

IP Exercise Checklist

❏ Open the *EE2_IP03* workbook and immediately save it as **Sales_FormatProtect**.

❏ Open the Research task pane and use the thesaurus to find an alternative word for *target*.

❏ Find the two occurrences of *target* in the worksheet, and replace them with an appropriate substitute from the thesaurus search results. Make sure that your edits produce correct capitalization, and close the Research task pane.

❏ Apply an AutoFormat of your choice to the range A10:F16.

❏ Apply cell protection in such a way that you can change existing content and objects except for the cells containing formulas and the chart. Do not set up a password for the worksheet.

❏ As you save your changes to the *Sales_FormatProtect* workbook, require the password **Ab1Cd2** to open the workbook.

❏ Close the *Sales_FormatProtect* workbook.

4 INSERTING A DIAGRAM, SUMMARIZING DONATION DATA, AND EMBEDDING DATA IN A WORD DOCUMENT

Based on Projects 1, 3, 5, 6, and 7

You maintain a worksheet that tracks donations to the Music Forever Foundation. You plan to add a diagram to improve visual appeal. You also want to compare two ways to summarize donations according to giving level—using the SUMIF function, and creating a pivot table. Finally, you want to use Microsoft Word as you begin an article on making donations that will be included in the foundation's next newsletter. You plan to embed the data on giving levels from the Excel worksheet.

IP Exercise Checklist

❏ Open the *EE2_IP04* workbook and immediately save it as **Donate_SumEmbed**.

❏ To the right of the giving levels and donation list, insert a radial diagram.

❏ Enter and bold **Giving Levels** in the center circle.

❏ Use the Diagram toolbar to add four outside circles—for a total of seven circles surrounding the center circle.

❏ Enter the name **Maestro** in the top outside circle; then press ⏎Enter and type **$10,000**.

❑ Enter the name **Conductor** in the next outside circle to the right; then press ⏎Enter and type **$5,000**.

❑ Continue in a clockwise fashion to enter the remaining giving levels and associated donation levels.

❑ Resize the diagram to fit between rows 1 and 14 to the right of the giving levels data.

❑ Apply a different fill color to each circle.

❑ Below the diagram and to the right of the donation data, set up a well-labeled SUMIF function to total the amount donated for any specified level.

❑ To the right of the diagram, generate a pivot table that sums the amount donated for each level and the grand total for all donations.

❑ Apply a predefined AutoFormat to the pivot table, and apply a Currency with 0 decimal places format to entries in the Amount column.

❑ Save your changes to the *Donate_SumEmbed* workbook.

❑ Launch Microsoft Word and display a blank document.

❑ Type **Initial Draft of Donations Article**; then enter your name and the current date on the next two lines.

❑ Enter a blank line, type **Intro paragraph goes here**, and enter another blank line or two.

❑ Use Paste Special to embed the range A3:B10 from the Donations worksheet.

❑ Save the document as **GivingLevels**; then close the document and exit Word.

❑ Close the *Donate_SumEmbed* workbook.

5 APPLYING STYLES, USING VLOOKUP, AND TRACKING CHANGES IN CRUISE DATA

Based on Projects 3, 4, 6, and 8

You are working with an Excel list of the Year 2005 cruises that depart from Tampa, Florida, for locations in the Caribbean, Mexico, and Central America. These cruises return to the same port. You plan to apply a combination of formats to column headings using two newly created styles. You also want to insert a column for rating description and use a VLOOKUP function to assign the correct description for each current rating. After activating change tracking, you need to revise one record for a change in cruise line and rating.

IP Exercise Checklist

❑ Open the *EE2_IP05* workbook, and save it as **Cruises_StyleLookup**.

❑ Insert a column to the right of the Rating column; then enter the column heading **Rating Desc** in cell G4, and widen the column.

❑ Create a style named BlueColHead with the following attributes: bold, centered, Comic Sans MS font, with Pale Blue fill.

❑ Create a style named GreenColHead with the following attributes: bold, centered, Comic Sans MS font, with Light Green fill.

❑ Apply the styles to the column headings in row 4, alternating the colors. Reapply text wrapping and adjust column width, if necessary.

❑ Insert rows above the cruise data as needed to create the *Table_array* area for a VLOOKUP function. This area should identify the following descriptions for the level indicated in parentheses: Exceptional (6), Excellent (5), Very Good (4), Good (3), Fair (2), and Limited Appeal (1).

❑ Set up and execute a VLOOKUP function to assign the description in column G associated with the rating number in column F. Set up the function so that a rating of 3.5 is assigned the description Good and the rating 4.5 is assigned the description Very Good. Copy the function to the appropriate cells in column G, and make sure that the functions generate the correct results.

❑ Activate change tracking; then locate the only record for the cruise line *Water World.*

❑ Change *Water World* to **Luxury Unlimited**, and change the associated rating to **5**.

❑ Assume that you received final information about the changes; accept the change to the name of the cruise line, but reject the change to the rating; then remove the workbook from Shared mode.

❑ Save your changes to the *Cruises_StyleLookup* workbook, and close the workbook.

CREATIVE SOLUTION

Based on Projects 1, 2, 3, and 4

6 CREATING AND PROTECTING A TRAINING QUOTE TEMPLATE

You work for Software Solutions, Inc., a firm that provides training in a variety of software, including Excel 2003. Your responsibilities include developing and distributing quotes for computer training. To make the process more efficient and consistent, you want to develop a custom template that you can use for any quote.

You have some ideas as to content and design. An area suitable for printing and faxing to a client should comprise most of the template. This section should be eye-catching and include some visual effect, such as WordArt or a clip. There should be three sections in this printed area: (1) data about you and your company—such as your company's name and address, your name and contact information, the date the bid was prepared, and the length of time the bid is valid; (2) data about the client—such as the person and firm requesting the bid, contact information, the type of training, desired number of training hours, and the number of people to be trained; and (3) the cost of training—in total, and per person. The total cost of training takes into account training materials per person trained, instructor's fee per hour of training, and a general administrative fee applied to every training session. The per-person cost of training materials, the instructor's fee per hour, and the general administrative fee should be placed outside of the area that is printed and distributed to the client.

IP Exercise Checklist

❑ Open a new workbook in Excel; then delete all but one worksheet, and rename that worksheet **Quote**.

❑ Plan the layout and content of the standardized quote; then enter the numbers, labels, and formulas needed to produce the template described in the introductory paragraphs. Remember to avoid using raw numbers in formulas.

❏ Enter test data to make sure that the formulas produce correct results; then delete the test data.

❏ Save the file as a template in the folder you are using to store your solutions for this text. Use the name **QuoteTraining**.

❏ Apply formatting and visual effects—such as clip art or WordArt—as desired.

❏ Set up a print area that encompasses the portion of the template to be viewed by a client.

❏ Unlock the cells used to enter data that change from quote to quote; also apply a light-colored fill to those cells.

❏ Enable worksheet protection.

❏ Save your changes to the *QuoteTraining* template, and close it.

FILE GUIDE

Guide to Files in Essentials: Microsoft Excel 2003 (Level 2)

Excel Level 2	Original Student File	Student File Saved As	Related Solution Notes
Project 1			
P1-L1 thru L7	EE2_0101.xls	LeaseOptions.xls	
P1-L8	EE2_0102.xls	HMBstaff.xls	
P1-SD1 thru SD6	EE2_0103.xls	EE2_P1drill.xls	
P1-CH1 thru CH6	EE2_0104.xls	EE2_P1challenge.xls	**CH3 and CH5 are Creative Solution exercises**
P1-DZ1 thru DZ3	EE2_0105.xls	EE2_P1discovery.xls	**DZ2 and DZ3 are Creative Solution exercises**
Project 2			
P2-L1 thru L6	EE2_0201.xls	Protection.xls	
P2-L7	EE2_0202.xls	RangeCode.xls	
P2-L8	EE2_0203.xls	BookCode.xls	**Passwords set to open (abc123) and modify (xyz999) the workbook**
P2-SD1 thru SD4	EE2_0204.xls	EE2_P2drill.xls	
P2-SD5			**View file properties of two unopened files**
P2-SD6		EE2_P2drill.xls	**File saved with the password drill6**
P2-CH1 thru CH4	EE2_0205.xls	EE2_P2challenge.xls	
P2-CH5			**No files; Onscreen Help exercise**
P2-DZ1 thru DZ4	EE2_0206.xls	EE2_P2discovery.xls	**Worksheet saved with the password FWFwages in DZ3; DZ1 and DZ4 are Creative Solution exercises**
Project 3			
P3-L1 thru L5	EE2_0301.xls	SFP12_31_04.xls	
P3-L6	EE2_0302.xls	BayshoreFees.xls	
P3-L7		BayshoreFees2.csv	*BayshoreFees* workbook saved in another format
P3-SD1 thru SD5	EE2_0303.xls	EE2_P3drill.xls	
P3-CH1 thru CH5	EE2_0304.xls	EE2_P3challenge.xls Baseball.mht	**#1-FlipClip worksheet copied to a new workbook, then saved as a single file Web page named *Baseball.mht***

P = Project   L = Lesson   SD = Skill Drill   CH = Challenge   DZ = Discovery Zone   IP = Integrating Projects

Creative Solution exercises permit individual choices that produce unique solutions

Excel Level 2	Original Student File	Student File Saved As	Related Solution Notes
P3-DZ1 thru DZ3	EE2_0305.xls EE2_0306.gif	EE2_P3discovery.xls	Insert the .gif file into the first sheet within *EE2_P3discovery.xls*; DZ3 is a Creative Solution exercise

Project 4

Excel Level 2	Original Student File	Student File Saved As	Related Solution Notes
P4-L1 thru L4	EE2_0401.xls	MS165grades.xls	
P4-L5		MS165grades.xlt MS165grades_Spr05.xls	*MS165grades.xls* saved as a template using the same name; template modified and saved as a workbook for Spring 2005
P4-L6		LoanSchedule.xls	Built-in Loan Amortization template modified and saved as a workbook
P4-L7		MS165grades_Spr05.xls	Workbook from Lesson 5 modified to include a second worksheet; used to illustrate hiding and unhiding a worksheet
P4-L8	EE2_0402.xls	GLrev2004.xls GLrev2005.xls GLrev2006.xls	Original workbook saved three times; *GLrev2005* and *GLrev2006* edited while all three workbooks are open and tiled
P4-SD1 thru SD5	EE2_0403.xls	EE2_P4drill.xls ExperiencedCars.xlt	In SD4, copy the #4-CustomTMP sheet to a new workbook and save as a template
P4-CH1 thru CH3	EE2_0404.xls	EE2_P4challenge.xls	
P4-CH4		MySalesInvoice.xlt	Creative Solution exercise; modify the Sales Invoice built-in template and save it as a custom template
P4-DZ1	EE2_0405.xls	EE2_P4discovery.xls	
P4-DZ2		GLrev.xlw	Open and arrange three workbooks (*GLrev2004, GLrev2005,* and *GLrev2006*); then save as a workspace
P4-DZ3		FromOnlineTemplate.xls	Creative Solution exercise; choose an online template, modify it, and save it as a workbook

Project 5

Excel Level 2	Original Student File	Student File Saved As	Related Solution Notes
P5-L1	EE2_0501.xls	LotSale.xls	
P5-L2	EE2_0502.xls EE2_0503.doc	SalesData01.xls SalesReport01.doc	Link data from the *SalesData01* workbook to the *SalesReport01* document
P5-L3	EE2_0502.xls EE2_0503.doc	SalesData02.xls SalesReport02.doc	Embed data from the *SalesData02* workbook to the *SalesReport02* document
P5-L4 and L5	EE2_0502.xls EE2_0504.ppt	SalesData03.xls SalesReport03.ppt	Link data and a chart from the *SalesData03* workbook to slides in the *SalesReport03* presentation
P5-L6	New workbook EE2_0505.txt	Manatee_Fund.xls	Import data from the text file (.txt) to a new workbook named *Manatee_Fund*

P = Project   L = Lesson   SD = Skill Drill   CH = Challenge   DZ = Discovery Zone   IP = Integrating Projects

Creative Solution exercises permit individual choices that produce unique solutions

Excel Level 2	Original Student File	Student File Saved As	Related Solution Notes
P5-L7	EE2_0506.xls EE2_0507.mdb	Clients.xls	Import data from the Access database (.mdb) to a workbook named *Clients*
P5-L8	New workbook	WebQueries.xls	Import data from the Web: currency rates into World Rates sheet, and Microsoft financial data into MS Data sheet
P5-SD1 thru SD5	EE2_0508.xls	EE2_P5drill.xls	
P5-SD2	EE2_0509.doc	GLmemo.doc	Link a range in #2-LinkView sheet within *EE2_P5drill.xls* to *GLmemo.doc*
P5-SD3	EE2_0510.txt	Not saved	Import data from the text file to the #3-ImportTXT sheet within *EE2_P5drill.xls*
P5-SD4	EE2_0511.ppt	Mileage.ppt	Link a range and chart in #4-LinkBoth sheet within *EE2_P5drill.xls* to a PowerPoint presentation named *Mileage.ppt*
P5-CH1 thru CH4	EE2_0512.xls	EE2_P5challenge.xls	CH3 and CH4 are Creative Solution exercises
P5-CH1	EE2_0513.doc	ReviewExp.doc	Embed in *ReviewExp.doc* a range from the #1-Embed sheet within *EE2_P5challenge.xls*
P5-CH2	EE2_0514.mdb	Not saved	Import data from the Access database (.mdb file) to the #2-FromAccess sheet within *EE2_P5challenge.xls*
P5-DZ1 and DZ2	EE2_0515.xls	EE2_P5discovery.xls	DZ1 is a Creative Solution exercise

Project 6

Excel Level 2	Original Student File	Student File Saved As	Related Solution Notes
P6-L1	EE2_0601.xls	VLOOKUP.xls	
P6-L2	EE2_0602.xls	HLOOKUP.xls	
P6-L3 thru L6	EE2_0603.xls	Indy500functions.xls	
P6-SD1 thru SD6	EE2_0604.xls	EE2_P6drill.xls	
P6-CH1 thru CH4	EE2_0605.xls	EE2_P6challenge.xls	CH1 and CH2 are Creative Solution exercises
P6-DZ1 and DZ2	EE2_0606.xls	EE2_P6discovery.xls	DZ1 is a Creative Solution exercise

Project 7

Excel Level 2	Original Student File	Student File Saved As	Related Solution Notes
P7-L1 thru L6	EE2_0701.xls	SalaryPivots.xls	
P7-SD1 thru SD6	EE2_0702.xls	EE2_P7drill.xls	
P7-CH1 thru CH4	EE2_0703.xls	EE2_P7challenge.xls	
P7-DZ1 thru DZ3	EE2_0704.xls	EE2_P7discovery.xls	DZ1, DZ2, and DZ3 are Creative Solution exercises
P7-DZ4			No files; Onscreen Help exercise

P = Project   L = Lesson   SD = Skill Drill   CH = Challenge   DZ = Discovery Zone   IP = Integrating Projects

Creative Solution exercises permit individual choices that produce unique solutions

Excel Level 2	Original Student File	Student File Saved As	Related Solution Notes
Project 8			
P8-L1	EE2_0801.xls	Annual_Report.xls	
P8-L2	EE2_0802.doc EE2_0803.xls	WordLink.doc	Set a link in the Word document to the Excel workbook
P8-L3	EE2_0804.ppt EE2_0805.xls	PPTlink.ppt	Set a link in the PowerPoint presentation to the Excel workbook
P8-L4 thru L6	EE2_0806.xls	Inventory.xls	
P8-L7	EE2_0807.xls EE2_0808.xls EE2_0809.xls EE2_0810.xls	Store_A.xls Store_B.xls Store_C.xls Merge_Workbooks.xls	Merge workbooks named *Store_A, Store_B,* and *Store_C* into *Merge_Workbooks*
P8-L8	EE2_0811.xls	Signature.xls	View a digital signature, and save the file to remove the digital signature
P8-SD1 thru SD6	EE2_0812.xls	EE2_P8drill.xls	
P8-CH1 thru CH4	EE2_0813.xls	EE2_P8challenge.xls	CH3 is a Creative Solution exercise
P8-CH5			No files; Online Help exercise
P8-DZ1	EE2_0814.xls	EE2_P8discovery1.xls	
P8-DZ2	EE2_0815.xls	Edit1.xls Edit2.xls EE2_P8discovery2.xls	Exercise for two people: Initially *Edit1* and *Edit2* are copies of *EE2_0815;* Person 1 makes changes to the *Edit1* workbook and Person 2 makes changes to the *Edit2* workbook; merged results are saved in *EE2_P8discovery2*
P8-DZ3	EE2_0816.xls EE2_0817.ppt EE2_0818.doc	EE2_P8discovery3.xls EE2_P8discovery4.ppt EE2_P8discovery5.doc	Creative Solution exercise; set up hyperlinks to easily navigate between a Word cover letter, a PowerPoint presentation, and the underlying Excel data; solution not provided

Integrating Projects

IP-1	EE2_IP01.xls	Cruises_FormatCount.xls	Creative Solution exercise
IP-2	EE2_IP02.xls	Cruises_FreqPivot.xls	Creative Solution exercise
IP-3	EE2_IP03.xls	Sales_FormatProtect.xls	Creative Solution exercise; requires the password Ab1Cd2 to open
IP-4	EE2_IP04.xls	Donate_SumEmbed.xls GivingLevels.doc	Creative Solution exercise; embedding a range from the workbook into a Word document
IP-5	EE2_IP05.xls	Cruises_StyleLookup.xls	
IP-6	New workbook	QuoteTraining.xlt	Creative Solution exercise

P = Project   L = Lesson   SD = Skill Drill   CH = Challenge   DZ = Discovery Zone   IP = Integrating Projects

Creative Solution exercises permit individual choices that produce unique solutions

MICROSOFT EXCEL 2003 TASK GUIDE (LEVEL 2)

A book in the *Essentials* series is designed to be kept as a handy reference beside your computer even after you have completed all the projects and exercises. Any time you have difficulty recalling the sequence of steps or a shortcut needed to achieve a result, find your task in the alphabetized listing that follows. If you have difficulty performing a task, turn to the page number listed in the second column to locate the step-by-step exercise or other detailed description.

Excel Task	Page	Mouse	Menu Bar	Shortcut Menu	Shortcut Keys
Arrow or line, color	14	Select object; [icon] on Drawing toolbar	Select object; Format | AutoShape; Colors and Lines tab	Right-click object; Format AutoShape; Colors and Lines tab	Select object border; Ctrl+1; Colors and Lines tab
Arrow or line, insert	15	[icon] or [icon] on Drawing toolbar			
Arrow or line, move or copy	15	Select object; [icon] or [icon] on Standard toolbar; select destination; [icon] on Standard toolbar *or* Drag and drop at new location	Select object; Edit | Cut or Copy; select destination; Edit | Paste	Right-click object; Cut or Copy; right-click destination; Paste	Select object; Ctrl+X to cut or Ctrl+C to copy; select destination; Ctrl+V
Arrow or line, resize	15	Select object; drag sizing handles	Select object; Format | AutoShape; Size tab	Right-click object; Format AutoShape; Size tab	Select object; Ctrl+1; Size tab
Arrow or line, style	16	Select object; [icon], [icon], or [icon] on Drawing toolbar	Select object; Format | AutoShape; Colors and Lines tab	Right-click object; Format AutoShape; Colors and Lines tab	Select object border; Ctrl+1; Colors and Lines tab
AutoFormat, apply	113		Select cell(s); Format | AutoFormat; select predefined style		
AutoFormat, remove	116		Select cell(s); Format | AutoFormat; select *None*		
AutoShape, add or edit text	7			Right-click object; Add Text or Edit Text	
AutoShape, create	6	AutoShapes ▾ on Drawing toolbar; point to category; point to specific shape and click it; draw the shape	Insert | Picture | AutoShapes; point to category; point to specific shape and click it; draw the shape		Alt+U; arrow to category; press →; arrow to desired shape; press Ctrl+↵Enter

Excel Task	Page	Mouse	Menu Bar	Shortcut Menu	Shortcut Keys
AutoShape, fill color	8	Double-click object; Colors and Lines tab; select Fill options		Right-click object; Format AutoShape; Colors and Lines tab; select Fill options	
AutoShape, flip	7	Select object; Draw ▾ on Drawing toolbar; Rotate or Flip; Flip Horizontal or Flip Vertical			
AutoShape, format	7	Double-click object; Colors and Lines tab	Select object; Format | AutoShape; Colors and Lines tab	Right-click object; Format AutoShape; Colors and Lines tab	Select object; Ctrl+1; Colors and Lines tab
AutoShape, move or copy	6	Select object; ✄ or 🗐 on Standard toolbar; select destination; 🗐 on Standard toolbar or Drag to move, or hold down Ctrl and drag to copy	Select object; Edit | Cut or Copy; select destination; Edit | Paste	Right-click object; Cut or Copy; right-click destination; Paste	Select object; Ctrl+X to move or Ctrl+C to copy; select destination; Ctrl+V
AutoShape, replace	8	Select object; Draw ▾ on Drawing toolbar; Change AutoShape; select new shape			
AutoShape, rotate	6	Select object; Draw ▾ on Drawing toolbar; Rotate or Flip; select rotate option or Select object and drag green rotate handle			
Callout, add 3D or shadow effects	19	Select object; ▢ or ▢ on Drawing toolbar			
Callout, create	18	AutoShapes ▾ on Drawing toolbar; Callouts; select callout; position pointer and drag to create			

Excel Task	Page	Mouse	Menu Bar	Shortcut Menu	Shortcut Keys
Callout, resize	19	Select object; drag sizing handles	Select object; Format | AutoShape; Size tab	Right-click object; Format AutoShape; Size tab	Select object; Ctrl+1; Size tab
Cell(s), delete	74		Select cell(s); Edit | Delete; Shift cells left or Shift cells up	Select cell(s); right-click; Delete; Shift cells left or Shift cells up	
Cell(s), insert	74		Select cell(s); Insert | Cells; Shift cells right or Shift cells down	Select cell(s); right-click; Insert; Shift cells right or Shift cells down	
Clip art, add border	24			Right-click object; Format Picture; Colors and Lines tab; select line thickness, style, and color	
Clip art, crop	23	Select object; ⊹ on Picture toolbar; drag to desired cropping			
Clip art, insert	21	🖼 on Drawing toolbar	Insert | Picture | Clip Art		
Clip art, resize	22	Select object; drag sizing handles	Select object; Format | AutoShape; Size tab	Right-click object; Format AutoShape; Size tab	Select object; Ctrl+1; Size tab
Clip art, show or hide Picture toolbar	20		View | Toolbars | Picture	Right-click object; Show Picture Toolbar or Hide Picture Toolbar	
Clip, change brightness	84	Select clip; ☼↑ or ☼↓ on Picture toolbar	Select clip; Format | Picture; Picture tab; Brightness	Right-click clip; Format Picture; Picture tab; Brightness	
Clip, change color	84	Select clip; ▥ on Picture toolbar	Select clip; Format | Picture; Picture tab; Color	Right-click clip; Format Picture; Picture tab; Color	
Clip, change contrast	84	Select clip; ◑↑ or ◑↓ on Picture toolbar	Select clip; Format | Picture | Picture tab; Contrast	Right-click clip; Format Picture; Picture tab; Contrast	

Excel Task	Page	Mouse	Menu Bar	Shortcut Menu	Shortcut Keys
Clip, flip	85	Select object; Draw ▾ on Drawing toolbar; Rotate or Flip; Flip Horizontal or Flip Vertical			
Clip, rotate	85	Select object; Draw ▾ on Drawing toolbar; Rotate or Flip; Rotate Left 90° or Rotate Right 90° *or* Select ▦ on Picture toolbar, or drag using rotation handle			
Comment, attach	46		Select cell; Insert | Comment; type comment	Right-click cell; Insert Comment; type comment	
Comment, change font	47	If comment is visible, drag over text and apply buttons on Formatting toolbar		Right-click comment border; Edit Comment; select text and apply buttons on Formatting toolbar or right-click within comment box; Format Comment	
Comment, copy	47	Select cell with comment; ▦ on Standard toolbar; select destination cell(s); Edit | Paste Special; Comments	Select cell with comment; Edit | Copy; select destination cell(s); Edit | Paste Special; Comments	Right-click cell with comment; Copy; select destination cell(s) and right-click; Paste Special; Comments	
Comment, delete all	47		Edit | Go To | Special | Comments; click OK; Edit | Clear | Comments		
Comment, delete one	47		Click cell with comment; Edit | Clear | Comments	Right-click cell with comment; Delete Comment	
Comment, edit	47	Click within visible comment box; change text		Right-click cell with comment; Edit Comment; change text	
Comment, move	48	Drag border of visible comment to new location			

Excel Task	Page	Mouse	Menu Bar	Shortcut Menu	Shortcut Keys
Comment, resize	48	Click border; drag sizing handles			
Comment, turn on indicator only	46		Tools | Options; select View tab; select Comment indicator only		
Comment, view all	46		View | Comments		
Comment, view one	46	Position pointer on cell with red comment indicator			
Comments, print	48		File | Page Setup; Sheet tab; display Comments drop-down list box; select print choice		
COUNTIF, enter function	200		Insert | Function; open Function Arguments dialog box for COUNTIF; complete *Range* and *Criteria* text boxes		
Custom number format, create	110		Select cell; Format | Cells; Number tab; Custom in Category list; enter format in *Type* box	Right-click cell; Format Cells; Number tab; Custom in Category list; enter format in *Type* box	Select cell; Ctrl+1; Number tab; Custom in Category list; enter format in *Type* box
Diagram, add borders	26		Select object; Format | Diagram; Colors and Lines tab	Right-click object; Format Diagram; Colors and Lines tab	Select object; Ctrl+1; Colors and Lines tab
Diagram, insert	25	on Drawing toolbar	Select cell; Insert | Diagram; select diagram style		
Diagram, modify	26		Select object; Format | Diagram; select a tab	Right-click object; Format Diagram; select a tab	Select object; Ctrl+1; select a tab
Digital signature, view	269		Tools | Options; Security tab; Digital Signatures button; View Certificate button		
Drawing toolbar, show or hide	3		View | Toolbars | Drawing	Right-click any toolbar; Drawing	

Excel Task	Page	Mouse	Menu Bar	Shortcut Menu	Shortcut Keys
Embed Excel data in Word	155	Select cell(s); [icon] on Standard toolbar; open Word document; Edit | Paste Special; Paste; select Microsoft Office Excel Worksheet Object in As list box	Select cell(s); Edit | Copy; open Word document; Edit | Paste Special; Paste; select Microsoft Office Excel Worksheet Object in As list box	Right-click selected cell(s); Copy; open Word document; Edit | Paste Special; Paste; select Microsoft Office Excel Worksheet Object in As list box	
Export data, from Excel to Access	166		With Excel data in list format and the workbook closed, launch Access; File | Open; select All Files from the *Files of type* drop-down list and open the Excel file in Access; follow directions in the Link Spreadsheet Wizard		
File properties, view and set, any workbook	55		File | Open; select filename then Tools | Properties or right-click filename; Properties		
File properties, view and set, current workbook	54		File | Properties; select tab		
Find, cell contents	76		Edit | Find; type contents to find; Find All or Find Next		Ctrl+F; type contents to find; Find All or Find Next
Find, cell formats	79		Edit | Find; Options | Format; set format(s) to find; click OK; Find All or Find Next		Ctrl+F; set format(s) to find; click OK; Find All or Find Next
Format, apply special number format	112		Select cell(s); Format | Cells; Number tab; Special in Category list; select format	Right-click selected cell(s); Format Cells | Number tab; Special in Category list; select format	Select cell(s); Ctrl+1; Number tab; Special in Category list; select format
Frequency distribution, create with FREQUENCY function	196		Insert | Function; open Function Arguments dialog box for FREQUENCY; complete *Data_array* and *Bins_array* text boxes; press the three-key combination Ctrl+◆Shift+↵Enter		

Excel Task	Page	Mouse	Menu Bar	Shortcut Menu	Shortcut Keys
HLOOKUP (approximate match), enter function	195		Insert	Function; open Function Arguments dialog box for HLOOKUP; complete *Lookup_value, Table_array,* and *Row_index_num* text boxes		
HLOOKUP (exact match), enter function	193		Same process as approximate match with one addition: specify False in *Range_lookup* box		
Hyperlink, change appearance	252			Right-click hyperlink; Format Cells; select formatting changes	
HYPERLINK, enter function	252		Insert	Function; open Function Arguments dialog box for HYPERLINK; complete *Link_location* and *Friendly_name* text boxes		
Hyperlink, insert	250	on Standard toolbar; select from *Link to* options; complete other settings in Insert Hyperlink dialog box (includes optional ScreenTip)	Insert	Hyperlink; select from *Link to* options; complete other settings in Insert Hyperlink dialog box (includes optional ScreenTip)	Right-click blank cell; Hyperlink; select from *Link to* options; complete other settings in Insert Hyperlink dialog box (includes optional ScreenTip)	Ctrl+K; select from *Link to* options; complete other settings in Insert Hyperlink dialog box (includes optional ScreenTip)
Hyperlink, move or copy	252			Right-click the hyperlink to be moved or copied; Cut or Copy; position the pointer at the new location and right-click; Paste	
Hyperlink, redirect	252			Right-click hyperlink; Edit Hyperlink; change link destination	
Hyperlink, remove (eliminate associated text)	252			Right-click hyperlink; Clear Contents	

Excel Task	Page	Mouse	Menu Bar	Shortcut Menu	Shortcut Keys
Hyperlink, remove (retain associated text)	252			Right-click hyperlink; **R**emove Hyperlink	
Import data, from Access database	162		**D**ata | Import External **D**ata | **N**ew Database Query; select MS Access Database; check *Use the Query Wizard to create/edit queries* and click OK; select database file , and click OK; select table and columns; click Next; filter data or click Next; sort data or click Next; select **R**eturn Data to Microsoft Office Excel and click Finish; specify **E**xisting worksheet, click destination cell, and click OK		
Import data, from text file	159	; open text file; enter specifications in Text Import Wizard dialog box; click **F**inish; **F**ile | Save **A**s; Microsoft Office Excel Workbook; click **S**ave	**F**ile | **O**pen; open text file; enter specifications in Text Import Wizard dialog box; click **F**inish; **F**ile | Save **A**s; Microsoft Office Excel Workbook; click **S**ave		Ctrl+O; open text file; enter specifications in Text Import Wizard dialog box; click **F**inish; **F**ile | Save **A**s; Microsoft Office Excel Workbook; click **S**ave
Import data, from Web	167		**D**ata | Import External **D**ata | Import Data; select a source and click **O**pen; choose **E**xisting worksheet or **N**ew worksheet; click OK		
Link Excel chart to PowerPoint	158	Select chart; on Standard toolbar; open PowerPoint and choose slide; **E**dit | Paste **S**pecial; Paste **l**ink; select Microsoft Office Excel Chart Object in **A**s list box; check or uncheck *Display as icon*	Select chart; **E**dit | **C**opy; open PowerPoint and choose slide; **E**dit | Paste **S**pecial; Paste **l**ink; select Microsoft Office Excel Chart Object in **A**s list box; check or uncheck *Display as icon*	Right-click selected cell(s); **C**opy; open PowerPoint and choose a slide; **E**dit | Paste **S**pecial; Paste **l**ink; select Microsoft Office Excel Chart Object in **A**s list box; check or uncheck *Display as icon*	

Excel Task	Page	Mouse	Menu Bar	Shortcut Menu	Shortcut Keys
Link Excel data to PowerPoint	157	Select cell(s); [icon] on Standard toolbar; open PowerPoint and choose slide; Edit | Paste Special; Paste link; select Microsoft Office Excel Worksheet Object in As list box; check or uncheck Display as icon	Select cell(s); Edit | Copy; open PowerPoint and choose slide; Edit | Paste Special; Paste link; select Microsoft Office Excel Worksheet Object in As list box; check or uncheck Display as icon	Right-click selected cell(s); Copy; open PowerPoint and choose slide; Edit | Paste Special; Paste Link; select Microsoft Office Excel Worksheet Object in As list box; check or uncheck Display as icon	
Link Excel data to Word	151	Select cell(s); [icon] on Standard toolbar; open Word document; Edit | Paste Special; Paste link; select Microsoft Office Excel Worksheet Object in As list box; check or uncheck Display as icon	Select cell(s); Edit | Copy; open Word document; Edit | Paste Special; Paste link; select Microsoft Office Excel Worksheet Object in As list box; check or uncheck Display as icon	Right-click selected cell(s); Copy; open Word document; Edit | Paste Special; Paste link; select Microsoft Office Excel Worksheet Object in As list box; check or uncheck Display as icon	
Merge workbooks	264		Tools | Compare and Merge Workbooks; in the Select Files to Merge Into Current Workbook dialog box, hold down Ctrl and click workbooks to merge		
Object, move in small increments	16				Select object; hold down Ctrl; click arrow key that points to direction you want to move object—left, right, up, or down
Objects, change order of stacked objects	12	Select object; Draw ▼ on Drawing toolbar; Order; choose order action		Right-click object; Order; choose order action	
Objects, group	12	Hold down ⇧Shift and select objects; Draw ▼ on Drawing toolbar; click Group		Hold down ⇧Shift and select objects; right-click; Grouping | Group	

Excel Task	Page	Mouse	Menu Bar	Shortcut Menu	Shortcut Keys
Objects, move grouped	13	Click within group; drag to new destination			Click within group; Ctrl+X; select destination; Ctrl+V
Objects, regroup	14	Select object in group; Draw ▼ on Drawing toolbar; Regroup		Right-click object in group; Grouping | Regroup	
Objects, ungroup	14	Select object; Draw ▼ on Drawing toolbar; Ungroup		Right-click grouped object; Grouping | Ungroup	
Password, create for worksheet	55		Tools | Protection | Protect Sheet; enter password to unprotect sheet		
Password, create for worksheet range	55		Tools | Protection | Allow Users to Edit Ranges; New; type name in *Title* text box; type password in *Range password* text box, click OK; follow instructions to reenter password		
Password, create or delete for workbook	58		File | Save As; Tools drop-down list; General Options; enter or delete password to open or modify workbook		
Password, open workbook with assigned	58		File | Open; select a password-protected file; Open; type password(s) when prompted		
Paste special	87		Copy or cut text or object; Edit | Paste Special; select option	Copy or cut text or object; right-click; Paste Special; select option	
Picture, insert from file	21	⊞ on Picture toolbar	Insert | Picture | From File		
Pivot chart, create from pivot table	229	⊞ on PivotTable toolbar		Right-click pivot table; PivotChart	

Excel Task	Page	Mouse	Menu Bar	Shortcut Menu	Shortcut Keys
Pivot table, add field	223	From PivotTable Field List, drag and drop field name to Row Area, Column Area, Page Area, or Data Area	Click field name in PivotTable Field List box; display area drop-down list to right of Add To button; select Row Area, Column Area, Page Area, or Data Area; click Add To button		
Pivot table, apply predefined format	231	[icon] on PivotTable toolbar; select format	Format | AutoFormat; select format		
Pivot table, change row or column field to page field	225	Drag field name up off the pivot table			
Pivot table, create	218		Click any cell in list; Data | PivotTable and PivotChart Report; verify location; select type of report and click Next; select range for data and click Next; specify where to put report; Finish; drag data, row, column, and page fields as desired from PivotTable Field List		
Pivot table, delete	222		Use mouse pointer to select entire table; Edit | Clear | All	Right-click table; Select | Entire Table; Edit | Clear | All	
Pivot table, hide or show field list	224	[icon] on PivotTable toolbar		Right-click pivot table; Hide Field List or Show Field List	
Pivot table, hide or show toolbar	227		View | Toolbars | PivotTable	Right-click pivot table; Hide PivotTable Toolbar or Show PivotTable Toolbar	
Pivot table, refresh	228	[icon] on PivotTable toolbar	Data | Refresh Data	Right-click pivot table; Refresh Data	
Pivot table, remove field	225		Drag field name left, right, or down off the pivot table		

Excel Task	Page	Mouse	Menu Bar	Shortcut Menu	Shortcut Keys
Pivot table, remove predefined format	234	on PivotTable toolbar; select *None*	**F**ormat	**A**utoFormat; select *None*		
Protection, turn off for current sheet	51		**T**ools	**P**rotection	**U**nprotect Sheet		
Protection, turn on for current sheet	50		**T**ools	**P**rotection	**P**rotect Sheet		
Protection, turn on or off for workbook	53		**T**ools	**P**rotection	Protect **W**orkbook or Unprotect **W**orkbook		
Protection, unlock cell(s)	51		Select cells to unlock; F**o**rmat	**C**ells; select Protection tab; uncheck *Locked* check box	Select cells to unlock; right-click; **F**ormat Cells; select Protection tab; uncheck *Locked* check box	Select cells to unlock; Ctrl+1; select Protection tab; uncheck *Locked* check box
Protection, unlock object	51	Double-click object; Protection tab; uncheck *Locked* check box	Select object; **F**ormat; select object type; Protection tab; uncheck *Locked* check box	Right-click object; specific Format option; Protection tab; uncheck *Locked* check box	
Range name, create	43	Select cell(s); click name box at left end of Formula bar; type range name; ↵Enter	Select cell(s); **I**nsert	**N**ame	**D**efine		
Range name, delete	45		**I**nsert	**N**ame	**D**efine; select name; **D**elete		
Range name, view	45		**I**nsert	**N**ame	**D**efine; select a name		
Range names, list	45		Select upper-left cell in blank area; **I**nsert	**N**ame	**P**aste; Paste **L**ist		
Replace, cell contents	76		**E**dit	Re**p**lace; type contents to find; type replacement; Replace **A**ll or **R**eplace		Ctrl+H; type contents to find; type replacement; Replace **A**ll or **R**eplace

Excel Task	Page	Mouse	Menu Bar	Shortcut Menu	Shortcut Keys
Replace, cell formats	79		Edit	Replace; specify format(s) to find; specify replacement formatting; Replace All or Replace		Ctrl+H; specify format(s) to find; specify replacement formatting; Replace All or Replace
Research task pane, open	145	on Standard toolbar	View	Task Pane; Research		Ctrl+F1; drop-down arrow by name of task pane; Research
Row height, change	109	Drag bottom boundary of row in worksheet frame or double-click bottom boundary	Select any cell in row; Format	Row	Height	Right-click row in worksheet frame; Row Height	
Save As, different file format	91		File	Save As; specify file type in Save as type text box; Save		
Style, copy between workbooks	119		Open both workbooks; Format	Style in the workbook you want to copy styles to; click Merge button; click name of source workbook		
Style, create	116		Apply desired formatting to a cell; Format	Style; enter name for style		
Style, delete	118		Format	Style; select style name; Delete button		
Style, modify	118		Format	Style; select style name; Modify button		
Style, remove style effects	118		Select cell(s); Format	Style; select Normal from style name list		
SUMIF, enter function	202		Insert	Function; open Function Arguments dialog box for SUMIF; complete Range, Criteria, and Sum_range text boxes		
Template, create custom template	120		File	Save As; select Template from the Save as type list; Save		

Excel Task	Page	Mouse	Menu Bar	Shortcut Menu	Shortcut Keys
Template, create default workbook	121		Create workbook with desired settings; **File** | Save **As**; save as Template in Microsoft Office XLStart folder using name *Book*		
Template, create default worksheet	121		Create workbook with one worksheet; **File** | Save **As**; save as Template in Microsoft Office XLStart folder using name *Sheet*		
Template, use built-in template	122		**File** | **New**; click *On my computer* under Templates; select Spreadsheet Solutions tab; click desired template		
Template, use custom template	120		**File** | **New**; click *On my computer* under Templates; select General tab; click desired template		
Text box, create	9	[icon] on Drawing toolbar; click cell and type text for box without border, or draw box and type text for box with border			
Text box, edit	9	Click inside object; select text; type changes			
Text box, exit edit mode	10	Click outside object		Right-click object; select Exit Edit Te**x**t	
Text box, format	11	Select object border; [fill icon], [line icon], or [font color icon] on Drawing toolbar	Select object border; **Format** | Text Bo**x**; Colors and Lines tab or Font tab	Right-click object border; Format Text Bo**x**; Colors and Lines tab or Font tab	Select object border; Ctrl+1; Colors and Lines tab or Font tab
Text box, link text to	11	Click inside text box; click formula bar, type =; click cell containing text to link to box; ↵Enter			

Excel Task	Page	Mouse	Menu Bar	Shortcut Menu	Shortcut Keys
Text, rotate in cell	107		Select cell(s); Format | Cells; Alignment tab; specify Degrees	Select cell(s); right-click; Format Cells; Alignment tab; specify Degrees	Select cell(s); Ctrl+1; Alignment tab; specify Degrees
Track changes, accept or reject changes	260		Tools | Track Changes | Accept or Reject Changes; specify When and Who box options; accept or reject each change		
Track changes, remove workbook from shared use	261		Tools | Share Workbook; Editing tab; uncheck Allow changes by more than one user at the same time		
Track changes, set number of days to track	258		Tools | Share Workbook; Advanced tab; type the desired number of days in the Keep change history for spinner box		
Track changes, turn on	258		Tools | Track Changes | Highlight Changes; check Track changes while editing		
Transpose, rows and columns	91	Select cells to be transposed; [icon] on the Standard toolbar; select first destination cell; Edit | Paste Special; Transpose	Select cells to be transposed; Edit | Copy; select first destination cell; Edit | Paste Special; Transpose	Select cells to be transposed; right-click; Copy; select first destination cell; right-click; Paste Special; Transpose	
VLOOKUP (approximate match), enter function	189		Insert | Function; open Function Arguments dialog box for VLOOKUP; complete Lookup_value, Table_array, and Col_index_num text boxes		
VLOOKUP (exact match), enter function	187		Same process as approximate match with one addition: specify False in Range_lookup box		
WordArt, delete	5	Select object; [icon] on Standard toolbar	Select object; Edit | Cut	Right-click object; Cut	Select object; Ctrl+X or press Del

Excel Task	Page	Mouse	Menu Bar	Shortcut Menu	Shortcut Keys
WordArt, format	5	Select object; [icon] on WordArt toolbar; Colors and Lines tab	Select object; Format | WordArt | Colors and Lines tab	Right-click object; Format WordArt; Colors and Lines tab	Select object; Ctrl+1; Colors and Lines tab
WordArt, insert	3	[icon] on the WordArt or Drawing toolbars	Insert | Picture | WordArt		
WordArt, move or copy	4	Select object; [icon] or [icon] on Standard toolbar; select destination; [icon] on Standard toolbar *or* Drag to move, or hold Ctrl and drag to copy	Select object; Edit | Cut or Copy; select destination; Edit | Paste		Select object; Ctrl+X to move or Ctrl+C to copy; select destination; Ctrl+V
WordArt, resize	5	Select object; drag sizing handles	Select object; Format | WordArt | Size tab	Right-click object; Format WordArt | Size tab	Select object; Ctrl+1; Size tab
Workbook, arrange	130		Window | Arrange; select desired arrangement		
Workbook, hide	129		Window | Hide		
Workbook, unhide	129		Window | Unhide; select workbook to unhide		
Worksheet, hide	127		Format | Sheet | Hide		
Worksheet, unhide	128		Format | Sheet | Unhide; select sheet(s)		

GLOSSARY

All key terms appearing in this book (in bold italic) are listed alphabetically in this Glossary for easy reference. If you want to learn more about a feature or concept, use the Index to find the term's other significant occurrences.

array   In computing terms, an arrangement of data in a tabular form.

array formula   A formula that you must enter by pressing the three-key combination Ctrl+Shift+Enter. The FREQUENCY function is an array formula.

array range   A rectangular area of cells that share a common formula.

AutoFormat   A feature that enables you to apply a predefined format to a list, pivot table, or range of cells.

AutoShape   A predefined shape that you create using the AutoShapes menu from the Drawing toolbar.

bin   A predetermined category used to analyze data, such as the number of survey respondents in each age range (20–29, 30–39, and so forth).

built-in template   A template provided by Excel that contains content and formatting designed to meet a common business need.

callout   A text-filled object that points to other text or another object.

change tracking   An Excel feature that records row and column insertions and deletions, moves and copies, and changes to cell contents.

clip   A drawing, photograph, or other media type such as sound, animation, or movies.

clip art   Drawings as well as photographs that you can insert in a document.

comment   An annotation attached to a cell that displays within a box whenever the mouse pointer rests on the cell.

comment indicator   A small red triangle in a cell's upper-right corner, indicat-

ing that a comment is attached to the cell.

COUNTIF function   A function used to count the number of cells within a range that meet the specified criteria.

custom number format   A number format that you can create for a unique situation, when a predefined format does not meet your needs.

custom template   A template that you create and save with your preferred content and/or formatting in one or more worksheets.

default workbook template   The template controlling the workbook that opens when you start Excel or open a new workbook without specifying a template.

default worksheet template   The template controlling the worksheet that displays when you insert a worksheet in a workbook.

destination file   A file that contains linked or embedded data. (*See also* **source file**)

diagram   A drawing that generally illustrates relationships.

digital certificate   A feature confirming that a document originated from the signer.

digital signature   A feature confirming that a document has not been altered since the document was signed.

embedded object   An object in a destination file that does not update when the data in the source file change.

file property   A characteristic of a file, such as file type, file size, storage location, author's name, and date last revised.

frequency distribution   The results of a calculation that counts how often specific values occur within a set of values.

FREQUENCY function   A function that calculates how many times values occur within a range.

grouped objects   Two or more objects that can be manipulated as a single object.

History worksheet   A temporary worksheet that provides—in a list, one change per row—detailed information about tracked changes.

HLOOKUP function   A function that is used to search for a value in the topmost row of a table array. If found, the function displays the contents of another cell in that same column for the row you specify.

hyperlink   Text or an object that you can click to jump to another location, to open another file, or to start a process.

indented format   A format that supports the presentation of pivot table data in categories and subcategories. (*See also* **nonindented format**)

linked object   An object in a destination file that updates whenever the data in the source file change.

nonindented format   A format that doesn't offset subcategories within categories in a PivotTable report. (*See also* **indented format**)

object   In Excel, a workbook, worksheet, range of cells, chart, clip art, or WordArt element that has properties and can be referenced and used by another program.

Object Linking and Embedding (OLE)   A method of sharing data that is supported by many different programs, including all Microsoft Office 2003 applications.

page field   A specification that adds a third dimension to a pivot table by allowing you to filter all of the data in a report by one or more fields.

password   A set of case-sensitive characters that must be known to access a password-protected element, such as an Excel range, worksheet, or workbook.

pivot table   An interactive table that quickly summarizes large amounts of data from a data source such as a list or another table.

PivotTable and PivotChart Wizard   A wizard that guides you through the steps to summarize data in a table layout with or without an accompanying chart.

range name   An English-like name applied to a cell or range of cells.

read-only   A file attribute that enables you to view, but not change, a file that you save under the same name. (*See also* **write access**)

refresh   A necessary action to recalculate the data in a pivot table after you change data in a worksheet and the new figures impact a summary calculation in the pivot table.

Research task pane   A tool for looking up words and phrases in more than a dozen resources, including a dictionary, encyclopedia, translation service, thesaurus, and news service.

shared workbook   An Excel file that is set up to enable multiple users to make changes.

source file   The file providing the data you want to link or embed. (*See also* **destination file**)

style   A means of combining more than one format—such as font type, size, and color—into a single definition that can be applied to one or more cells.

SUMIF function   A function that adds the contents of cells within a range that meet the specified criteria.

template   A workbook containing standardized content and/or formatting that you can use as the basis for other workbooks. A template file has an .xlt extension.

text box   An object shaped like a square or rectangle that contains words.

thesaurus   A tool that enables you to look up alternative words—synonyms—for a specified word.

third-party service   When working with Microsoft Office applications, a

term applied to a resource provider other than Microsoft Corporation.

thumbnail   A miniature representation of an image.

translate   The act of changing a word or phrase from one language to a different language.

transpose   To copy in a special way so that the data from the top row of the copied range appear in the left column of the destination area, and data from the left column of the copied range appear in the top row of the destination area.

unlock   To remove the default locked setting that prevents change to a cell or object when worksheet protection is active.

VLOOKUP function   A function that is used to search for a specified value in the leftmost column of a table. If found, the function displays the contents of another cell in that same row for the column you specify.

Web query   A means to retrieve data stored on the Internet or a firm's intranet or extranet.

WordArt   A special effect that displays user-specified text in one of 30 predefined styles.

write access   The capability to modify a file. (*See also* **read-only**)

INDEX

NUMERICS

3-D effects, adding, 19

A

accepting changes in workbooks, 259–262, 279
access
  passwords, 55–60, 66
  thesauruses, 149
Access, importing databases, 162–166, 179–180
adding
  borders to clip art, 24
  callouts, 34
  cells, 46–47
  clip art, 20–23
  colors to text boxes, 11
  comments, 65
  diagrams, 24–28, 38
  emphasis
    to callouts, 18–19, 34
    to shapes, 14–17, 33–34
  images, 24, 38
  shapes, 34, 37
  special effects, 40
  text
    AutoShapes, 7
    shapes, 36
  text boxes, 35
Allow Users to Edit Ranges dialog box, 55
analysis
  COUNTIF function, 200–201, 209, 212
  FREQUENCY function, 198. *See also* FREQUENCY function
  multiple pivot tables, 244
  SUMIF function, 202–203, 210–212
applying
  AutoFormat, 113–115, 135
  built-in templates, 122–125, 139
  range names, 42–45, 64–70
  styles, 116–119
approximate matches, 195. *See also* **HLOOKUP function; VLOOKUP function**
Arrange Windows dialog box, 130

arrays
  formulas, 196
  ranges, 195
arrows
  formatting, 17
  highlighting, 14–17, 33–34
aspect ratios, 5
AutoFormat, 113–115, 135
AutoShapes. *See also* **shapes**
  banners, 32
  colors, 8
  deleting, 8
  text, 7
  unlocking, 65

B

banners, creating, 32
bins
  charting, 199
  FREQUENCY function, 195–198, 209–211
borders, adding to clip art, 24
brightness, modifying, 83–84, 99, 103–104
built-in templates, 122–125, 139. *See also* **templates**

C

calculating. *See also* **formulas**
  charting, 199
  FREQUENCY function, 195–198, 209–211
  pivot tables, 227–228
  summary data, 243–244
callouts
  editing, 34
  highlighting, 18–19, 34
categories
  charting, 199
  FREQUENCY function, 195–198, 209–211
cells
  AutoFormat, 113–115, 135
  circling, 37
  comments, 46–47
  COUNTIF function, 200–201, 209–212
  deleting, 73–75, 97

hiding, 139
  inserting, 73–75
  protecting, 50–53
  ranges
    charting, 199
    FREQUENCY function, 195–198, 209–211
  searching/replacing, 76–82, 96–98, 101
  styles, 116–119
  SUMIF function, 202–203, 210–212
  unlocking, 69
Cells command (Insert menu), 74
change tracking, 257
charts
  creating pivot tables, 229–230, 241
  drawing lines, 37
  embedding
    deleting, 68
    unlocking, 70
  FREQUENCY function, 199
  linking slides (PowerPoint), 158. *See also* OLE
Choose Columns dialog box, 163
Choose Data Source dialog box, 162
circling cell contents, 37
clip art
  adding, 20–23
  borders, 24
  brightness/contrast, 83–84, 99, 103–104
  flipping/rotating, 85–86, 101
  shapes, 5–7
Clip Art task pane, 20
Clip Organizer, 36
colors
  AutoShapes, 8
  diagrams, 28
  text boxes, 11
columns
  headings, 135
  HLOOKUP function, 192–195, 208, 214
  transposing, 91
  VLOOKUP function, 185–191, 207–214
commands
  Data menu
    Import External Data, 162, 167, 168, 171